Coproduction and Coarticulation in IsiZulu Clicks

Coproduction and Coarticulation in IsiZulu Clicks

by

Kimberly Diane Thomas-Vilakati

University of California Press

Berkeley   Los Angeles   London

UNIVERSITY OF CALIFORNIA PRESS, one of the most distinguished university presses in the United States, enriches lives around the world by advancing scholarship in the humanities, social sciences, and natural sciences. Its activities are supported by the UC Press Foundation and philanthropic contributions from individuals and institutions. For more information, visit www.ucpress.edu

University of California Press
Berkeley and Los Angeles, California

University of California Press, Ltd.
London, England

Volume 144

Coproduction and Coarticulation in IsiZulu Clicks
by Kimberly Diane Thomas-Vilakati

ISBN 978-0-520-09876-3 (pbk. : alk. paper)

Library of Congress Control Number: 2010922226

The paper used in this publication meets the minimum requirements of ANSI/NISO Z39.48-1992 (R 1997) (*Permanence of Paper*).

Dedication

This study is dedicated to the following individuals:

To my loving father, who sacrificed his life to work hard in order to educate me and who, through his loyalty and devotion, made this all possible.

To my loving mother, who gave selflessly to seven children and many grandchildren, whose confidence in me never waivered and who gave me the fortitude to compete in the international arena.

To my loving grandmother, Amelia, who instilled a wonderful love of language in me through her poetry, and whose protection and love I carry with me and still feel to this day.

To my loving husband, who has been my chief counselor and guide for the last nine years of my life, and whose emotional support of me in this task was truly divine
And especially the following:

To Mateu, my loving son, who has brought so much joy into my life, and whose unconditional love gives me the strength to be a better person and to pursue and succeed in such a difficult endeavor, and from whom I gained the desire and motivation to continue to better myself for the sole purpose of setting for him a good example.

To Simanga, my daughter, who is such a breathe of fresh air in my life. May your light continue to shine. Let it shine.

To all those children of mine who call me mother but have never been nurtured by me on a day-to-day basis, this too is for you.

It is through the dedication of this book to my children that I wish to bless them, such that they may always strive to be the best that they can be.

Contents

Figures

Tables

Acknowledgements

This study took nearly three years to complete, and during that time there were many people who contributed valuable assistance in various ways. I would like to thank my dissertation committee Professors Peter Ladefoged, Ian Maddieson, Thomas Hinnebusch, Sun-Ah Jun, Christopher Ehret, and Asif Agha. Their masterful guidance was of the utmost importance to me, and they were always encouraging, positive and ready to help.

Much needed technical assistance with data collection was provided by Henry Tehrani, Ian Maddieson and Peter Ladefoged. Many thanks to Nomsa Khumalo, Caseline Kunene, Nhlanhla Thwala and George Vilakati for their enthusiasm during the data collection process. They definitely went out of their way to help me record data. Many thanks to the members of the UCLA phonetics lab for providing a stimulating work environment. I would especially like to thank Aaron Shryock and Bonny Sands, who gave me a lot of encouragement over the years.

There were many personal friends who provided much needed emotional support and, in some cases, hours of babysitting. They are: Oleg and Lidia Vassiliev, Angaluki and Hulda Muaka, Nhlanhla Thwala and Auntie P, The Horga Family, Magdalena Guerrero, Anna Szabolsci, Rose Letsholo, Ruth and Glen Light, Cheryl Harris and her mother Juanita and husband Willie Kgositsile. I would especially like to thank those families who graciously and unconditionally opened their homes to us during the last stages of the dissertation process. We can never thank you enough for coming to our aid when we truly needed support. I must also thank the following children who were wonderful companions to Mateu and whom I have grown to love: Karabo, Simanga, Andrusha, Thebe, Kiyanna, Dennis and Stephanie and the others at University Village

I deeply thank Professor Ian Maddieson, who has been a powerful motivating force from the moment I entered graduate school and who has guided me at every stage in the production of this research project. His patience and expert guidance, and his gracious and dignified character have greatly affected my development as a person and as a linguist.

Much thanks to the Linguistics Department of UCLA, the Phonetics Lab and UCLA graduate studies for financial assistance in the way of generous fellowships, TAships, phonetics training grants, and a dissertation fellowship award. Many thanks to Peter Ladefoged,who provided generous technical support in the way of research materials and who also provided the initial funding to begin this project.

To my mother and sister Evonne for the many ways they supported me in the last weeks of this project. A special thanks to my sister Evonne, who helped me pack my boxes for international shipping. I would also like to thank my brothers Wes, Alan, and Keith, for co-parenting Mateu.

Many thanks go to my Kimbark family for their support during the final phases of this project. Your many words of encouragement spurred me on to completion.

There are many others to thank who are unlisted here, but you know who you are.

Abstract

Although clicks are widely considered to be among the most interesting classes of segments, many aspects of their phonetics are little known. This book examines how the three different click types of IsiZulu differ from each other in their production in both spatial and temporal dimensions, and considers the question of how these complex segments are integrated into the stream of speech.

In order to produce a click the tongue must create a sealed cavity along the palate, and rarefaction of the trapped air inside this cavity must occur. Thus, all parts of the tongue are active in click production. Strong claims have been made in the literature that clicks, due to their complex nature, do not coarticulate, but there is little articulatory evidence to support this claim. Coproduction of the dental, palato-alveolar and lateral clicks of IsiZulu was examined using three different techniques for the collection of physiological phonetic information: static palatography and linguography, dynamic palatography, and aerodynamic records. Four native IsiZulu speakers provided controlled data sets of real IsiZulu words in three symmetrical environments, /a__a/, /e__e/ and /o__o/.

Results indicated that the characteristics of the front closure release are markedly different for the three click types. Dental clicks are released through a narrow fricative-like escape channel. The frication of their release is therefore an explicit part of the motor program for their production. The release of lateral clicks is also through a narrow channel whose position is also held for some time. This channel is located far back on the releasing side. In palato-alveolar clicks the location of the front contact slides back considerably before release, creating an abrupt non-affricated release.

The total (dorsal) closure durations of the three click types are very similar, but there are differences in their internal timing patterns. The cavity is sealed later and held for a shorter period in palato-alveolars. Rarefaction in all three click types is achieved by lowering the tongue center, with the greatest proportional change in cavity volume occuring in palato-alveolar clicks and the least with laterals. Palato-alveolar clicks supplement tongue center lowering with some retraction of the location of the dorsal closure.

Quite extensive adaptation of both spatial and timing properties of clicks to the different vowel contexts is observed. For example, the dorsal closure is fronted in front vowel contexts, and before mid vowels the click cavity contracts from its maximum size before the tongue blade/tip release, indicating a rise of the tongue center in preparation for the upcoming mid-vowel. Clicks are indeed complex articulations but they have less resistance to coarticulation than has been previously reported.

CHAPTER 1: INTRODUCTION TO ORAL INGRESSIVES

1.0 Introduction

Clicks are fascinating complex multi-gestural segments. Yet, many aspects of their phonetics are little known. This study examines how the three different click types of IsiZulu differ from each other in their production, in both their spatial and temporal dimensions, and considers the question of coarticulation, or how these complex segments are integrated into the stream of speech.

1.1 Theoretical Framework: Coarticulation

Coarticulation is a phenomenon of spoken language that has been a major research topic for at least a century. Since the late 1800's phoneticians have been aware that, in the flow of speech, segments overlap in time and are not produced as though they are in isolation (Daniloff and Hammarberg 1973, Hardcastle 1981, Farnetani 1997). The term "coarticulation" has been used to refer to the complex interactions involved in multiply-articulated segments as well as the interplay between a single segment and its surrounding segments. In the same vein, "coproduction" has been used to refer to overlapping gestures involved in multiply-articulated segments as well as referring to one of the possible mechanisms by which coarticulation is effected. In this study, we use the term "coproduction" to refer to the internal coordination between different aspects of the tongue involved in the production of the click. Coarticulation is used in this study to refer only to the influence of vowels on any aspect of click production. Vowel-to-vowel coarticulation and the effects of clicks on adjacent vowels are not considered in this study.

Fowler (1993) states that the articulatory organization of multi-gestural segments involves the creation of transient dependencies among articulators. The function of creating these transient dependencies is to reduce the degrees of freedom of the individual movements in such a way that the articulators function together to reach an intended goal. These dependencies are not hardwired but are flexible and able to respond to perturbations in order to reach their intended goal. Fowler cites evidence from speech production studies where one articulator is unexpectedly perturbed and compensatory responses from other articulators are observed (e.g. Shaiman 1989). In natural language, changes in phonetic context are analogous to external perturbations. Click production involves coordinated movements among articulators, and though we expect clicks to be lexically specified for a certain degree of overlap, we should none-the-less expect them to exhibit the same compensatory action as other complex segments.

Though much research has been done on the topic of coarticulation, no one model exists which has been able to capture all the various kinds of coarticulatory behavior known to exist in human language. Two general classes of timing models exist which attempt to capture coarticulatory behavior. These two classes of timing theories may be referred to as extrinsic timing models and intrinsic timing models. Extrinsic timing models view segments as feature bundles that are serially ordered. Coarticulation results from the spreading of features to neighboring segments, modifying the canonical target. An example of a "feature-spreading" model of coarticulation is the model proposed by Daniloff and Hammarberg (1973) and Hammarberg (1976). Henke (1966) is another classic example of a feature-spreading model that incorporates a "look-ahead" mechanism.

Intrinsic timing approaches define a segment by both its spatial and temporal characteristics. Thus, the movement towards a constriction, in addition to the place of constriction, is an inherent specification of a segment. In intrinsic timing approaches to coarticulation, targets are invariant and coarticulation results from the overlapping of these dynamically specified units. Thus, these models are sometimes referred to as "gestural" or "coproduction" models. Browman and Goldstein (1986, 1992), Fowler (1980, 1981), drawing heavily from Öhman's work (1966), represent examples of "coproduction" models of coarticulation. Fowler (1983) provides an adequate review of the empirical evidence supporting "coproduction" models of coarticulation while Fowler (1980) reviews extrinsic timing theories and why they fail as a class in capturing coarticulatory behavior.

This study uses the term gesture to refer to the dynamic, target-intentioned coordinative movements of articulators involved in producing a speech-relevant goal. This definition follows Saltzman and Munhall (1989) and Fowler (1993). According to this definition, a gesture may consist of several articulatory movements, but all movements are not considered to be gestures. Fowler exemplifies the term gesture in the following way:

> Although gestures are composed of articulatory movements, not all movements can be interpreted as gestures or gestural components. For example, when the vertical distance between the upper and lower lips changes due to the active coordination of the lips and jaw to produce a bilabial closure the resultant movement pattern is considered to be a gesture. However, when the interlip distance changes as the passive consequence of the jaw's active participation in

a different gesture (e.g., an alveolar gesture), the bilabial movement pattern
would not be called a gesture. (Fowler 1993, p.172)

From Fowler's example, the active control of articulator movement is the primary standard for deciding whether articulatory movements constitute a gesture. It is in this sense that gestures are considered to be "goal-intentioned" combinations of movement. This study will take a dynamic gestural perspective of speech production but will not offer a specific model of click production in gestural terms.

1.2 Clicks and Coarticulation

Few articulatory studies have addressed the coarticulation of clicks. Early information on clicks and coarticulation mainly consisted of anecdotal descriptions of click production, coming typically from pedagogical instructions directed at students attempting to learn a click language. As a result, the earliest approaches to understanding coarticulation in clicks have been from an "ease-of-articulation" perspective. For example, Doke (1926) explained how to produce a click with a vowel. He wrote:

> The greatest difficulty is experienced when trying to combine the vowel with the click. Usually the click is enunciated, and then a considerable space intervenes before the vowel. This is due to a silent release of the velar part considerably after the plosion of the incomplete click. It must be the aim of the student to eliminate this space altogether, in other words, to make the click complete instantaneously; and then the vowel will follow on normally. Perhaps the following exercise will prove helpful in this connexion...Many students find it easier to learn the nasal forms first, as they find very little difficulty in eliminating the space in nasal clicks; and, having once mastered the method of elimination with nasals, they are able to apply the same principles to the other forms...(p. 131).

Doke's explanation on how to produce a click with a following vowel describes my own experience, in both learning to produce clicks and teaching others how to make them as well. His comments on the easy production of nasalized clicks are particularly insightful in light of aerodynamic data from Sandawe clicks.

Wright, Maddieson, Ladefoged and Sands (1995) analyzed clicks in Sandawe, an East African click language spoken in Tanzania, using nasal and oral airflow measurements. They looked at clicks in both word initial position and intervocalic position. They reported that the voiced clicks are allophonically prenasalized in intervocalic position as a way of allowing continuous voicing during its early formation, when the click cavity is still being created. This mechanism makes the production of a click easier to integrate into the stream of speech because voicing does not have to be discontinued and then resumed again within a very short span of time. As this paper points out:

The study of clicks in word-medial environments provides some new insights into certain aspects of their integration into the flow of speech (Wright et al., 1995, p. 3)

In addition to work done on intervocalic clicks in Sandawe, there is one study that specifically addresses the effect of changes in vocalic context on clicks, namely Sands (1991). Sands used both acoustic and perception data to address the coarticulation of clicks in IsiXhosa. She observed the spectral charateristics of clicks before the five vowels /a, e, i, o, u / in order to determine if there was anticipatory coarticulation of the upcoming vowel on the preceding click. She concluded that there were no consistent differences in the burst characteristics of the clicks that could be attributed to vowel quality, other than that of lip rounding.

Sands also did a perception study to test whether fronting of the dorsal gesture before front vowels occured in clicks as it does for pulmonic velars in many languages (Keating 1993, Ladefoged 1993a). The perception tests included the edited tokens from 7 Xhosa speakers in which the coronal burst was removed, leaving the velar burst in front of the five phonemic vowels. These edited tokens were tested on six phoneticians in a forced choice task to determine if these sounds were velar, uvular or coronal. The results indicated that front vowel environments seemed to yield a uvular interpretation, quite the opposite of the expected results. Sands explained this result by suggesting that listeners were expecting to hear fronted-velars in the front vowel context. When this did not occur, then they interpreted the stimuli as uvular. The other hypothesis, that dissimilation occurs, was disregarded because clicks in the contexts of /i/, heard as uvular, and /a/, heard as velar, had identical F2 values at the onset of the following vowel. If dissimilation had occurred, F2 values should have been lower in the front vowel context, indicating a backer tongue body position. Sands's comments on clicks and coarticulation are as follows:

So there is no perceptual evidence indicating that the type of back click closure varies due to the type of front click closure or to that of a following vowel. (p. 30)

Coarticulatory relations between clicks and vowels are less extensive than those between other consonants and their following vowels. However, this is not surprising, considering that the tongue body cannot so freely vary its position in clicks. Presumably both the front and the back of the tongue have to be in particular positions to produce the consonant. Coarticulation involving the tongue position of vowels must be limited...The only coarticulation effect seen is that due to the anticipation of vowel rounding, since this does not involve a gesture used in the click production. (p.35)

Sands points out that the tongue body is constrained in the production of a click. However, it is precisely this point that has yet to be fully explored using articulatory data.

Traill's (1985) cinematography study emphasized the different articulatory positions that the tongue center achieved at the end of the rarefaction gesture, just prior to the anterior release. For the palatal and dental clicks, the tongue center was in a higher postion relative to the lateral and alveolar clicks, which had relatively low tongue center positions. (The click described as alveolar by Traill is most similar to the IsiZulu palato-alveolar click). Traill's study pointed out that the clicks with high tongue center positions are incompatible with the desired shape needed to produce a low vowel and clicks with low tongue center positions are incompatible with high vowels. This concern was merely noted by Traill, and he does not suggest how these competing demands between click and vowel might be resolved and indeed, this apt observation was a motivating factor in the design of the present study.

One articulatory study that specifically addressed the coarticulatory behavior of a multi-gestural single segment is Maddieson's work on labial-velars. Previous work on labial-velars by Ladefoged (1968) showed that an element of rarefaction may be present in these doubly-articulated sounds, making them somewhat similar to clicks. Maddieson (1993) investigated the doubly-articulated labial-velar stops of Ewe, a West African language, using electromagnetic articulography (EMMA). He demonstrated that, while labial-velar stops require a crucial timing mechanism of the tongue body and a second oral closure that is more forward in the mouth, the dorsal component in labial-velars did indeed coarticulate with the surrounding vocalic environment (see Maddieson and Ladefoged 1989, Ladefoged 1968 for more on labial-velars). He comments:

> This analysis shows that the degree of coarticulatory adjustment of the tongue back
> to surrounding vowels is equal in simple velar stops and labial-velars. (p. 205)

We suppose that clicks also require crucial temporal organization of the multiple gestures involved in their production. This does not necessarily mean that these segments are rigidly articulated and incapable of coarticulating with surrounding segments, or unable to adapt to contextual variation. It is quite possible that these segments may respond as a unit to contextual influences, utilizing slightly different production strategies in order to contend with changes in context (Fowler 1993). Understanding the coordination of a multi-gestural segment and how it responds to contextual variation is important in the overall study of speech production. Since click production involves the use of the tongue body as well as the tongue blade, while vowel production involves a particular tongue body configuration as well, understanding how the tongue body resolves the competing demands between a click and adjacent vowels will likely elucidate the underlying *principles* of multi-movement coordination as it pertains to speech production.

1.3 About IsiZulu

IsiZulu is a Bantu language of the Nguni cluster, closely related to IsiXhosa and SiSwati. IsiZulu has the typical characteristics of a Bantu language, being poly-morphemic and having both a rich system of noun class markers and concordial agreement between nouns and verbs. One outstanding aspect of IsiZulu is the presence of clicks in its phonological inventory. Clicks are typologically rare, found only in languages of Southern Africa and a trio of East African languages (see Sands, Maddieson and Ladefoged 1996; Wright, Maddieson, Ladefoged and Sands 1995; Maddieson, Spajič, Sands and Ladefoged 1993; Tucker, Bryan and Woodburn 1976).

The phonological inventory of IsiZulu contains a diverse inventory of sounds, encompassing segments from all the possible airstream mechanisms, which include pulmonic egressives, glottalic egressives, glottalic ingressives and, of course, oral ingressives or clicks. Table 1 details the IsiZulu phonemic inventory, based in part on Khumalo (1981), Doke and Vilakazi (1958) and Maddieson (1984).

Traditionally, clicks have been described by the place of articulation of the anterior closure as well as the place and manner of release of the back closure along with accompanying laryngeal and velo-pharyngeal settings. These two sets of properties were referred to in the early literature on clicks as the influx and the efflux, respectively (Beach 1938). Current terminology refers to these articulations as the click type and the click accompaniment, respectively. Various click accompaniments combine with any one particular click type to create phonemic distinctions. For example, clicks can be contrastively nasalized, voiced, voiceless aspirated, voiceless unaspirated or glottalized (as well as combinations of these laryngeal and velo-pharyngeal settings); the back closure may be either velar or uvular. In IsiZulu, place of articulation of the back click closure has always been described as velar. Accompaniments in IsiZulu may be voiceless unaspirated, aspirated, breathy-voiced and nasalized. Three click types, discussed below, combine with each of four accompaniments to create twelve contrastive clicks in IsiZulu.

Historically, the place descriptions of the three click types in IsiZulu have been varied. In older place descriptions i.e. Doke (1926), they have been described as dental, palato-alveolar and alveolar lateral. The dental and lateral clicks are invariably affricated while the palato-alveolar click is abruptly released, without affrication. Modern descriptions show some variation from Doke in their place descriptions of IsiZulu clicks. Maddieson (1984) refers to the dental click as alveolar. Taljaard and Snyman (1990) classify them as apico-lamino-dental, apico-palatal palatal (for Doke's palato-alveolar) and apico-alveo-palatal (for Doke's lateral). Ladefoged and Traill (1994) suggest that the classification of clicks has been confusing due to focus on different aspects of the closure and movement of the anterior edge of the front closure. They also state that the articulatory descriptions of click consonants should focus on the point of articulation at the moment of release since the acoustic characteristics of any click type are determined by the location of the closure just prior to release. Analyzing movement during the front closure necessitates the use of dynamic palatography and, in classifying the place of articulation using this technique, we also adhere to the idea that the position of the tongue blade/tip just prior to release is important in determining click type.

This study refers to IsiZulu clicks as dental, palato-alveolar and lateral. Data from Chapters 2 and 3 provide evidence to support this choice. In this study, clicks are referred to using the orthographic symbols of IsiZulu. Specifically, /c/, /q/ and /x/, are substituted for the IPA symbols k |, k !, k ‖, respectively. Note that the use of the velar stop, representing the back closure, is used as a written convention, and represents a general back closure. That is, place of articulation should not be interpreted as strictly velar. Data from this study strongly suggest that the back closure is more dynamic than originally thought. Sands (1991) and Miller *et al* (2007) suggest that the click release is uvular in other click languages.

Table 1: Phonological Inventory of IsiZulu

clicks:

k‖	k‖	k!
k‖^h	k‖^h	k!^{h}
g‖	g‖	g!
ŋ‖	ŋ‖	ŋ!

Stops:

p	t		k
p^h	t^h		k^h
b̤			
ɓ			

nasals:

m	n		ɲ	ŋ

affricates:

tʃ'	ʤ	kɬ'

fricatives:

f	s	ɬ	ʃ		h
v	z	ɮ			ɦ

liquids:

l
r

glides

j	w

vowels

i	u
e	o
a	

 This study investigates the articulation of only the voiceless unaspirated clicks, i.e those in the first row of Table 1, as produced in the symmetrical vowel contexts of /a__a/, /e__e/ and /o__o/.

We now turn to the description of general aspects of click production, as the understanding of the production of IsiZulu clicks will obviously be enhanced by considering what is known about click production in other languages.

1.4 Basic Click Production

Click consonants in general have been characterized by acoustic data (Kagaya 1978, Sands 1991, Jakobson 1968, Jessen 2002, Nakagawa 1996, Miller-Ockhuizen 2003), aerodynamic data (Ladefoged and Traill 1984, 1994; Wright, Maddieson, Ladefoged and Sands 1995, Nakagawa 1995), static palatography and linguography (Doke 1926, Sands, Maddieson and Ladefoged 1993, Nakagawa 2006, Sands et al 2007), perception studies (Sands 1991, Traill 1994) and x-ray cinematography (Traill 1985). Acoustic data has provided invaluable information on the acoustic characteristics of the click bursts while aerodynamic data has elucidated details on the timing of various click accompaniments using primarily pharyngeal pressure and oral and nasal airflow data. Prior to the present study, no empirical aerodynamic data on the intraoral cavity has been available. Kagaya (1978) estimated the intraoral pressure of !Xóõ clicks based on Traill (1985). Static palatography and linguography have provided information on the tongue blade/tip articulations as well as place of articulation. But little attention has been devoted to understanding the basic rarefaction mechanism or the spatio-temporal organization of the dorsal and coronal gestures, their internal organization as well as how the segment as a whole adapts to changes in phonetic context.

Clicks are indeed stop consonants and should be considered to have the same structure as pulmonic stops, namely a "shutting" period, a closure period, and a release as well (Abercrombie 1967, Johnson 1997). Given that clicks are complex stops these phases are more complicated. Figure 1 depicts the steps in click production, based in part on Ladefoged (1993a) and Ladefoged and Maddieson (1996). In general, we know that clicks are made by creating a chamber in the mouth between the front portion of the tongue and the back of the tongue. Both a portion of the back of the tongue and the tongue blade/tip make contact with the palate, shown in Step 1. The sides of the tongue also touch along the sides of the roof of the mouth, leaving a small area in the center where the tongue does not make any contact with the palate[1]. This initial phase of click production—cavity formation—is referred to in this study as the "tongue dorsum lead" phase. Next, there is a decrease in linguopalatal contact, increasing the volume inside the sealed cavity, thereby rarefying the trapped air, as shown in Step 2. We refer to this stage of click production as the "overlap" phase. When the front of the tongue releases contact from the palate, a popping or clicking sound occurs due to the influx of atmospheric air, as depicted in Step 3. Finally the tongue dorsum is released, as illustrated in Step 4. Steps 3 and 4 together depict what we refer to as the "tongue dorsum lag" phase of click production.

---

[1] In the case of bilabial clicks, the primary front closure is made by lip compression as in a "kissing" gesture. IsiZulu does not have bilabial clicks as part of its phonemic inventory.

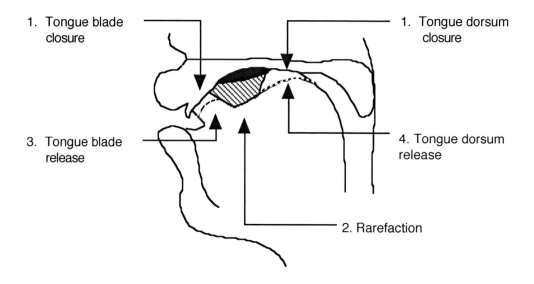

Figure 1: Basic mechanism used in click production. The black area depicts the cavity formed when the initial closures are made, while the striped lines show the cavity just prior to the anterior release. (Figure 1 is based on Ladefoged and Maddieson 1996).

This description of click production does not specify the order in which the dorsal and front closures are formed. Ladefoged (p.c. 1995) depicted them as occurring simultaneously as their order was unknown to him. Essential details of the rarefaction mechanism are also sketchy. This description also implies that all click types are produced using the exact same mechanism. (It is also apparent from Figure 1 that we must consider the tongue blade/tip, the tongue dorsum and the tongue center as separate articulators). The releases must follow in the order as described since, if the dorsal closure were released first, the sound created would be muffled by the front closure, preventing much of the acoustic energy from radiating out of the mouth.

We will now discuss some of the previous work on click production, focusing on issues relating to rarefaction and the coordination of the tongue blade/tip and tongue dorsum articulations.

1.5 Dynamic Articulatory Studies

There has been one major dynamic articulatory study on clicks, namely Traill's x-ray cineradiology study, which has provided some insight into the details of the internal organization of the various click types. Traill's (1985) cinematography study on clicks is essentially the only comprehensive dynamic study of clicks to date. !Xóõ is a Khoisan language which has five click types referred to as bilabial, dental, alveolar, lateral and palatal. Traill's (1985) !Xóõ x-rays showed that the front margin of the click cavity was not static during the closure portion of the consonant. This movement was especially observable for the palatal click, but for all click types there was a change in the position of the anterior edge of the cavity. Traill's study provided the first indication that click production was more dynamic than previously assumed.

Two electropalatographic studies have been done on clicks. Both of these studies were done by Roux—one on IsiXhosa (1993) and the other being a pilot study on IsiZulu (p.c.1995). Roux's (p.c. 1995) electropalatography observations of IsiZulu clicks describe distinctive dynamic movements of the anterior closure for the dental, palato-alveolar and lateral clicks. Roux describes the place of the anterior closure of dental clicks as extremely variable. The palato-alveolar and lateral clicks are described by Roux as having distinct movement from the alveo-palatal region to the dental and then back to the alveo-palatal region. Though the movement patterns described by Roux and Traill differ, the results from both Roux's EPG data and Traill's x-ray data provide evidence that the articulations of clicks are not static during the closure. More recently, Miller *et al* (2007), Miller (2008) and Miller *et al* (2009) have provided ultrasound data on click cavity formation, as well as data on differences in tongue body constriction of different click types, and differences in the posterior place of articulation. These dynamic articulatory studies, while yielding much new insight into the intricacies of click production, also highlight the need for more dynamic articulatory studies on this complex segment type.

1.6 Static Palatography and Linguography

Most studies on click production did not collect linguographic data showing the tongue blade/tip postures. Typically the tongue blade/tip postures have been inferred from the shape of the palatogram. For example, claims that !Xũ has a retroflex click (e.g. Doke 1925) or that the alveolar click in !Xóõ has a retroflex variant (Ladefoged and Traill 1994, see also Ladefoged and Maddieson 1996) have never been supported by linguographic data. Traill's (1985) x-ray cinematography study of !Xóõ clicks made strong inferences about the tongue blade/tip postures based on cine x-rays. He combined the linguographic data with cine x-rays from the same speakers. He showed that the two laminal clicks—the dental and palatal—had the smallest cavity area while the lateral and alveolar clicks, which had thinner, more apical-like contact patterns, had larger cavity areas. Traill concluded from these results that the click cavity area is correlated with the type of tongue blade articulation used, not with the place of articulation, which he showed was variable, especially in the case of the lateral clicks. Traill ultimately concluded that the apical/laminal distinction, rather than place of articulation, is most important in characterizing the click types, especially for click languages that have dental, alveolar, palatal and lateral click types. This study re-evaluates this claim based on articulatory data from IsiZulu. It should be noted that this study only cnsiders IsiZulu and the apical/laminal distinction may be relevant in languages with a greater number of click contrasts.

1.7 Order of the closures, Order of the releases

At the present, strong conclusive evidence does not exist which has verified the order of the closures. Doke (1923) made x-rays of IsiZulu clicks in order to confirm the presense of a velar closure. He fashioned a thin lead chain which could be placed on the center of the tongue and down the throat of the subject. X-rays of the production of clicks could then be made. Doke viewed the production of clicks during the x-ray session and concluded that there is indeed a velar closure and it is formed after the tongue blade/tip closure was made. Though he observed the x-ray production of clicks in real time, observing the closures in this way is not the most reliable method of verifying their order because it is difficult to follow the rapid closure movements with the naked eye. Roux's dynamic palatography study of IsiZulu clicks disagreed with Doke's conclusion. Roux concluded that the dorsal closure preceeds the coronal closure. Traill's x-ray cinematography study did not capture separate frames showing the dorsal and coronal closures. However, acoustic records from Traill (1993) on IsiZulu show that F2 and F3 converge at the onset of the click closure, consistent with a velar closure. (His records also show that, at the dorsal release, F2 and F3 are no longer converged. He concludes that the back click closure may be modified during the course of the closure).

Note that in click production, the tongue blade release must precede the dorsal release in order for the click sound to radiate out of the mouth. However, the order of the closures is not crucial in the same way, though the order of the closures may be important in planning for the release gesture. Clearly, more needs to be learned about the coordination of the gestures internal to the various click types.

1.8 Rarefaction Mechanism

Clicks are stop consonants that are produced using an oral ingressive airstream mechanism, often referred to as the velaric airstream mechanism. The term "velaric" was principally used in reference to the tongue dorsum, as dorsal retraction was considered to be the initiator of movement of air inside the oral cavity. Abercrombie (1967), following Beach (1938) and Catford (1939), states that the tongue dorsum is pulled back along the palate to create an oral ingressive sound. Abercrombie's claim that rarefaction was accomplished by retraction of the tongue dorsum was based on his knowledge of the mechanism that smokers use to inhale smoke from a cigarette into their mouth. His claim is that smokers retract the tongue dorsum in order to inhale warm smoke into the mouth, where it cools before being sucked into the lungs by a pulmonic ingressive airstream mechanism. Abercrombie does not cite references or show data to support either the claim made about clicks or smokers.

Current descriptions (i.e. Traill 1985) of the rarefaction mechanism used in click production suggest that the center of the tongue is lowered to produce rarefaction; tongue dorsum retraction does not play a role in rarefaction, at least not in !Xoõ clicks. Other descriptions of click consonants found in dictionaries or phonetic textbooks often suggest that one or the other, (or both) of these rarefaction mechanisms is involved in click production (e.g. Catford 1977).

1.9 Overview of the Study

The complex overlapping articulatory movements involved in click production warrants the use of several different experimental techniques. This study used electropalatography or dynamic palatography (EPG), static palatography (SPG), linguography and aerodynamic data. Acoustic data was used to determining timing information as well. These techniques were used in combination to offset some of their inherent individual weaknesses apparent in each of the techniques when used alone. EPG offers an excellent opportunity to view time-sensitive data on linguopalatal contact during the closure portion of the consonant while static palatography, linguography and pressure and airflow measurements provide reliable bases for inferring the nature of some aspects of click articulations that cannot be observed by EPG alone. While all three techniques offer a unique perspective on the articulation of this complex segment type when used separately, the true import of this study is the multi-dimensional perspective that the techniques provide when used in combination.

This book is organized as follows: Chapter 2 presents the static palatographic and linguographic results. Chapter 3 presents EPG data, while Chapter 4 compares simple pulmonic consonants with their counterpart gestures in clicks. Chapter 5 discusses the results of the aerodynamic data. Each of these chapters describes in detail the corpus, methodology and measurements specific to that particular technique. Chapter 6 discusses the inferences that may be drawn when the confluence of all data types is brought to bear on the issues under consideration, namely the coproduction and coarticulation of this complex segment type.

CHAPTER 2: STATIC PALATOGRAPHY AND LINGUOGRAPHY

2.0 Introduction

Static palatography (SPG) is an older but still common technique used to collect information about contact patterns of the tongue as it touches the palate (Abercrombie 1957, Ladefoged 1957, 1997, Dart 1991); this technique has been used extensively in the study of coronal articulations. With respect to click consonants, it has been the main technique used in obtaining reliable articulatory data. Static palatography is a method that allows the researcher to obtain an imprint of the contact made on the upper palate and teeth by the tongue. This type of imprint is referred to as a palatogram. An imprint of the tongue's contact with the upper palate and teeth, referred to as a linguogram, is also useful to obtain. This latter technique is referred to as linguography. Static palatography and linguography complement each other and, in fact, inferences with respect to tongue blade articulation based solely on static palatograms can be misleading (Dart 1991). Static palatography and linguography were used in this study on click consonants as supplementary techniques to further aid in the interpretation of dynamic palatography, as well as to provide an added dimension of interpretive power in the investigation of this complex segment type.

Unlike dynamic palatography, which shows the tongue's varying contact with the palate over an entire utterance (at ten millisecond intervals), static palatography depicts a time-smear of the entire contact of a single consonantal gesture on the upper palate. That is, the observed contact pattern on the palate cannot be assigned to any single time point during the course of the utterance. Static palatography does, however, provide more precise boundaries for the contact area than electropalatography since the data are not quantized into discrete electrode positions. This advantage of SPG over EPG is not a trivial one, as shall be discussed in greater detail later in this work. Electrode placement on the EPG pseudopalate is rarely symmetrical and varies in density across articulatory regions of the palate. As a result, interpreting EPG contact patterns (with respect to place of articulation) can be misleading without reference to more precise articulatory boundaries such as those obtained from static palatography.

2.1 Methodology

2.1.1 Speakers

Data for this study was collected from four native IsiZulu speakers, two male and two female. The speakers in this study are referred to as Speakers GV, NT, NK and KK. The two male speakers, GV and NT, both grew up in the Kingdom of Swaziland, a small land-locked country (about the size of Rhode Island) which is bordered on the north, south and west by South Africa and on the east by Mozambique. Both GV and NT were raised in the Shiselweni region of Southern Swaziland, which borders Zululand in South Africa. As a result of Shiselweni's proximity to Zululand, many Swazis from this region speak fluent Zulu. In addition to IsiZulu being spoken in the community in this particular region of Swaziland, IsiZulu was also taught as a class in primary and secondary schools in Swaziland until 1972, when SiSwati was introduced (English was still the medium of instruction in all other classes). Speaker GV, who was in his forties at the time of the recording, studied IsiZulu from primary school through college. Speaker NT, who was in his early thirties at the time of the recording, studied IsiZulu through standard six (seventh grade), until SiSwati replaced IsiZulu as a language requirement. Both speakers have taught IsiZulu at the university level in the United States.

NK and KK, the female speakers, are both first language IsiZulu speakers who grew up in Springs near Johannesburg, South Africa. Speakers NK and KK both speak fluent SeSotho and some Afrikaans. Both of these speakers were in their twenties when the data for this study was recorded.

All four speakers in this study were educated at UCLA and speak fluent English. Despite their language diversity and their long stints in the United States, all have maintained their native IsiZulu pronunciation and have the full range of expected distinctions among the click consonants of IsiZulu.

2.1.2 Corpus

Table 2 lists the corpus of test utterances for this portion of the study. The test utterances consisted of the three voiceless unaspirated dental, palato-alveolar and lateral clicks in the symmetrical vowel contexts of /a/, /e/ and /o/, uttered as citation forms. These utterances represent real IsiZulu words except in two instances, marked by an asterisk in Table 2. Appendix A lists the test utterances and their morphemic composition. The corpus of words used here closely resembles the test utterances used in the EPG and aerodynamic parts of the study, with one exception, discussed below.

Table 2: Test utterances used in SPG and linguographic data collection. Test utterances consisted of the three click types—dental, palato-alveolar and lateral—in symmetrical vowel contexts of /a/, /e/ and /o/, uttered in isolation.

Click type⇒ Vowel ⇓	Dental	Palato-alveolar	Lateral
/a/	ab<u>ac</u>aba	ab<u>aq</u>apha	ab<u>ax</u>aba
/e/	bab<u>ec</u>eba	bab<u>eq</u>eba*	bab<u>ex</u>eba*
/o/	bab<u>oc</u>oba	bab<u>oq</u>oba	bab<u>ox</u>ova

Note that the first syllable of words in the /a/ vowel context consists only of the vowel /a/. The initial syllable /be-/ that is included in the EPG and aerodynamic test utterances for this particular vowel context could not be used here because the linguopalatal contact for /e/ is greater than the contact for /a/. Since static palatograms represent a time-smear of the overall contact of an utterance, then contact of the mid vowel /e/ from the first syllable would overshadow contact made from the test sequence located in the following syllable. Note that test utterances in the /e/ and /o/ contexts have /a/, a more open vowel, as the surrounding vocalic environment[2]. All other consonants besides the click are bilabial or labiodental and therefore have no palate contact.

2.1.3 Data Collection Procedure

In order to make a palatogram, a 1:1 mixture of charcoal and olive oil was used to coat the surface of the tongue (Dart 1991). Once the tongue was thoroughly covered with the mixture, the subject was instructed to relax and say the target word once, after which a dental mirror, warmed to prevent it from becoming foggy, was inserted into the mouth. The reflection of the upper palate was observed and filmed using a video camcorder. Corresponding linguograms were collected by painting the surface of the palate and teeth, having the subject say the target word once, and then filming the tongue, with a video camcorder, as it protrudes out of the mouth. One palatogram and one linguogram were made for each of these nine test utterances

---

[2]For dynamic palatography this does not present a problem because one can scroll through the utterance as it occurred at ten millisecond intervals, thereby distinguishing contact made from the 'e' in the first syllable from the test sequence /...aca.../ beginning in the second syllable.

for Speakers GV, NT, NK and KK. Two linguograms for each of these test utterances were made for Speaker GV in order to look at variation in tongue blade/tip articulations.

Video clips of the linguograms and palatograms were captured using a PC equipped with a video-capture card and Adobe Premiere 4.0, a software program which permits the extraction of individual frames from a video clip. Individual frames of palatograms and linguograms were converted to Macintosh files. The linguograms were printed out and filed in a notebook for later qualitative assessment. Quantitative analysis was done on the palatograms using Image 1.61, which reports distances and areas in terms of pixels. Section 2.2 describes the qualitative analysis of the linguograms while the remaining part of this chapter is devoted to the static palatographic analysis.

2.2 Linguographic Analysis

Given the fluid-like nature of the tongue, it is not possible to do quantitative analysis on linguograms. Still qualitative generalizations of linguographic data have proven useful in previous studies on coronal articulations. Qualitative analysis of linguograms involves classifying tongue blade articulations into discrete categories in order to make meaningful generalizations about the tongue blade usage of the segments under examination. These types of tongue blade classifications are more powerful when combined with palatographic data.

It should be emphasized that, like palatograms, information obtained in linguograms represents a time-smear of the total area of tongue/palate contact for an entire utterance so information on the time sequence of tongue blade/tip contact with the palate cannot be determined from this type of data.

2.2.1 Classification of Linguograms

In order to obtain reliable and indisputably objective classifications of the linguographic data, two phoneticians, IM and VA, at the UCLA Phonetics Lab, were asked to classify the data. One phonetician is a Professor of Linguistics at UCLA while the other is a Ph.D. Candidate in Linguistics who is working on palatographic and linguographic data of an aboriginal Australian language, and therefore experienced in classifying such data. The classifications were done "blind", that is, the classifiers did not know which utterance was represented in any token, nor how any tokens had been classified by the other judge. Classification of the linguograms was also done by the author, KT, though the classification was not blind as it was for IM and VA.

Linguograms of the nine test utterances for the four subjects were printed and randomized. Each linguogram was labeled with a number in order to disguise the identity of the test utterance. IM and VA were given four sets of linguograms, one set for each speaker, and asked to classify the tongue blade articulations and to add parenthetical notes if they deemed necessary in order to further clarify any important distinctions they observed. Comparison of the classifications done by IM and VA showed good agreement. Both phoneticians used a three-way classification system—apical, apico-laminal and laminal— but added parenthetical notes to further distinguish one class or another. For example, VA made a distinction between 'broad apico-laminals' and 'narrow apico-laminals' while IM made a distinction among laminal articulations, noting them as either 'laminal', 'front laminal' or 'broad laminal'.

Although the terminology adopted by IM and VA differed, some clear correspondences were evident. For every case in which VA classified a linguogram as 'narrow apico-laminal', IM classified the same linguogram as 'apical'. In addition, every linguogram classified as 'broad apico-laminal' by VA was classified simply as 'apico-laminal' by IM. For IM, tongue tip articulations with a more narrow contact were considered apicals while the apico-laminal designation for IM was reserved for tongue tip articulations with a much broader contact. What is evident here is that both IM and VA agree that the tongue *tip* was used in these articulations and disagreed only on whether or not the contact was broad enough to also be considered laminal. Given these obvious classification correspondences, linguograms classified as 'narrow apico-laminals' by VA have been re-categorized as 'apicals', thereby reserving the category 'apico-laminal' for tongue tip articulations whose broader contact pattern is considered to have unequivocally extended onto the tongue blade as well.

Both IM and VA differentiated laminals into several types using parenthetical notations. VA referred to laminals as either 'narrow', 'medium' or 'wide' while IM used notations of either 'front' or 'broad'. Whenever IM classified a laminal as 'broad' VA classified it as 'wide'. This classification correspondence occurred only in Speakers KK, NK and NT. KT classified all 'broad' or 'wide' laminals of IM and VA as 'apico-laminals', as these articulations were quite a bit more anterior than some of the other more obviously laminal articulations observed in this data. For Speaker GV, IM classified his laminals in several instances as 'front' while VA noted these laminals as 'narrow' in two instances and 'medium' in one instance. In one of these three instances, KT classified a 'front, narrow laminal' as an apical.

The apparent discrepancies in categorizing the linguograms are understandable given the variety of width types found among the laminals in this set of data. For three speakers, what IM and VA term 'broad' or 'wide' laminals are much more anterior than contact seen in other linguograms that are more obviously categorized as laminal given the posteriority of the front edge of the tongue blade/tip contact. The broadness of these laminals coupled with their more anterior articulation makes them difficult to distinguish from apico-laminals. (Note that KT classified these broad, anterior laminals as 'apico-laminals'). These broad more anterior laminals were considered to form a separate class which will be referred to as *Front -Laminal*, in order to distinguish them from more 'posterior' or 'true' laminals as well as the apico-laminals. The *Front -Laminal* category would also include 'narrow' Front-*Laminals* such as those noted by IM for Speaker GV.

Once these correspondences in nomenclature were resolved and more clearly defined categories set up, there were only 6 linguograms out of the 45 where IM, VA and KT showed discrepancies in classification. Two of these cases were from Speaker KK, whose linguograms were often times challenging to interpret due to smearing effects resulting from difficulties during data collection due to her very tight mouth opening. The final classification of these six linguograms was decided upon by consensus from IM, VA and KT. In addition, the author reviewed the linguograms in all six cases to make sure that the consensus reached was a reasonable conclusion and was consistent with the general classification rules laid out for the bulk of the linguograms. The final linguographic designations are summarized in Table 3. Prototypes of the four tongue blade/tip designations used in this study—*True Laminal, Front-Laminal, Apico-Laminal and Apical* —are depicted in Figures 2, 3, 4, and 5.

Dart (1991, 1998) used a similar system for classifying the coronal articulations of English and French. Based on the range of data found in her study, four categories of linguograms were defined for stop consonants. These classifications were designated as *apical, upper apical, apico-laminal* and *laminal*. Dart defines *apical* articulations as those having a very thin contact on the apex and along the rim of the sides of the tongue, as opposed to *upper apical* articulations, which have more contact on the upper surface of the apex and sides of the tongue. *Apico-laminal* articulations were designated as those linguograms which had contact on both the apex and the blade of the tongue, while linguograms classified as *laminal* had contact only on the blade of the tongue, with the apex remaining contact-free.

Table 3: Summary of Tongue Blade/Tip Classification

Laminal —	Two types of laminal articulations were defined—*True-Laminal* and *Front-Laminal*. In *True-Laminals*, the apex of the tongue is indisputably passive as the wipe-off medium from the palate onto the tongue is quite posterior to the apex, while *Front -Laminals* had contact medium very *near* the apex as well as behind it.
Apical —	Apical articulations are defined as those articulations which had contact on the vertical portion and/or upper surface of the apex and sides of the tongue.
Apico-laminal—	Apico-laminal articulations were designated as those linguograms which had contact on both the apex and the blade of the tongue. Typically tongue blade contact for this designation was quite broad.

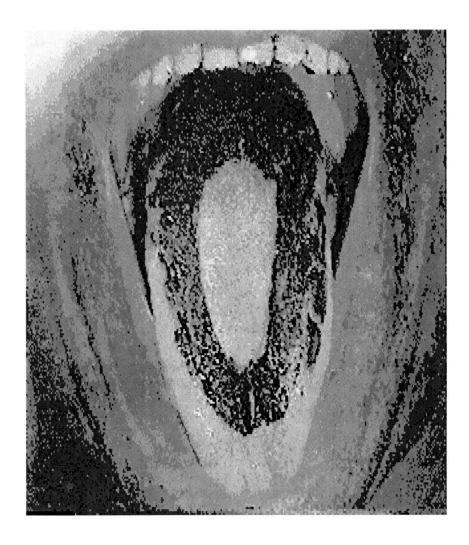

Figure 2: Linguogram of the lateral click, in the symmetrical vowel context of /e/ produced by Speaker GV, exemplifying the True-Laminal category.

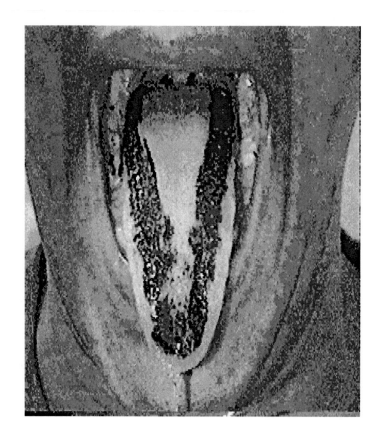

Figure 3: Linguogram of the lateral click, in the symmetrical vowel context of /e/, produced by Speaker NK, exemplifying the Front-Laminal category.

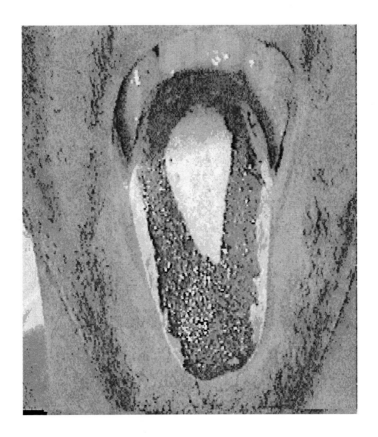

Figure 4: Linguogram of the lateral click in the symmetrical vowel context of /o/, produced by Speaker NT, exemplifying the Apico-Laminal category

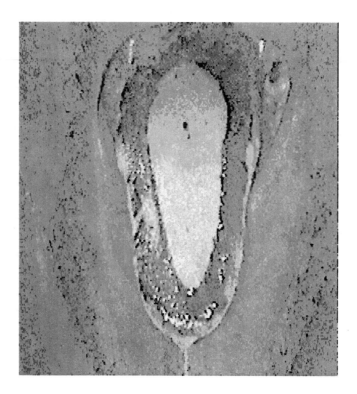

Figure 5: Linguogram of the palato-alveolar click in the symmetrical vowel context of /e/, produced by Speaker NT, exemplifying the Apical category

        In our study on clicks there were no linguograms that were strictly 'apical' according to Dart's definition. Accordingly, Dart's *upper-apicals* are simply referred to as *Apicals* in this study. Our system further classifies the laminals into two distinct types—*True-Laminal* (denoted simply as *Laminal* in Dart's study) and *Front-Laminal*. Based on previous linguographic analysis of click consonants (i.e. Hadza, see Sands, Maddieson and Ladefoged 1996) and Dart's systematic classification system of coronal articulations for French and English, the tongue blade/tip classification system adopted here seems adequate for describing the range of data encountered in this study.

2.2.2 Linguographic Results

Table 4 depicts the results of the linguographic data for the nine test utterances for all four subjects. For Speaker GV, recall that there were two linguograms for each test utterance while the other speakers had only one linguogram per test utterance. Linguograms for the palato-alveolar click type were unequivocally categorized as *Apical* for all speakers in all vowel environments. The dental clicks were predominately classified as *True-Laminal*, and the lateral clicks predominately as *Front-Laminal*. The three click types are therefore seen to be distinct in the part of the tongue used for the front closure. The dental and lateral clicks displayed some vowel and speaker-dependent variation, which will now be discussed in detail.

Table 4: Linguographic Results, tallied by Speaker

Click ⇓	Apical	Front-laminal	Apico-laminal	True laminal
aca				KK,NK NT,GV,GV
ece		KK		NK NT,GV,GV
oco		GV (n) NT	KK,NK	GV
aqa	KK,NK NT,GV,GV			
eqe	KK,NK NT,GV,GV			
oqo	KK,NK NT,GV,GV			
axa	KK	NK NT	GV	GV
exe		KK NK NT GV(n)		GV
oxo	GV	NK GV(n)	KK NT	

Vowel effects

One outstanding observation that should be noted with respect to the effect of vowel context on tongue blade/tip articulation is that the dental click in the context of /o/ showed a more extreme tongue tip articulation when compared to the /a/ and /e/ vowel contexts.

Speakers NK, NT and GV had true-laminal articulations in the /a/ and /e/ contexts but in the context of /o/ used either front-laminal (GV and NT) or apico-laminal (KK and NK) articulations. A true-laminal articulation might be enhanced by a more forward raised tongue body position, such as occurs in the /e/ context. In the /o/ context the more retracted tongue body might result in a more retracted tongue blade as well, making it difficult for the tongue tip to be placed against the lower incisors, as is typical for laminal articulations. Under such conditions, the tongue tip may be placed along the surface of the palate itself, thereby creating a more retracted apical-like laminal articulation in this vowel context. Note once again that, in support of this claim of vowel effect on this click type, there were no instances of purely apical articulations. This fact could be interpreted in the following manner: dental clicks are primarily laminal articulations, with the use of the tongue tip being incidental, and resulting only from the need to resolve the competing demands placed on the tongue body for both click production and vowel production. The resolution of these competing demands would be to make a more forward 'true-laminal' articulation in the context of a front vowel, but a more retracted mixed-laminal articulation (either *front- or apico-laminal*) in the context of a back vowel. This analysis makes the prediction that the place of articulation of the tongue blade for the dental click in the context of /e/ is more anterior than in the context of /o/. This prediction is confirmed by the static palatographic data, presented in Section 2.6.

Interspeaker Variation

Speaker **KK** used a true-laminal articulation in the context of /a/ for the dental click. For the mid vowels, she used similar articulations, having a front-laminal articulation for the /e/ context and an apico-laminal articulation in the context of /o/. The lateral click showed a similar pattern for the mid vowels, being front-laminal in the context of /e/ but apico-laminal in the context of /o/. In the context of /a/, for the lateral click, this speaker used an apical articulation.

Speaker **NK** used a true-laminal articulation in the vowel contexts of /a/ and /e/ for the dental click. In the context of /o/ for this same click type she used an apico-laminal articulation. For the lateral click, NK used a front-laminal articulation in all vowel contexts.

Speaker **NT** used a true laminal articulation in the vowel contexts of /a/ and /e/ for the dental click, but used a front-laminal articulation in the /o/ vowel context for this same click type. He used a front-laminal articulation for the lateral click in the contexts of /a/ and /e/ but used an apico-laminal articulation in the context of /o/ for this same click.

Speaker **GV** used a fairly consistent true-laminal articulation for the dental click across all vowel contexts, except for one instance in the /o/ context, where he used a narrow front-laminal articulation. (Narrow front-laminal articulations are parenthetically noted as 'n' in Table 4. This type of front-laminal articulation was only observed for Speaker GV). Speaker GV displayed a great deal of variation in the production of the lateral click. In the context of /a/, he used both a true-laminal as well as an apico-laminal articulation. In the context of /e/, both a true-laminal and a narrow front-laminal articulation were used. In the context of /o/ he used more apical-like articulations, using, in one instance, a pure apical articulation and in the other instance, a narrow front-laminal articulation, closely resembling an apical articulation. The lateral click type shows quite a bit of intraspeaker (or within-speaker) variation based on the data for this one speaker. This is perhaps because the tongue blade/tip is not crucial in the production of the primary release, which is lateral, not central. Perhaps the main requirement of the tongue blade/tip in the production of the lateral click is for it to remain in a raised position until the lateral release has been effected.

Pooled Data

Table 5 depicts the pooled data across speakers and vowels for the three click types. Percentages were calculated for three tongue blade categories—*Apical, True-Laminal, and Mixed-Laminal*, which combined the *Front-Laminal* and *Apico-Laminal* designations, since these categories had some articulatory similarity. The pooled results show that the dental click was produced with a laminal articulation in 66% of the utterances. The remaining 33% of the articulations were produced with either a front-laminal articulation (20%) or an apico-laminal articulation (13%). As there were no instances of pure apical articulations for this click type, we adopt the strong conclusion that this click type is typically laminal in nature. The occurrence of the mixed-laminals for this click type can be viewed as a function of vowel context and was previously discussed at the beginning of this section.

The palato-alveolar click type showed absolutely no variation in tongue blade usage, and all three phoneticians who classified the linguograms were very confident in designating this click type as *Apical*. The lateral click showed the most variation of the three click types, showing both between speakers as well as within speaker variation. 73.3% of the linguograms for this click type were of the mixed-laminal variety, that is, either front-laminal, which comprised the greatest percentage at 53.3%, or of the apico-laminal variety, at 20%. Pure apicals and laminals were rarely produced for this click type. The overall conclusion that may be drawn from this data is that, while both the lateral and dental click types can be considered *Laminal*, the lateral click is more apical-like than the dental click. Whereas the majority of the articulations for the dental click cluster in the *True-Laminal* category, the lateral click clusters more in the *Front-Laminal* category, which by definition, is more apical-like than the *True-Laminal* category.

Table 5: Pooled Linguographic Results (%)

Ling category⟹ Click type⟱	Apical	Mixed-Laminal (apico- & front)	True-Laminal
Dental /c/	0	33.3%	**66.6%**
Palato-alveolar /q/	**100%**	0	0
Lateral /x/	13.3%	**73.3%**	13.3%

2.3 Static Palatographic Analysis

The upper palate is a non-malleable hard tissue structure which lends itself to much more reliable quantitative measurement when compared to soft tissue structures such as the tongue.

2.3.1 Defining reference lines

Although it would be possible to do any analysis in terms of relative pixel values, this study makes an effort to convert pixels to real-life centimeter values based on a stone-cast of the speaker's upper palate. In order to make the conversion from pixels to centimeters, a line drawn on the palatogram must be measured in both pixels and centimeters. In this way, any particular measurement made on a palatogram may be converted from pixels into centimeters. Figure 6 depicts a palatogram of the lateral click as uttered by Speaker GV while Figure 7 shows the scanned image of the stone casting of the upper palate for the same speaker. The contact area is shown in black for all palatograms. The same reference lines were drawn on both the palatogram and the stone casting for the purpose of making quantitative measurements. The purpose of these reference lines was to obtain a conversion factor in pixels/cm, which would allow any measured pixel value to be converted to real-life dimensions, expressed in centimeters.

Three reference lines were needed on the palatograms to obtain conversion factors that adjust for the distortion of the image in the mirror in both the horizontal and vertical dimensions. One reference line was drawn at the base of the front incisors and was referred to as 'reference line t'. This reference line served as an anchor point from which other reference lines and measurements could be fixed. A horizontal reference line, referred to as 'reference line x', was drawn from molar to molar. The endpoints of this line were always fixed between two (pre)molars at the gumline. The exact placement of reference line x between any two molars was dependent on the landmarks that were visible on a particular palatogram.

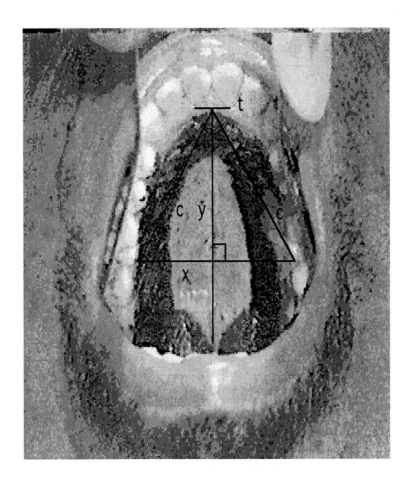

Figure 6: Sample palatogram from Speaker GV of the lateral click in the /a/ vowel environment. Reference lines have been drawn at the base of the teeth (t), horizontally from molar to molar (x). Reference line y was drawn vertically from 't' to 'x'.

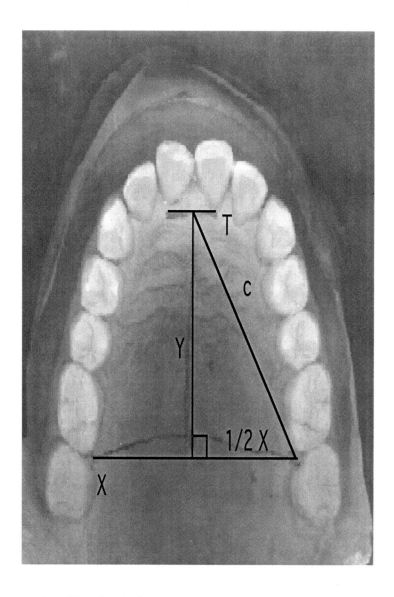

Figure 7: Stone casting of Speaker GV's upper palate, with reference lines, labeled in capital letters, corresponding to those in the palatogram in Figure 6.

In some cases the teeth were visible on only one side of the palatogram; in these cases any calculations were made using 1/2x as the reference distance. The vertical reference line, referred to as 'reference line y', was a mid-sagittal line drawn from reference line 't' to the intersection point with reference line x. Pixel values were obtained for reference lines x and y using Image 1.61 for the Macintosh. Reference lines x and y were drawn and measured (in pixels) separately for each palatogram in order to adjust for the varying angle of the mirror in the mouth, distortion of the image in the mirror, subject's neck angle and other factors, as these are known to differ from palatogram to palatogram. Figure 7 represents a stone casting of speaker GV's mouth. Note that the anchor points of the reference lines on this stone casting are the same as those on the palatogram in Figure 6. Centimeter measurements for reference line X were made in the 2-dimensional plane directly from the stone casting using a fine-adjustable compass. The points of the compass needles could easily rest between the crevice of two molars along the gumline. Anchoring the needles of the compass in this way ensured an accurate measurement of reference line X in the 2-dimensional plane. When 1/2x is the reference line on the palatogram, corresponding centimeter values were determined by measuring the entire horizontal line in centimeters and then dividing by 2, the assumption being that the palates of these speakers are symmetrical[3].

Determining reference line Y in centimeters proved to be more difficult because, although the leg of the compass at the anterior edge of the reference line was able to rest on the casting at the base of the front incisors, the intersection point of reference lines X and Y, at the posterior end of the palate, had no such natural landmark on which to rest the compass needle. In order to circumvent this problem, reference line Y was calculated using the Pythagorean theorem.

Reference line C, the hypotenuse of the right triangle, with reference lines X and Y as its legs, could be accurately determined by placing one compass needle on the base of the teeth, on reference line 't' while the other needle was placed along the gumline in between the appropriate (pre)molars. Reference line Y in centimeters was then calculated using Equation 1:

Equation 1: $\mathbf{Y(cm)} = \sqrt{C^2 - (\tfrac{1}{2}X)^2}$, where C and X were measured values from the stone casting[4].

---

[3]Direct measurement of 1/2X on the stone casting was never used due to the error involved in making a 2-dimensional measurement where one needle of the compass could not be reliably balanced on an articulatory landmark.

[4]Note that only half of reference line x constitutes a leg of the right triangle.

2.3.2 Conversion factors

Reference lines x and y on the palatogram, measured in pixels, now have corresponding centimeter values, such that any measured value in pixels in either the horizontal or vertical dimension may be converted to centimeters by dividing the number of pixels by the centimeter value obtained for the same distance on the stone casting.

For example, for the palatogram in Figure 6, as spoken by Speaker GV, x=170 pixels, y = 251 pixels and, from the stone casting X=4.8 cm, C=4.0 cm. Y was calculated as previously described using Equation 1 in Section 2.3.1, and was 3.2 cm. Calculations for the conversion factors for this **particular palatogram were:**

$$\frac{x}{X} = \frac{170 \text{ pixels}}{3.2 \text{ cm}} = 53 \frac{\text{pixels}}{\text{cm}} = \mathbf{X^c} \quad \text{and} \quad \frac{y}{Y} = \frac{251 \text{ pixels}}{4.8 \text{ cm}} = 52 \frac{\text{pixels}}{\text{cm}} = \mathbf{Y^c}$$

For simplicity, we may refer to the horizontal conversion factor as X^c and the vertical one as Y^c. **Using these** conversion factors, any measured pixel value in the horizontal or vertical dimension can be converted to centimeters. The "vertical" dimension is taken to be vertical on the photographs as shown here in the plane of the teeth (i.e. between reference lines 'T' and 'X'), not vertical in the sense of from the plane of the teeth to the roof of the mouth. It should be emphasized that these conversion factors must be determined independently for each palatogram, as various factors in the data collection procedure result in different distortions of the mirrored images under investigation.

2.4 Measurements

Seven measurements were made on each palatogram—four on the internal click cavity, two on the tongue blade articulation and one on the tongue dorsum articulation. Measurements were made in pixels and then converted to centimeters using the appropriate conversion factor. Dimensions in pixels were obtained by using tools from NIH Image 1.61 for the Macintosh. Using this software, distances in pixels could be measured by drawing lines, and an area could be measured by encircling a space, no matter how irregularly shaped, using the polygon tool.

2.4.1 Tongue blade measurements

<u>Tongue Blade Position</u> (TBL_p): measures the position of the front edge of the tongue blade closure relative to reference line t, as shown by the black vertical line in Figure 8. Articulations beginning posterior to the reference line were recorded as positive values while tongue blade articulations beginning anterior to the reference line were assigned negative values. Pixel values were converted to centimeters in the 2-dimensional plane using the length conversion factor Y^c .

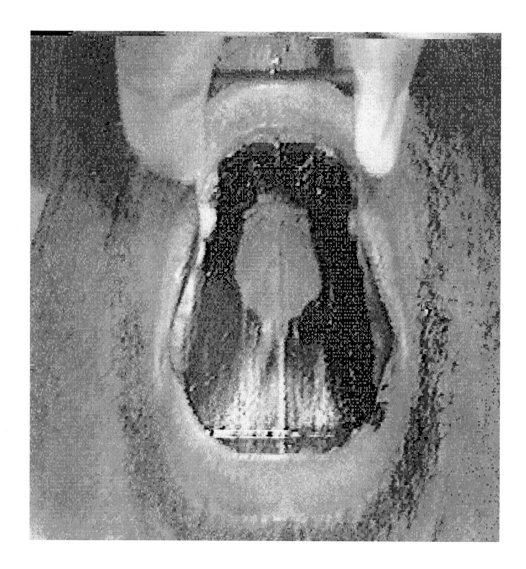

Figure 8: Palatogram of the dental click in the symmetrical vowel context of /a/, produced by Speaker GV, depicting the Tongue blade position measurement.

<u>Tongue Blade Width</u> (TBL$_W$): The width of contact of the tongue blade closure was measured in the midsagittal plane, depicted by the black vertical line in Figure 9. Pixel values were converted to centimeter values in the 2-dimensional plane using the length conversion factor Y^c . Measurements for the tongue blade articulations were adjusted for distance in the 3-dimensional plane in order to account for the sharp curvature of the sloping alveolar ridge and palatal area. The actual distance along the palate surface in the anterior portion of the plane between any two points might differ considerably from its 2-dimensional distance. For

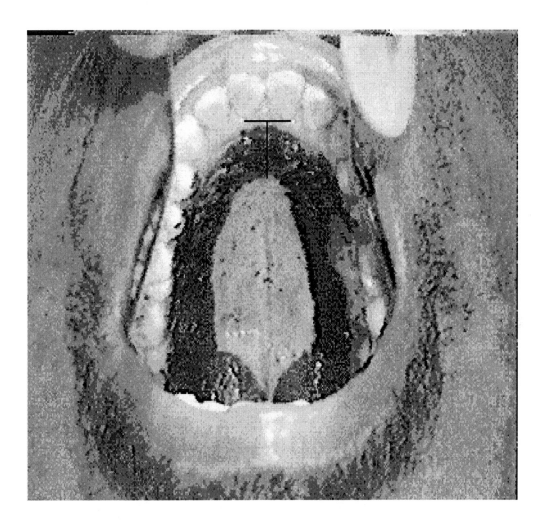

Figure 9: Palatogram of the lateral click in the symmetrical vowel context of /a/, produced by Speaker GV, depicting the Tongue blade width measurement.

this reason, the 3-dimensional distance of the vertical reference line was measured on the stone casting using a compass, and its percentage difference from the 2-dimensional measurement was calculated. The distance values for TBL_p and TBL_w were then scaled up by the same percentage factor. These adjusted values represent more accurate distances of position and width along the actual palate surface.

2.4.2 Tongue dorsum measurements

Tongue Dorsum Place (TD$_p$): The position of the tongue dorsum was measured by taking the distance along the midsagittal axis from reference line t to the back edge of the click cavity. TD$_p$ is depicted by the black vertical line in Figure 10. Pixel values were converted to centimeters by using the length conversion factor Y^c.

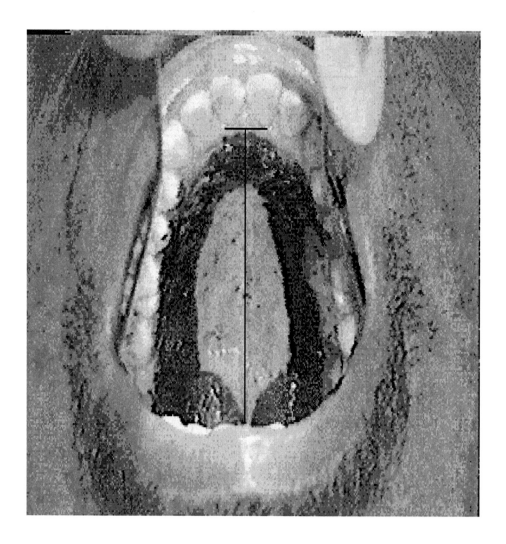

Figure 10: Palatogram of the lateral click in the symmetrical vowel context of /a/, produced by Speaker GV, depicting the Tongue dorsum place measurement (TDp).

2.4.3 Cavity measurements

Cavity Area (CA)

Figure 11 depicts the cavity area, outlined in black, as well as cavity length and cavity width, for the lateral click of speaker GV. With respect to cavity area, measured values were in pixels but were converted to centimeter values by taking the average of the horizontal and vertical conversion factors, previously calculated in Section 2.3.2, squaring this average, and then using this squared average to convert from pixels to centimeters. Steps 1-3 outline the calculations involved in converting CA from pixels to square centimeters, followed by a sample calculation for the palatogram in Figure 6.

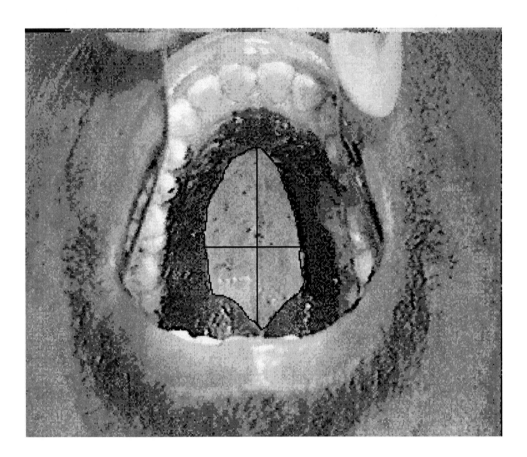

Figure 11: Palatogram of the lateral click in the symmetrical vowel context of /a/, produced by Speaker GV, depicting the measures of cavity area (enclosed space), cavity length (vertical line) and cavity width (horizontal line).

Step 1: calculation of linear conversion factor

$$\frac{(X^c \text{ pixels/cm} + Y^c \text{ pixels/cm})}{2} = \text{Avg. of two conversion factors, termed}$$

A^c (pixels/cm)

Step 2: convert to area factor

$$\text{squared average} = (A^c)^2 = \frac{\text{pixels}^2}{\text{cm}^2} = \text{area conversion factor}$$

Step 3: conversion to cm^2

measured area in pixels^2, as obtained from the palatogram using the polygon tool, was converted to centimeters by multiplying it by the inverse of the area conversion factor.

$$\frac{CA}{(A^c)^2} = \frac{\text{pixels}^2}{\text{pixels}^2/\text{cm}^2} = \text{pixels}^2 \times \frac{\text{cm}^2}{\text{pixels}^2} = \text{area (cm}^2)$$

Sample calculation:

1. $53\dfrac{\text{pixels}}{\text{cm}} = X^c$ and $52\dfrac{\text{pixels}}{\text{cm}} = Y^c$ so, $A^c = \dfrac{53 + 52}{2} = 52.5\dfrac{\text{pixels}}{\text{cm}}$

2. Area conversion factor: $(A^c)^2 = 2756.25\dfrac{\text{pixels}^2}{\text{cm}^2}$

3. The measured cavity area from the palatogram in Figure 2 was 19,842 pixels^2.

$$19{,}842 \text{ pixels}^2 \times \frac{1}{2756.25}\frac{\text{cm}^2}{\text{pixels}^2} = \text{Cavity Area (CA)} = 7.2 \text{ cm}^2$$

<u>Total Cavity Width</u> (CW): Cavity width was measured at it widest, as shown by the horizontal line in Figure 11. Pixel values were converted to centimeter values by using the calibration conversion factor X^c.

<u>Total Cavity Length</u> (CL): Cavity length was measured in the midsagittal plane from the back edge of the tongue blade contact to the beginning of tongue dorsum contact in the posterior region of the palate. Pixel values were converted to centimeters using the conversion factor Y^c.

<u>Cavity Width Difference</u> (CW_d): Asymmetry in cavity width was calculated by measuring the widths of the left and right sides of the palate, divided along the midsagittal plane. The pixel value for CW_d was obtained by subtracting the right side from the left side. This difference in cavity widths was then converted from pixels to centimeters using the width calibration conversion factor X^c. In addition, we look at the absolute value of this measurement, termed Absolute Cavity Width difference, or $ABCW_d$. This alternative way of analyzing this measurement puts the focus only on the magnitude of the asymmetry, regardless of which side had more contact.

2.5 Statistical Analysis

A two-way Analysis of Variance was performed on each of the eight dependent variables— TBL_p, TBL_w, TD_p, CA, CW, CL, CW_d and $ABCW_d$— with SPEAKER and CLICK as the independent factors. Note that this analysis conflates vowel environment across click types.

In order to analyze the effect of vowel context on these same dependent variables, a separate two-way ANOVA was performed with CLICK and VOWEL as the main independent variables. The emphasis here will be to report significant main effects of VOWEL as well as significant interactions and interesting trends of the interaction between CLICK and VOWEL. Note that the speaker effect could not be analyzed here because only one repetition exists for each click in the various vowel contexts. Post hoc analysis was performed using Fisher's PLSD, at a 95% confidence level. All significant results and marginally significant trends are reported.

In addition to Analysis of Variance tests, simple linear regression analysis was done on measurements of the cavity dimensions. In separate analyses, the independent variables of Cavity Length (CL) and Cavity Width (CW) were regressed against Cavity Area (CA) in order to determine the strength their relationship. Significant and marginally significant results are reported.

2.6 Palatographic Results

Figures 12, 13 and 14, respectively, depict typical articulations of the dental, palato-alveolar and lateral clicks. The dental and lateral clicks are depicted in the /e/ context while the palato-alveolar click is shown in the /a/ context. Note that for the dental click, depicted in Figure 12, contact on the palate from the tongue blade/tip extends from nearly the top of the upper incisors onto the alveolar ridge. This articulation can accurately be referred to as *dental*

Figure 12: Palatogram of the dental click in the symmetrical vowel context of /e/, as produced by Speaker GV

Figure 13 depicts what has been referred to as the 'palato-alveolar' click in IsiZulu. The contact pattern for this click type extends from the alveolar to the palato-alveolar region. Note that the contact is quite broad for what we now know to be an apical articulation, and the fading out of contact medium along the mid-sagittal axis produces a smearing effect, indicative of movement. EPG data presented in Chapter 3 discusses the tongue blade/tip articulations for all the clicks in more detail.

Figure 13: Palatogram of the palato-alveolar click in the symmetrical vowel context of /a/, as produced by Speaker NT

Figure 14 depicts the lateral click. It is essential to note that this click type seems to be the most variable click with respect to its tongue blade articulation, as described in the linguographic results. Palatographic data also shows that the tongue blade position of this click type varies across speakers. For this speaker, the front edge of the closure was typically near the base of the upper incisors and extended beyond the alveolar ridge. Also note that for this speaker, the right side has more contact on the palate than the left side.

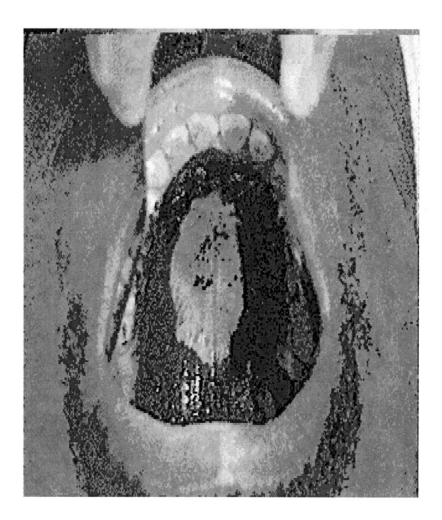

Figure 14: Palatogram of the lateral click in the symmetrical vowel context of /e/, as produced by Speaker GV.

2.6.1 Position and Width of Front Contact

Measurements of the position (TBLp) of the front edge of the closure as well as the width of contact (TBLw) along the midsagittal axis were made in order to quantify these obvious qualitative differences among the click types. Figure 15 depicts the mean tongue blade positions for the three click types for four speakers, pooled across vowel contexts. Recall that zero on the vertical axis corresponds to reference line t, located at the base of the upper incisors. Negative values indicate contact on the teeth, while positive numbers indicate contact posterior to the base of the teeth, near and posterior to the alveolar ridge.

All speakers show negative TBLp values for the dental click while the palato-alveolar click type shows positive values for all speakers. Tongue blade place for the lateral click is variable. It rests very near the baseline for Speaker GV, patterns more like the dental click for Speakers NT and NK, while KK's lateral click patterns like the palato-alveolar click, using a more retracted tongue blade/tip position for the lateral click than the other three speakers.

A two-way ANOVA with the main effects of SPEAKER and CLICK on TBLp was performed. There was a significant main effect of CLICK on TBLp $[F(2, 24) = 3.3, p<.01]$. Post-hoc analysis showed that all three clicks types were significantly different from each other at $p<.01$. The interaction between SPEAKER and CLICK was not at all significant. Except in the case of the lateral click for Speaker KK, all speakers behaved similarly.

The results also showed a highly significant main effect of SPEAKER $[F(3,24 = 8.4), p<.01]$ of TBLp. This effect of SPEAKER on TBLp primarily results from two sources of variation. Firstly, there are speaker differences in the overall magnitude of contact arising perhaps from differences in palate morphology among the various speakers. Secondly, the lateral click for Speaker KK patterns in the opposite direction from the other three speakers, resulting in a significantly different mean.

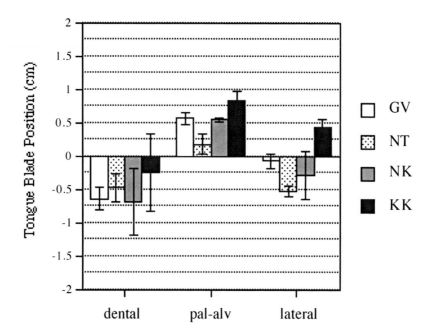

Figure 15: Mean results of the tongue blade position measurement (TBLp) for the dental, palato-alveolar and lateral click types, pooled across vowel contexts, for Speakers GV, NT, NK and KK.

Figure 16 depicts the results of the TBL_W measurements for the various click types, pooled across speakers and vowel contexts. The dental click has the greatest contact width, and the width of the palato-alveolar click is greater than the lateral click. However these differences are not large enough to be significant. A two-way ANOVA with the main independent variables of SPEAKER and CLICK on TBL_W yielded a non-significant effect for both CLICK and SPEAKER. The interaction between CLICK and SPEAKER on TBLw was not significant either. Based on the linguographic results for the three click types, we might expect the palato-alveolar click, which we now know to be apical for all speakers, to have the thinnest contact compared to the lamino-dentals or the laterals, which were mainly *Front-Laminal* or *Apico-Laminal* and typically had broad tongue blade contact. However, this expectation was not born out. The absence of this expected difference is quite important and is fully addressed in the EPG data.

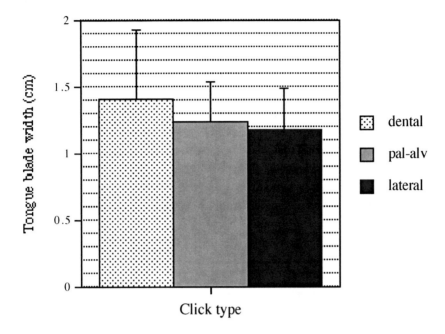

Figure 16: Mean results of the tongue blade width measurement (TBLw) for the dental, palato-alveolar and lateral clicks, pooled across speakers and vowel contexts.

Tongue blade/tip: Vowel Effects

In order to determine the effect of vowel context on the position and width of the front contact on the various click types, a two-factor ANOVA was done with the main independent variables of CLICK and VOWEL on both TBLp and TBLw. The main effect of VOWEL on TBLp was not significant nor was the interaction between CLICK and VOWEL for this same variable, but post-hoc analysis showed a marginal effect for the comparison of /e/ and /o/, at p<.1, when all click types were pooled. Figure 17 depicts the mean front contact position for the three click types in the vowel contexts of /a/, /e/ and /o/. Note that for both the palato-alveolar and lateral click types the means in the three vowel contexts are similar. However, the dental click shows greater differences among the vowel contexts than the other click types. The marginal significance observed in the pooled data results mainly from the dental click. In order to assess the dental click separately from the other click types, a separate one-factor ANOVA was done on TBLp, with VOWEL as the main independent variable. The main effect of VOWEL on TBLp for the dental click was not significant. However, post-hoc analysis showed that the comparison of /e/ and /o/ was significant, at p<.05. No other vowel comparisons were significant. The results indicate that the mid vowels affect the tongue blade/tip articulation for the dental click. The more positive TBLp value in the context of /o/

indicates that the tongue blade/tip articulation may be more posterior when compared to its position in the front vowel context.

The two-way ANOVA with the independent variables of CLICK and VOWEL on width of the front contact (TBLw) was also done. There was a marginally significant main effect of VOWEL on TBLw [$F(2, 27) = 2.98$), $p<.07$]. Post-hoc analysis showed that the comparison of /e/ and /o/ was significant, with $p<.03$. Figure 18 depicts TBLw for the dental, palato-alveolar and lateral click types in the vowel contexts of /a/, /e/ and /o/. Note that, just as for TBLp, the marginal significance obtained from the post-hoc comparison in the two-way ANOVA analysis is due to the behavior of the dental click. Note that the width of contact for the dental click in the context of /e/ is much greater than in the context of /o/. The palato-alveolar and lateral click types have similar means for all three vowel contexts.

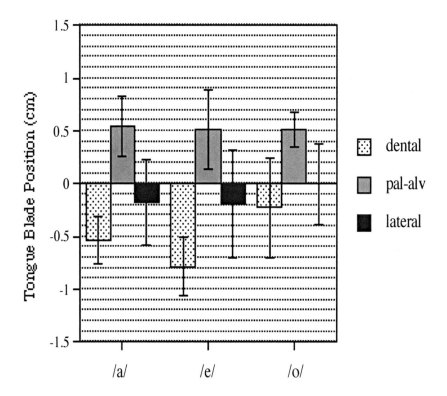

Figure 17: Mean results of the tongue blade position measurement (TBLp) for the dental, palato-alveolar and lateral click types in the vowel contexts of /a/, /e/ and /o/, pooled across speakers.

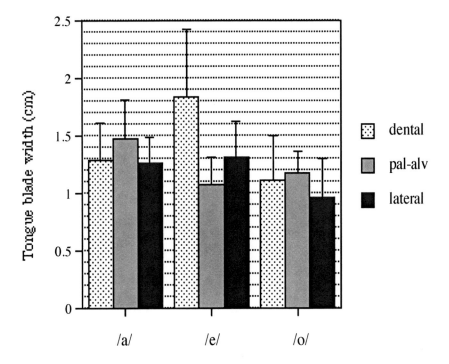

Figure 18: Mean results of the tongue blade width measurement (TBLw) for the dental, palato-alveolar and lateral click types in the vowel contexts of /a/, /e/ and /o/, pooled across speakers.

In order to assess TBLw more thoroughly for the dental click, a one-way ANOVA on this variable was done for the dental click, with VOWEL as the main independent variable. The main effect of VOWEL on this variable was not significant but post-hoc analysis showed that the comparison of /e/ and /o/ was significant, at p<.05. For the dental click, it appears that the tongue blade articulation is greater in width in the context of /e/ than /o/.

2.6.2 Tongue Dorsum Results

The position of the front edge of the contact of the tongue dorsum (TDp) was measured along the midsagittal plane, from reference line 't', located at the base of the upper incisors, to the back edge of the click cavity. Figure 19 presents the results for the TDp for the three click types, pooled across speakers and vowel contexts, while Figure 20 depicts the mean results for the same measure for the three click types for each of four speakers, pooled across vowel contexts.

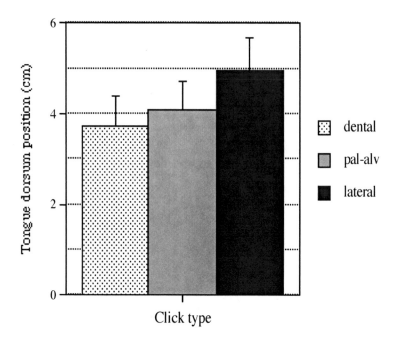

Figure 19: Mean results of the tongue dorsum position measurement (TDp) for the dental, palato-alveolar and lateral click types for data pooled across speakers and vowel contexts.

The results indicate that the dental click has the most anterior tongue dorsum, followed by the palato-alveolar click while the lateral click has the most posterior tongue dorsum position of the three click types. A two-factor ANOVA with CLICK and SPEAKER as the main independent variables was performed. A highly significant main effect of CLICK was observed [$F(2,24)=4.74$, $p<.001$]. Post-hoc comparisons of the dental and palato-alveolar clicks with the lateral click were highly significant at $p<.001$, while the comparison of the dental and palato-alveolar clicks was only marginally significant, at $p<.08$. A significant main effect of SPEAKER was also observed [$F(3,24)=4.89$, $p<.01$]. Post-hoc comparisons showed that Speaker KK differed significantly from NK and NT at $p<.01$ but differed only marginally when compared to Speaker GV, at $p<.09$. These speaker differences probably arise from differences in palate dimensions, as Speaker KK has the smallest palate, while the other three speakers' palates are comparable in size.

The interaction between SPEAKER and CLICK yielded a significant main effect on TDp [$F(6,24)=4.852$, $p<.01$]. Speaker NT deviates from the pooled pattern shown in Figure 19 in that the tongue dorsum position of the lateral click, at 4.6 cm, is intermediate between the dental and palato-alveolar click types, with TDp values at 4.3 cm and 4.7 cm, respectively.

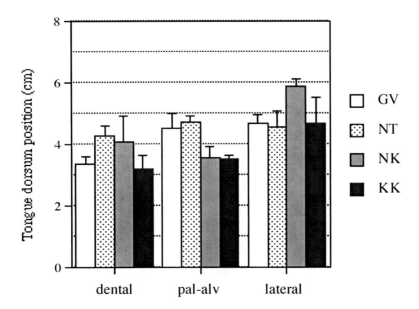

Figure 20: Mean results of the tongue dorsum position measurement (TDp) for the dental, palato-alveolar and lateral click types for Speakers GV, NT, NK and KK, pooled across vowel contexts.

Tongue Dorsum: Vowel effects

Given that the TDp measurement was taken from a fixed point on the anterior part of the palate, the changes in measured distances are the result of differences in position of the back edge of the click cavity, resulting from the tongue dorsum gesture. The effect of vowel context on the tongue dorsum gesture can be assessed from this measurement. The expectation is that front vowels should have a more forward tongue dorsum position, or a shorter TDp value than back vowels, which should have more posterior tongue dorsum positions. Figure 21 depicts the TDp measurements for the dental, palato-alveolar and lateral click types for the vowel contexts of /a/, /e/ and /o/. Note that in every vowel context the lateral click is more posterior than the dental and palato-alveolar clicks. In the contexts of /a/ and /o/ the dental click has the shortest TDp. These results reflect the magnitude differences inherent in the click types, as was observed for the pooled data in Figure 19. In the contexts of /a/ and /o/ a similar pattern is observed. The dental click has the smallest TDp value, the lateral click the largest, with the palato-alveolar click being intermediate between the two. However, the dental click noticeably deviates from this pattern in the context of /e/, with a mean equivalent to the palato-alveolar click. Also note that the palato-alveolar and lateral clicks have their smallest means in the context of /e/ while the dental click has its greatest

TDp value in the context of /e/. A two-factor ANOVA with CLICK and VOWEL as the main independent variables yielded no significant main effect of VOWEL on TDp. However, this result should be noted even though the observed trends are non-significant, given the vowel effects reported for the tongue blade articulation and the tongue blade position for the same click type in exactly the same vowel environment.

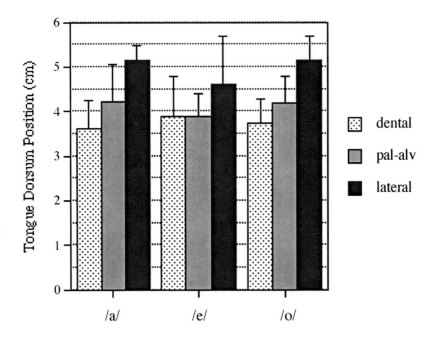

Figure 21: Mean results of the tongue dorsum position measurement (TDp) for the dental, palato-alveolar and lateral click types in the vowel contexts of /a/, /e/ and /o/, pooled across speakers.

2.6.3 Cavity Dimensions

Cavity Length and Width

Figure 22 depicts both the cavity length (CL) and cavity width (CW) results of the dental, palato-alveolar and lateral click types, pooled across speakers and vowels contexts. Note that for CL, the lateral click has the greatest value, the palato-alveolar the smallest with the dental intermediate between the two. A two-way ANOVA was performed with SPEAKER and CLICK as the main independent variables on CL. There was a significant main effect of CLICK on CL [F(2, 24)=27.37, p<..001]. Post hoc analysis showed that the lateral click differed significantly from both the dental and palato-alveolar clicks at p< .001. The dental and palato-alveolar clicks were only marginally differentiated, at p< .06. There was also a significant main effect of CLICK on CW [F(2, 24)=45.23, p< .001]. Post hoc comparisons on CW showed that the dental click differed significantly from both the palato-alveolar and lateral clicks. Comparison of the latter two clicks showed the difference was only marginally significant, at p< .07.

Individual speaker differences with respect to cavity length and cavity width are depicted in Figure 23 and Figure 24, respectively. Figure 23 shows the cavity length results of the three click types for each speaker. The general trend that is expected, as previously exemplified in Figure 22, is for the lateral click to have the greatest CL, the palato-alveolar the smallest CL and the dental click to be slightly greater than the palato-alveolar click.

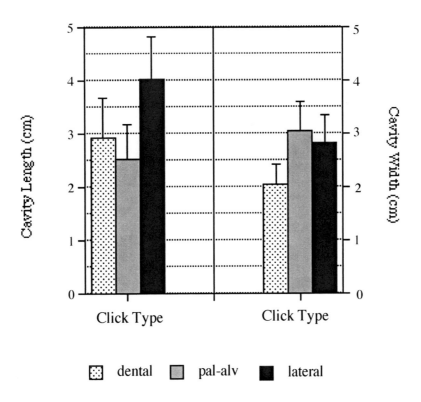

Figure 22: Mean results of the Cavity Length and Cavity Width measures for the dental, palato-alveolar and lateral click types, pooled across speakers and vowel contexts.

Speakers NT, NK and KK follow this pattern while GV shows a different pattern. For GV, the palato-alveolar click has a greater mean value for CL than the dental click, deviating from the overall trend observed in the pooled data. The lateral click for GV has greater cavity length than both the dental and palato-alveolar clicks, as for the other speakers.

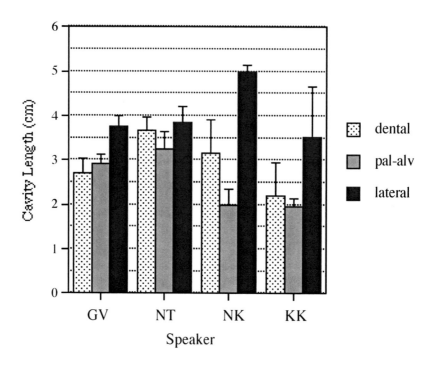

Figure 23: Mean results of the Cavity Length measure for the dental, palato-alveolar and lateral clicks, for Speakers GV, NT, NK and KK, pooled across vowel contexts.

Figure 24 depicts the cavity width of the three click types for each speaker. Note that the general trend observed in the pooled data, shown in Figure 22, is for the dental click to be significantly smaller in width than the palato-alveolar and lateral click types, while the comparison of the palato-alveolar and lateral clicks was only marginally significant. Marginal significance between these two click types is primarily due to Speaker GV, who shows a large difference between the means for the palato-alveolar and lateral click types, while the other speakers have nearly equal means for these click types. For each speaker, the dental click has a smaller CW than both the other click types. For Speakers NT and NK the difference is large enough to be significant while Speakers GV and KK show smaller differences between the dental and lateral clicks.

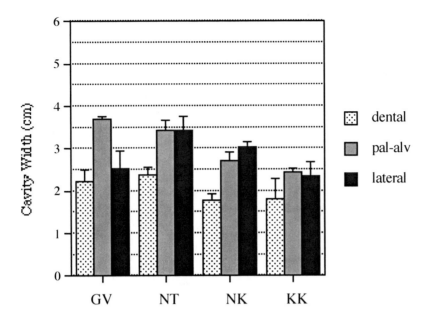

Figure 24: Mean results of the Cavity Width measure for the dental, palato-alveolar and lateral clicks, for Speakers GV, NT, NK and KK, pooled across vowel contexts.

Cavity Area (CA)

Figure 25 depicts the results of the cavity area measurements for the three click types, pooled across vowel contexts and speakers. The dental click had the smallest cavity area at 5.0 cm^2, followed by the palato-alveolar and lateral clicks, at 6.55 cm^2 and 9.23 cm^2, respectively. A two-factor ANOVA with the main independent variables of CLICK and SPEAKER on CA was performed. The results indicate that the click types differ significantly with respect to this variable [F(2, 24)= 30.07, p<.001]. Post hoc analysis showed that the comparisons of /c, x/ and /q, x/ were significant at p<.001, while the comparison of /c, q/ was significant at p<.01. Figure 26 depicts the results for CA for the three click types for all four speakers. A significant main effect of SPEAKER on CA was found [F(3, 24) = 12.19, p<.001]. Post hoc comparisons showed that Speaker KK differed from the other three speakers, having a lower mean CA at 4.77 cm^2 as compared with speakers GV, NK and NT, who had larger cavity areas of 6.9, 7.6 and 8.5 cm^2, respectively. Also note that Speaker GV differed significantly from speaker NT. A highly significant main effect of the interaction between SPEAKER and CLICK was observed [F(6, 24) = 7.08, p<.001] on CA. Speakers NT, NK and KK follow the expected rank order for click types previously exemplified in Figure 25, although NK has a larger than average cavity area for the lateral click. Speaker GV displays a different pattern.

For this speaker, the palato-alveolar click has a larger cavity area than the lateral click. The dental click patterns as expected, having the smallest cavity area.

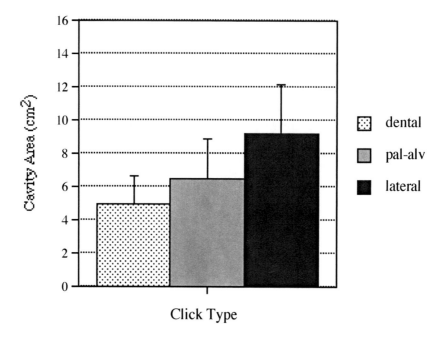

Figure 25: Mean results of the Cavity Area measure for the dental, palato-alveolar and lateral clicks, for data pooled across speakers and vowel contexts.

Relationship between the Cavity Dimensions

In order to determine the strength of the relationship between CW and CL with respect to CA, simple regression was done with CA as the dependent variable. Simple linear regressions were performed separately for cavity length and width, for each click type, pooled across speakers and vowel contexts. Given the need to control for the variations in palate sizes and idiosyncratic speaker strategies, the raw values for cavity length, cavity width and cavity area were converted to percentage values for each speaker. These percentage values were obtained by taking the average of the nine test utterances, and then expressing the raw values of each of the variables as a percentage of this mean. Conversion of raw values for CL, CW and CA to percentages preserves the relationship between the variables and abstracts away from differences in magnitude of the measures that might result from differences in overall palate size and/or differences in individual speaker strategies of certain types.

The results showed primarily weak relationships for nearly all test cases except when CL was regressed against area for the dental click [$F(1,10)=14.55$, $p<.01$]. The R^2 value was

.593. The palato-alveolar click showed nearly equal contributions of length [$F_{(1,10)}=9.68$, p<.02] and width [$F_{(1,10)}=8.9$, p< .02] as regressed against cavity area. However, the relationship in both cases was weak, with R^2 values of .492 and .472 for cavity length and width, respectively. For the lateral click, simple regression of cavity width versus cavity area yielded marginal significance [$F_{(1,10)}=5.19$, p<.05]. The relationship between the variables was extremely weak, with an R^2 value of .342. When cavity length was regressed against cavity area for the lateral click, the result was not even marginally significant. Linear regression analysis on the cavity dimensions shows that, in general, the relationship between either length or width in predicting cavity area for any given click type is weak. This result is somewhat surprising, but given the irregularly shaped areas observed for the click cavities as well as differences in palate morphology, which might affect production strategies for a given speaker, it is none-the-less understandable.

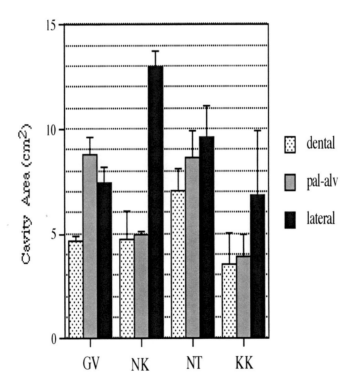

Figure 26: Mean results of the Cavity Area measure for the dental, palato-alveolar and lateral clicks, for Speakers GV, NT, NK and KK, pooled across vowel contexts.

Cavity Dimensions: Vowel Effects

Figures 27 and 28, respectively, depict the results for CW and CL, showing the three click types in the vowel contexts of /a/, /e/ and /o/, pooled across speakers. Note that in the context of /e/, the dental click has a smaller cavity width than in the contexts of either /a/ or /o/. For the palato-alveolar click all three vowel contexts are similar. For the lateral click, the /o/ context has a greater width than in the other vowel contexts.

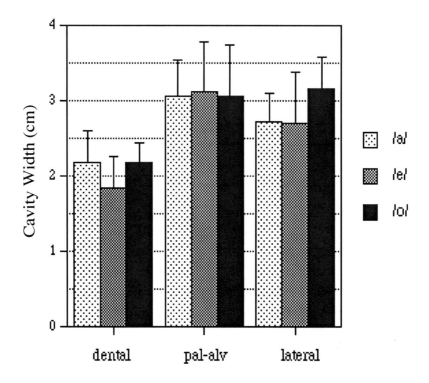

Figure 27: Mean results of the Cavity Width measure for the dental, palato-alveolar and lateral click types in the vowel contexts of /a/, /e/ and /o/, pooled across speakers.

With respect to CL, the lateral click has a shorter cavity length for /e/ when compared to the contexts of /a/ and /o/. The dental clicks have similar length for all vowel contexts. The palato-alveolar click in the context of /a/ has the shortest value for CL, an intermediate value in the context of /e/ and the greatest value in the context of /o/, but the differences are small. A two-way ANOVA with CLICK and VOWEL as the main independent variables was performed on CL and CW. There was a non-significant main effect of vowel on both CL and CW. Interactions between CLICK and VOWEL on CL and CW were not significant either.

However, these results are depicted because they are believed to represent trends in the data that reflect reasonable predictions about how we might expect vowel environment to affect the measures of CW, especially in the case of the dental click, and for CL, especially in the case of the lateral click.

Figure 29 depicts the results of CA for the dental, palato-alveolar and lateral click types in the contexts of /a/, /e/ and /o/, pooled across speakers. The results presented in this graph show that, for each click type, the cavity area is smallest in the /e/ vowel context. A two-way ANOVA with the main independent variables of CLICK and VOWEL on CA was done in order to look at the effect of vowel environment on each click type.

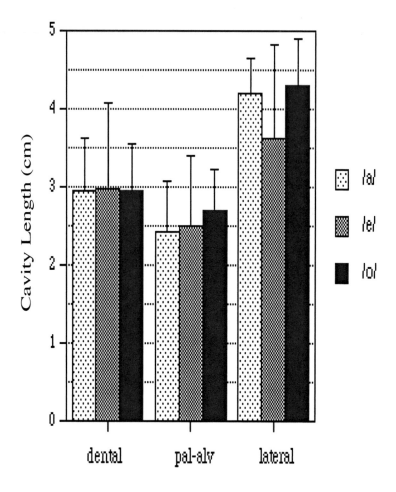

Figure 28: Mean results of the Cavity Length measure for the dental, palato-alveolar and lateral click types in the vowel contexts of /a/, /e/ and /o/, pooled across speakers.

The results yielded a non-significant main effect of VOWEL on CA. However, the observed results, although they are not significant, depict a trend in the expected direction. That is, we might expect mid front vowels to induce more contact on the palate at the lateral margins as well as a more forward raised tongue dorsum position, both of which would effectively reduce the cavity area in comparison to the other vowel contexts. Note that the difference is greatest for the lateral click, which has the largest mean area. In the dental clicks, the difference may be reduced since a minimum area is being approached. The non-significant trends observed here with respect to CL, CW and CA might indeed be significant if the data set were expanded to include more speakers and increased numbers of repetitions for each test utterance.

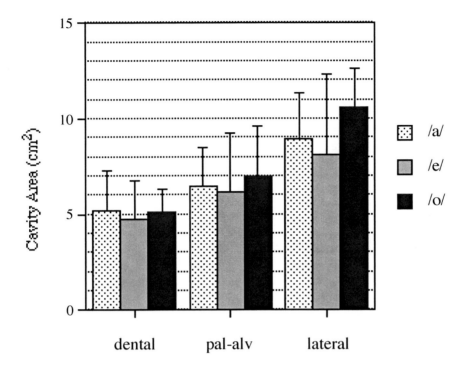

Figure 29: Mean results of the Cavity Area measure for the dental, palato-alveolar and lateral click types in the symmetrical vowel contexts of /a/, /e/ and /o/, pooled across speakers.

2.6.4 Cavity Width Asymmetry

Figure 30 presents the cavity width asymmetry of the three click types for each speaker. Recall that this measurement was calculated by subtracting the cavity width on the right of the median line from that on the left. Positive values indicate a greater cavity width on the left while negative values are indicative of a larger cavity width on the right.In general, the greater the cavity width on a particular side, the less contact there was from the tongue touching the palate and teeth on that side. A two-factor ANOVA of CLICK and SPEAKER on CWD was performed. There was a main effect of SPEAKER on this variable [$F(3,24)=$ 14.6, p<.001]. Speaker GV has a larger mean cavity width on the right for all three click types, Speaker NK has a larger mean on the left for all three click types, while Speakers NT and KK show no consistent pattern across the click types.

Given the large variation observed in the click types for all speakers, the main effect of the interaction between SPEAKER and CLICK was not significant.

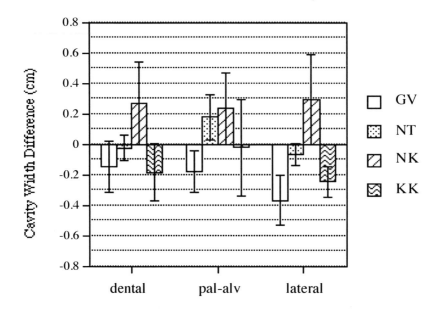

Figure 30: Mean results of the Cavity Width Asymmetry measure for the dental, palato-alveolar and lateral click types for Speakers GV, NT, NK and KK, pooled across vowel contexts.

Absolute Cavity Width Difference (ABCW$_d$): Magnitude Effects

The measure of ABCW$_d$ was used as a way of abstracting away from the preference for left versus right side, and instead shifts the focus to the magnitude of the asymmetrical contact. Figure 31 depicts the ABCW$_d$ results for the dental, palato-alveolar and lateral click types, pooled across vowels. The lateral click has the greatest magnitude followed by the palato-alveolar click and then the dental click. A two-factor ANOVA of CLICK and SPEAKER on ABCW$_d$ showed non-significant differences for the main effects of CLICK and SPEAKER. The interaction of CLICK and SPEAKER was not significant either. Although the click types are not significantly different, the greatest asymmetry for the lateral click is surely related to preparing for the release to one side or the other. Individual speaker exceptions to the general pattern are as follows: The palato-alveolar click for Speaker NT has the greatest ABCW$_d$, while the dental and lateral clicks have nearly equal values for this variable. Speaker NK shows greater magnitude of asymmetrical contact for the dental click than for the palato-alveolar click. Although the main effect of Speaker on ABCW$_d$ was not significant, post hoc analysis showed that, for the comparison of Speakers NT and NK, there was a significant effect at $p < .05$, with NK having the greatest value for this measure, and NT the least. Other speaker comparisons were not significant.

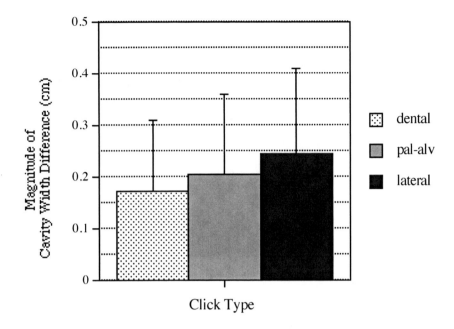

Figure 31: Mean results of the Absolute Cavity Width Asymmetry measure for the dental, palato-alveolar and lateral click types, pooled across speakers and vowel contexts.

Absolute Cavity Width Difference (ABCW$_d$): Vowel Effects

Vowel effects on ABCW$_d$ were assessed using a two-factor ANOVA with CLICK and VOWEL as the main independent variables. The results, depicted in Figure 32, showed a greater magnitude of asymmetry in the context of /e/ than /a/ and /o/. This trend was consistent for all click types. The fronter, higher tongue position of /e/ allows more asymmetry to be registered on the palate. While the main effects of CLICK, VOWEL, as well as their interaction were not significant, post hoc analysis of VOWEL on this variable showed the comparisons of /a, e/ and /o, e/ to be marginally significant, at p<.07 and p<.1, respectively. The comparison of /a, o/ was not at all significant.

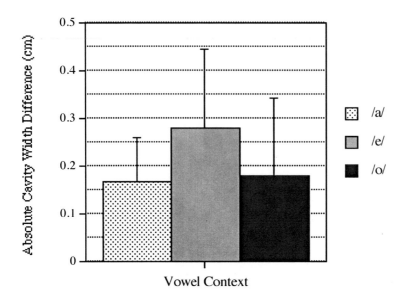

Figure 32: Mean VOWEL results for the Absolute Cavity Width Asymmetry measure, for speaker- and click-pooled data.

2.7 Summary of the Palatographic Results

Figure 33 provides a simple schematic diagram of palatograms for the dental, palato-alveolar and lateral click types based on the palatographic results of pooled data of four measures, namely the cavity width measure, tongue dorsum position measure and the tongue blade/tip width and position measures (that is, the schematic reflects the means across speakers and vowel contexts). The diagrams are idealized in that cavity asymmetry is not illustrated nor is the exact shape of the cavity area shown. The front incisors are represented by the square at the top of each diagram. Reference line 't' is drawn at the base of the front teeth. The relative position of the tongue dorsum is indicated by reference line 'z'. The figure illustrates the difference in the cavity sizes for the various click types, the differences in their lateral contact and the breadth and position of the anterior articulation, as previously discussed. As Figure 33 shows, the position and shape of the cavity show important differences across click type.

2.8 Discussion

This chapter lays the initial groundwork for discussing some important aspects of click consonant articulation. Historically, the articulatory phonetic classification of clicks has been confusing (Ladefoged and Traill 1994 p. 35). So, establishing tongue blade/tip articulation as well as place of articulation facts for a particular set of speakers of a given language becomes extremely critical. Results from this chapter suggest that the variations in tongue blade articulation and tongue blade/tip position are not totally random but vary according to vowel context or for other principled reasons.

Specifically, Traill (1985) and Ladefoged and Traill (1994) put forth the hypothesis that it is the shape of the tongue blade/tip articulator that is the invariant articulatory property in click production while specific place of articulation may be more variable and therefore less important in characterizing the various click types. Results from the static

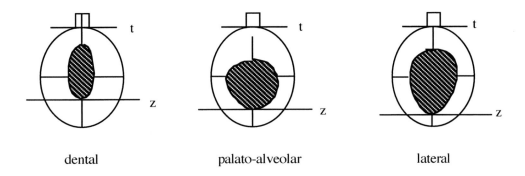

dental   palato-alveolar   lateral

Figure 33: Schematic palatograms for the dental, palato-alveolar and lateral clicks based on the mean results of pooled data for the tongue dorsum position, tongue blade position and tongue blade width and cavity width measures. Contact area is shown in white.

palatographic and linguographic data in this study show that the tongue blade / tip articulations are not invariant.

For example, the lateral click displayed both intraspeaker as well as interspeaker variation with respect to the tongue blade/tip articulation, being classified as apical, mixed-laminal and laminal. The dental click showed variation relating to vowel context, producing mixed-laminals in the /o/ context, while producing true-laminals in the contexts of /a/ and /e/. Only the palato-alveolar click type exhibited invariant tongue tip articulation.

Place results showed some variability, but as a function of either vowel context or specific qualities inherent within the click type that make this variation feasible. While the palato-alveolar click showed very consistent place results, with all speakers showing tongue tip contact posterior to the base of the teeth, place results for the dental click showed vowel dependent effects, with the dental click in the context of /e/ being more fronted and laminal, and in the context of /o/ having a more posterior tongue blade position. The lateral clicks were the most variable of the click types, showing both intraspeaker and interspeaker variation, with the tongue blade/tip articulation extending from the dental to the post-alveolar region. This variation probably results from the unspecified nature of the tongue blade/tip, since for the lateral click, the position of the tongue blade/tip does not characterize the acoustic release. It is the configuration of the lateral margins in forming the release channel that is primary for this particular click type. From this vantage point, it is not surprising that the tongue blade/tip shows the greatest amount of variation for this particular click type.

The apical/laminal distinction is also thought to play an important role in shaping the size of the cavity and therefore in the overall dynamics of click production (Traill 1985). For example, the broad laminal contact of the dental click is thought to create an initially smaller cavity area than the thin apical contact of the palato-alveolar click. The data from this study points out that although the width and position of the tongue blade/tip contact are important delimiters of the cavity space, the cavity area is also defined by the position of the tongue dorsum, the width of contact of the lateral margins, as well as the height of the tongue body. Changes in any of these variables would affect the cavity volume. More specifically, this study showed that differences in the width of the lateral margins for the dental and palato-alveolar clicks are very important, much more so than the apical/laminal distinction. Varying tongue dorsum positions for the three click types and how anterior the front closure is also contribute to cavity size differences. In addition, for the palato-alveolar click, the breadth of the anterior midsagittal contact was more extensive than expected for an apical articulation. Smearing on the palatograms for this click type suggests that there is movement during the closure, presenting an added dimension of complexity to interpreting the role of tongue blade/tip articulations. That is, assessing the effect of static apical contact compared to static laminal contact might be possible, but comparing the effects of *dynamic* apical contact and static laminal contact on the cavity area and overall changes in cavity volume is more difficult, and more information needs to be known before any conclusions can be drawn. The role of the lateral margins and their interaction with other variables that affect cavity volume should not be overlooked when considering rarefaction strategies for the various click types.

The static palatographic and linguographic data support taking as basic the apical nature of the palato-alveolar click, the laminal nature of the dental click and the mixed-laminal nature of the lateral click, keeping in mind the propensity of the tongue blade/tip articulation to vary for this particular click type. These conclusions regarding the tongue blade/tip articulations are specific to IsiZulu and not necessarily generalizable to all click languages. However, data collected here from IsiZulu clicks highlight the fact that there is a certain amount of variation in both tongue blade/tip usage as well as place of articulation; both of these factors are important in click production. Furthermore, much of this observed variation is not random but results from specific contextual variation or inherent segmental properties that make variation acceptable.

In the next chapter, the dynamic properties of click articulation will be examined using EPG, the results of which will be interpreted in the light of the conclusions drawn from static palatographic and linguographic data results from this chapter.

CHAPTER 3: ELECTROPALATOGRAPHY

3.0 Introduction

Electropalatograhy (EPG) is a powerful tool for studying some articulatory aspects of speech precisely because it allows for the in-depth analysis of linguopalatal contact during continuous speech. (Fletcher *et al* 1975, Hardcastle 1972). In EPG, contact patterns of the tongue on the hard palate are graphically displayed as a series of mini-palates, with darkened circles representing tongue contact along the surface of the palate. Data analysis methods involve making both qualitative assessments of these mini-palates at particular timepoints during the utterance as well as quantitative analyses, which normally consist of numeric indices based on mathematical computations of the contact patterns. Commercial software does exist for calculating some indices, but much of the data analysis techniques used in EPG today have not been fully automated, and the development of methods for processing EPG data still presents a formidable challenge.

3.1 Methods of Data Reduction in EPG

Electropalatographic data collection and analysis is relatively simple but vast amounts of data are generated for which automatic processing has yet to become available. For example, in just a 3 second sample, for a pseudopalate with 96 electrodes, approximately 28,000 data points are generated if one tracks all 96 electrodes independently at 100Hz sampling rate[5]. This example demonstrates the need for data reduction and/or automation in EPG data analysis, as a typical phonetics experiment consists of more than just one 3 second utterance.

---

[5]The calculation was derived as follows: 3 sec = 3000 msec. Sample rate = 1 frame every 10 msec. We will observe 300 frames. Each frame has 96 electrodes to track, resulting in 300*96 data points or 28,800 data points to analyze.

Both qualitative and quantitative analyses have been employed to make useful generalizations about the vast amounts of data that EPG generates.

3.1.1 Qualitative data reduction methods

Qualitative methods typically involve scrolling through the utterance, and perhaps several repetitions of the same utterance, on a frame-by-frame basis, and describing the most salient generalizations as observed across multiple repetitions of the same utterance. One type of qualitative data reduction could involve just looking at one particular articulatory configuration, that is, one frame per utterance, at a designated point during the utterance (such as the frame having maximum linguopalatal contact), and assigning that articulatory configuration to a specific articulatory category (Byrd 1995). In this way, each 3 second utterance would be reduced from 300 frames to 1 frame. Graphic representations of qualitative analyses frequently show a schematic of one particular frame at a crucial timepoint during the utterance. Or, the entire time-series of minipalates, which depicts the temporal progression of the utterance may be shown. Some examples of research using qualitative methods are Nolan (1992), Marchal (1988) and Barry (1985).

3.1.2 Quantitative data reduction methods

Much work has gone into developing mathematical computations of the observed contact patterns in both the spatial and temporal domains. These types of mathematical computations have been referred to as "indices" and can be calculated based on the contact pattern of activated electrodes, as defined across the entire palate or on just a sub-section of the total palate.

Sectioning off electrodes into sub-groupings has been referred to as "region definition." Region definition involves grouping together a portion of the electrodes into a single section or region, usually based on some articulatory principle, and then either counting the absolute number of activated electrodes or a percentage of the contacted electrodes for that particular region (Byrd 1995). As many regions as necessary may be defined. This type of region definition greatly reduces the amount of samples per utterance. For example, we calculated earlier that in a three second utterance, if all 96 electrodes on a psuedopalate were tracked independently, approximately 28,800 data points would be generated. However, if we defined two regions—for example, a FRONT one for alveolar stops and a BACK region for velar plosives, and calculated the percentage of contacted electrodes in each region —then the total number of data points generated would be reduced from 28800 points to 600 —a nearly 50-fold difference[6] , thereby rendering data analysis

---

[6]This new calculation assumes two regions, for example, a FRONT and a BACK region representing tongue blade and tongue dorsum activity, respectively. 300 frames * 2 regions = 600 data points.

more manageable. Several types of analyses may be used to analyze these 600 percentage values.

The percentage values obtained for the FRONT and BACK regions may be graphed as a function of time, providing a visual representation of the dynamics of tongue/palate contact. This type of graph has been called a "contact profile" (Byrd 1994) or a "totals" display (Hardcastle, 1989). These "contact profiles" not only depict tongue/palate contact over time for each defined region, but also provide a source for further analysis in that numerical calculations may be obtained from them (Barry 1991, Byrd 1994, 1995). For example, Byrd (1994, 1996), measured the skewness of the contact profile, the area under the contact profile, as well as the flatness of the curve in her efforts to quantify the coproduction of alveolar and velar consonants in sequence. In principle, these same measures of area, skew and flatness may also be applied to contact profiles generated in this study if their interpretation is relevant to the empirical questions being considered.

Byrd primarily used index measurements that focused on quantifying dynamic temporal patterns of coproduction. However, many indices listed in the literature focus on calculating index measurements at several crucial timepoints during the course of an utterance. The index measurements at these timepoints are then compared in order to better understand the temporal progression of the articulation. Some index measurements that have thus far been developed are the "asymmetry" index, "centre of gravity" index, "coarticulation" index, "trough" index and the "variability" index. Hardcastle (1984) and Hardcastle, Gibbon and Nicolaidis (1991) both provide sound reviews of some of the EPG data reduction methods developed thus far, and new methods are constantly being developed. Work by Recasens (1984, 1993), Farnetani, Hardcastle and Marchal (1989), Butcher and Weiher (1976), and Farnetani, Vagges and Magno-Caldognetto (1985) and Farnetani (1990) serve as examples of EPG studies on intervocalic plosives while work by Byrd (1996), Hardcastle (1985) and Gibbon, Hardcastle and Nicolaidis (1993) and Hardcastle and Roach (1979) serve as examples of EPG studies on consonant clusters. While numerous EPG studies and measurement techniques have been done on coarticulation of intervocalic plosives and complex consonant sequences, this study found it necessary to develop some new index measurements that specifically met the empirical goals of the present study as well as the segment type under investigation.

3.2   Advantages and Disadvantages of Dynamic Palatography

One of the major drawbacks with using EPG is the limited extent to which contact on the soft-palate can be recorded. The standard pseudopalate produced by Kay Elemetrics does not extend onto the soft palate because the gag reflex may be stimulated, which in turn would obviously make the palate very uncomfortable to wear. As a result, velar, back-velar and uvular articulations may not be observed on the standard artificial palate. Typically researchers have countered this problem by using front vowel environments in order to create fronted-velars, as in Byrd (1994). Given that this study looks at the influence of both front and back vowels on click production, Byrd's solution to this problem would be counter to the aims of this research. Instead, this study uses supplementary techniques such as pharyngeal pressure records and static palatographic data in order to assess tongue dorsum behavior in addition to any information obtained from EPG itself. Another drawback is that EPG gives no direct information about the tongue blade articulation used. Linguography must be used in order to obtain data on the tongue blade articulation. Thirdly, EPG does not provide information about the portions of the tongue body which do not contact the palate, i.e. overall tongue shape (Hardcastle 1991). Finally, data on the total gestural trajectory cannot be obtained from this method since EPG only provides information about the tongue as it contacts the palate, and gives no information regarding the approach to the palate from a neutral or resting position (Stone 1997).

    One advantage that EPG has over tongue tracking systems is that EPG does give information about the lateral edges of linguopalatal contact. Tongue tracking systems typically record data only in the midsagittal plane and therefore cannot detect linguopalatal contact which falls outside the median line.

    In spite of the drawbacks mentioned here, the wealth of information obtained from EPG data far outweighs these aforementioned difficulties. As shall become apparent later in this work, the specific idiosyncrasies of this technique must be taken into account during the data analysis and interpretation process.

3.3   Procedure

3.3.1 Equipment

This study uses the Kay Elemetrics Palatometer system, which consists of custom-made pseudopalates, a hardware interface to a PC, and software for data capture, display and analysis. This system is integrated with the Kay Computerized Speech Laboratory (CSL).

    EPG data collection requires custom-fitted pseudopalates for each subject. Custom-itted pseudopalates were created as follows. A dental impression of the upper palate for each of four speakers was made by a licensed technician, from which stone castings of the hard palate and teeth were fashioned. These stone castings were then sent to Kay Elemetrics in order to begin the process of creating the final product—a pseudopalate with embedded electrodes. Initially, Kay Elemetrics produces a small sample acrylic pseudopalate, without electrodes. The subject tries on this sample artificial palate in order to test whether the stone casting was an accurate enough replica to produce the final pseudopalate[7]. The artificial palates are vacuum-produced such that their dimensions and physiological detail are nearly identical to the stone cast of the live palate. The final custom-fitted pseudopalate contains 96 electrodes. Figure 34 depicts an example of an artificial palate made for a male subject— Speaker NT. The female subjects had a slightly different electrode configuration from the standard arrangement used for the male speakers in that an electrode from the lateral side was moved to the backmost row of electrodes in an attempt to see more of the back contact. Appendix B contains scanned images of the pseudopalates for each speaker; the difference in electrode configuration between the male and female speakers is readily apparent in these images. All pseudopalatas contain the same total number of electrodes. Kay attempts to place electrodes on protruding landmarks along the palate surface whenever feasible, and as a result, the electrodes are arranged in slightly irregular arcs along the teeth and palate. The leads from the electrodes are grouped into two relatively unobtrusive bundles that lead out of the mouth, which allow the artificial palate to interface with the host computer (via the palatometer unit).

---

[7]This same sample acrylic was used to measure intraoral pressure in the aerodynamic portion of this study, which is fully discussed in Chapter 4.

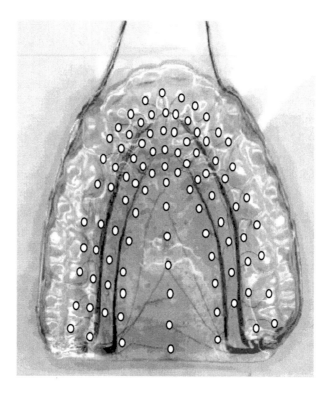

Figure 34: Acrylic pseudopalate with electrodes, for Speaker NT. White circles represent electrode locations.

It is evident from Figure 34 that electrode distribution across the palate is not equal. The density of electrodes in the anterior area is greater than in other regions of the palate. Also note the scarcity of electrodes between the
midsagittal line and the next column of electrodes on either side. Any linguopalatal contact between these two columns of electrodes would not be recorded.

The pseudopalate is sampled at 100Hz (producing one frame every ten milliseconds); it takes 1.7 milliseconds to acquire all 96 values. Simultaneous acoustic data was collected at a sample rate of 12.5 kHZ. It should be noted that due to the differences in sample rate, a specific acoustic event, such as a stop release, for example, is not exactly time-aligned with the EPG data.

EPG results are displayed as a series of mini-palates such that one can scroll through the articulation of the utterance as it had occurred, frame-by-frame. Figure 35 depicts a time-series of a dental click as produced by a male IsiZulu speaker. The electrode arrangement on the mini-palates does not mirror the exact placement of electrodes on the artificial palate itself, but represents an idealization in which electrodes are shown as much more symmetrical across the entire surface of the palate than they are on the actual pseudopalate. This point is important in the analysis of the data and should always be kept in mind when viewing palatograms.

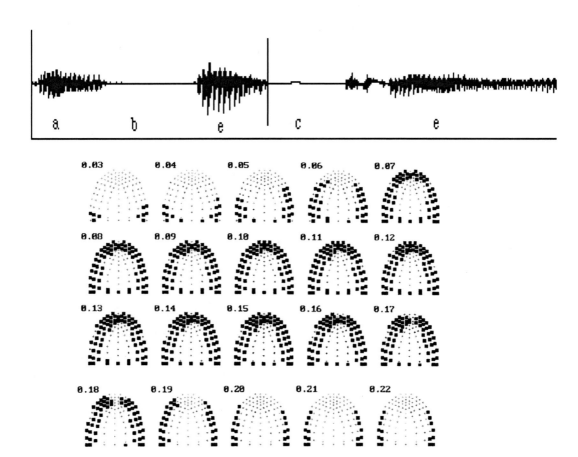

Figure 35: EPG frames of the dental click as spoken by a male IsiZulu speaker. Time-aligned waveform of same utterance, with time on the x-axis and amplitude on the y-axis. The first frame marks the acoustic closure, representing tongue dorsum contact. Subsequent frames occur every 10 msec. Overlap of tongue dorsum and tongue blade occurs from frames .07-0.16. Tongue blade release occurs at frame 0.17.

In Figure 35, the first frame is taken at the acoustic closure, marking tongue dorsum contact with the palate, followed by one frame every 10 milliseconds. Note that the tongue dorsum closure is not fully evident on the palate until frame 0.07. In many cases tongue dorsum closure cannot be viewed at all on the palate, but its presence can be determined from the acoustic record. In this example, full closure of both the tongue blade and tongue dorsum was observable on the palate from frame 0.07 to 0.16. The acoustic record, however, makes clear that the dorsal closure both begins earlier and ends later than these times.

3.3.2 Recording Set-up

Several days prior to the actual recording, each speaker had a training session where they were familiarized with the entire corpus. During this practice session, the semantic context of each word was clarified by using it in a sentence. Nonsense stems used in the study were also pointed out during this practice session. Appendix A provides a list of the corpus, an explanation of the morphological composition of the wordlist, as well as a sample sentence for each word.

On the day of the recording, the subject wore the artificial palate for at least 45-60 minutes prior to data collection in order to adjust their speech to the pseudopalate and to reduce the salivation response. The recording began when each speaker felt as though their speech was normal because the pseudopalate felt more natural.

Data collection took place at the UCLA Phonetics Laboratory. The subject sat at a table near the PC, close to the palatometer and CSL hardware units, facing away from the computer screen. The leads from the psuedopalate were attached to the palatometer unit. Wires from the pseudopalate that lead out of the mouth were taped to the subject's cheeks so as not to interfere with speech. The subject also wore a head-mounted microphone which was attached to the CSL unit, in order to simultaneously record the audio signal. At the time of the recording the subject was allowed to practice a list of words. The subject was also asked to talk at a consistent speaking rate. The instruction that was particularly emphasized at the time of the recording was the need to repeat an utterance if the artificial palate became separated from their upper palate. This was especially important because pilot aerodynamic data had shown the negative intraoral pressure to be much larger than previously estimated and possibly sufficient enough to weaken the seal between the pseudopalate and the live palate. Indeed, during the recording session for all speakers, the pseudopalate was occasionally sucked off of the palate. These files were discarded and the subject was asked to repeat the utterance.

The test utterances were collected directly onto the computer using CSL and stored as digital files for later analysis. Both acoustic and electropalatographic data were saved in a single digital file. The subject paused after each token in order to allow the data to be saved. Once the file was saved the subject was cued for the next utterance but was allowed to speak when ready. This ensured that the speaker had time to collect their thoughts and produce the correct click in its proper prosodic context.

3.3.3 Experimental Design

Corpus

The corpus of test utterances consisted of the voiceless dental, palato-alveolar and lateral clicks in symmetrical vowel contexts, said in the carrier phrase /bathi _____/ 'They say_____'. The three vowels /e/, /a/ and /o/ were used so that effects of variations in both vowel height and backness could be studied. High vowels were not used because the large amount of linguopalatal contact they have might be confounded with the contact patterns of the clicks. The test utterances are listed in Table 6. Each test utterance consisted of six syllables, with the test segment occurring in the penultimate syllable. All other consonants except the voiceless aspirated alveolar stop of the carrier phase were bilabial stops or fricatives. Labial segments were used to assure that the contact patterns associated with the test sequence were not influenced by other lingual consonants. Qualitative viewing of several tokens suggests that the alveolar stop in the carrier word was far enough from the test sequence such that it did not influence the test segment in any way.

The corpus also included selected examples of non-click consonants to which the more complex components of click articulations could be compared. For example, we would like to know whether aspects of the tongue dorsum articulation in a click consonant resemble that of simple pulmonic velar plosives, as produced in IsiZulu. The comparison of non-click consonants and clicks ensues in Chapter 4; the relevant test utterances are presented in that chapter as well. EPG data was collected from the same four speakers—NK, KK, NT and GV—who were in the SPG portion of this study. Relevant linguistic details on these speakers are listed in Chapter 2.

Table 6: Test utterances used in the EPG study. They consisted of the dental, palato-alveolar and lateral clicks in the symmetrical vowel contexts of /a/, /e/ and /o/, uttered in a carrier phrase.

Click type⇒ Vowel⇓	**Dental**	**Pal-Alveolar**	**Lateral**
/a/	bathi beb<u>ac</u>aba	bathi beb<u>aq</u>apha	bathi beb<u>ax</u>aba
/e/	bathi bab<u>ec</u>eba	bathi bab<u>eq</u>eba	bathi bab<u>ex</u>eba
/o/	bathi bab<u>oc</u>oba	bathi bab<u>oq</u>oba	bathi bab<u>ox</u>ova

3.4 Data Analysis: Methodology

3.4.1 Region Definition

In an attempt to describe the coordinated movements of the tongue blade and tongue dorsum gestures in click production, we initially divided the palate into a front region and a back region, following Byrd (1994). However, having defined these regions based on these control utterances, it became evident that this method was unsuitable for analyzing the component tongue blade and dorsum gestures of clicks for several reasons. First, the tongue dorsum closure was not always evident in the EPG frames, even when the acoustic record confirmed its presence. As a result, any timing information on the tongue blade and tongue dorsum based on EPG frames would be misleading. Vowel environment was an important independent factor in this study so it was not possible to use only a low front vowel to achieve a more forward velar articulation, which would in all likelihood be better represented on the pseudopalate.

Another problem in defining front and back regions was that component anterior and posterior gestures of clicks appeared to have different spatial configurations from their corresponding singleton alveolar and velar stops, making it difficult to define separate front and back regions exactly according to the simple pulmonic consonants. Byrd did not encounter this problem because the same consonants used to define front and back regions were also the test segments.

Region definition in this study was determined after viewing many repetitions of the various click types for all subjects. It was determined that approximately half of the anterior palate would be sufficient to characterize the tongue blade/tip for all speakers. This region was termed FRONT and included 54 electrodes. Figure 36 depicts the front region, and includes all electrodes anterior to line A as drawn in the figure. In addition to the FRONT region, the entire pseudopalate was considered to be a region, referred to as TOTALPAL, and included all 96 electrodes.

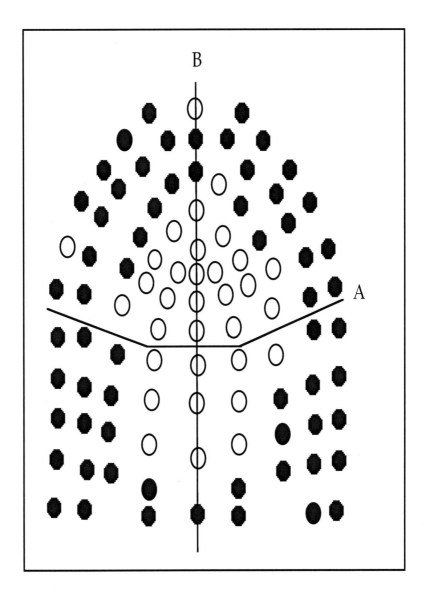

Figure 36: EPG frame of the dental click for Speaker NT at the frame just prior to the tongue blade release. Electrodes in the front of the dividing line A fall in the FRONT region. Those to the right of dividing line B are in the RIGHT region, and those to its left are in the LEFT region.

Two additional regions—LEFT and RIGHT—were defined in order to look at asymmetry in click articulations. Line B in Figure 36 separates the left and right sides of the palate. Midsagittal electrodes are excluded from these regions. A back region, which would represent the tongue dorsum articulation, was not defined because it was difficult to observe dorsal contact on the pseudopalate. Alternative means thought to be more accurate are adopted to characterize the tongue dorsum.

<u>Summary of Region Definition</u>

<u>TOTALPAL:</u> All 96 electrodes.

<u>FRONT:</u> the anterior region as demarcated along line A, which includes 54 electrodes.

<u>LEFT:</u> the 42 electrodes to the left of the midline.

<u>RIGHT:</u> the 42 electrodes to the right of the midline.

3.4.2 Quantitative Measurements

Contact profiles

Contact profiles of the FRONT and TOTALPAL regions for the various click types, pooled across speakers and vowel contexts where appropriate, are used to characterize the various click types and augment any qualitative descriptions based on general observations made of raw EPG time-series data. Figure 37 depicts a sample of the contact profiles.

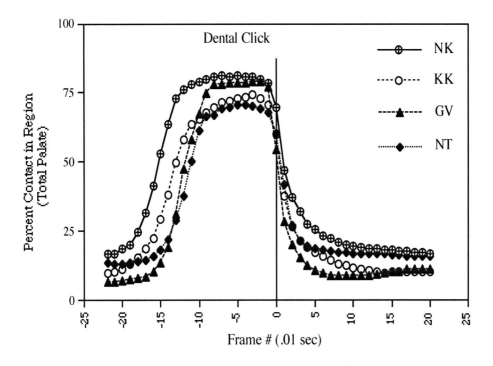

Figure 37: Mean contact profiles of the dental click type for each of four speakers as calculated for the total palate.

Each trace represents the average of 16-18 repetitions of the dental click for each speaker, pooled across the three vowel contexts. The values used to generate these traces were obtained by taking the individual means of 4-6 repetitions for each vowel context, and then taking the average across the three vowel contexts. The y-axis designates the percent of contacted electrodes across the region defined as TOTALPAL while the x-axis represents time, shown as frame numbers. All repetitions were aligned at the tongue blade release, as determined from the EPG frames and labeled time-zero on the x-axis. The time sampled extends from frames -23 to +20 in order to capture part of the preceding vowel and the entire click duration for all speakers. Analysis of the contact profiles focuses mainly on describing the shape, duration and peakedness of the profiles. Contact profiles for the regions defined as TOTALPAL and FRONT are graphed while the regions defined as LEFT and RIGHT are used in the "asymmetry" index calculation and are not presented as contact profiles.

Two types of measurements—index calculations and duration measurements—were made on the electropalatographic data. The following sections describe the criteria used for making these measurements.

Index Measurements

As previously mentioned, data reduction in electropalatographic data analysis is essential. One form of data reduction that has been proven to be useful in analyzing spatio-temporal patterns of articulatory behavior is arithmetic index calculations. Index measurements described in this section were specifically designed for capturing important articulatory spatial configurations of clicks at crucial time-points during their articulation.

Recall that click consonant production necessitates multiple closures at the velum, alveolar ridge and/or front teeth and the lateral margins of the palate, thereby creating a sealed chamber within the confines of these closures. During the rarefaction period, the cavity has been shown to expand in a manner that has been primarily attributed in the recent literature (Traill 1985) to the downward movement of the tongue body. The role of the lateral margins and tongue dorsum in rarefaction have yet to be clearly explicated. The following index measurements attempt to capture, in a more detailed way than previously addressed, the spatio-temporal progression of the multiple gestures involved in click consonant production by addressing the role of the tongue blade, the extent of lateral contact, tongue dorsum behavior and especially click cavity dynamics, as the area of the click cavity and its various spatio-temporal configurations are extremely important in understanding the overall dynamics of click production.

Six indices were developed specifically to meet these aforementioned goals. They are: Posteriority Index (EPI), Anteriority Index (EAI), Median Anteriority Index (EMAI), Width Index (EMAWI), Cavity Area Index (ECAI) and an Asymmetry Index (ABASI). *All* index values were calculated at three time-points during the consonantal closure. They were: 1. First frame of initial tongue blade closure (CLOS), 2. Frame at which maximum electrode activation across the region defined as TOTALPAL was reached (%MAX) and, 3. Frame just prior to the tongue blade/tip release (REL). Figure 38 depicts sample contact patterns for the dental click at CLOS, %MAX and REL.

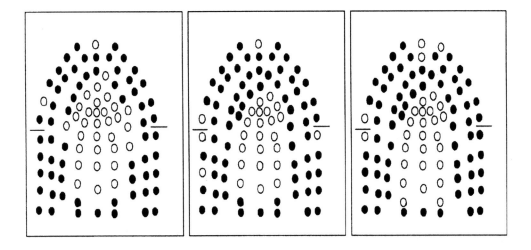

Figure 38: Speaker NT's dental click at initial onset of tongue blade closure, %MAX contact, and the frame just prior to the tongue blade release.

All index values except the Asymmetry Index were calculated by hand from printouts of the EPG time-series data. All hand-counted index values represent raw, unweighted counts of either uncontacted or contacted electrodes, as required by a particular index. Asymmetry index values are percentages obtained from computer calculations of the regions defined as LEFT and RIGHT. These indices are further explicated below and sample calculations provided in Table 7 for the three contact patterns of the dental click in Figure 38. Formula for the more complex index calculations are provided.

Total segment measurements

Cavity Area (ECAI): determined by counting the number of *unactivated* electrodes within the click cavity. A greater index value represents a larger cavity area. However, it should be noted that the actual cavity area may not be fully observable on the pseudopalate given that the back edge of the cavity is not always visible for every click type. In addition, the distance between the mid-sagittal row of electrodes and the column of electrodes adjacent, on either side of the median line, is great. It is possible that during click production, the lateral edges of tongue contact fell in this area but could not be detected, given that no electrodes were present to register linguopalatal contact in this area. This would mean that in some cases the actual cavity area is smaller than what is recorded by the index measure. Cavity area index values should not be misconstrued to mean overall cavity volume either. This index only reflects the upper surface of the cavity and does not take any account of the contribution of the tongue center to overall cavity volume.

<u>Peak Linguopalatal Contact (%MAX)</u>: the percentage value of maximum linguopalatal contact across the total palate region.

%MAX contact = #contacted electrodes/96 x 100

<u>Asymmetry Index</u> (ABASI): measures the magnitude of asymmetry by comparing the percentage of contact on the left and right sides. Recall that electrodes along the midline were excluded from the analysis (see Figure 36 for an explanation of the regions defined as LEFT and RIGHT). ABASI is calculated by taking the absolute value of the difference between the percentage of contacted electrodes on the right side and the percentage of contacted electrodes on the left side. The resulting index value gives an indication of the absolute magnitude of asymmetry for a given contact pattern, without reference to left/right dominance. This index is an adaptation of the Asymmetry index developed by Marchal and Expresser (1987).

Absolute Asymmetry Index = | %left side – %right side |

Tongue blade/tip measures:

<u>Anteriority Index</u> (EAI)[8]: calculated by counting the number of uncontacted electrodes in front of the tongue blade closure, and then subtracting this value from the total number of electrodes in the FRONT region i.e. 54 electrodes. This index gives a good indication of the overall posture of the anterior portion of the tongue. Larger index values depict more anterior tongue blade positions.

EAI = 54 – #uncontacted electrodes in front of the closure of the FRONT REGION

[8]Some index abbreviations are preceded by the letter 'E' to note that this measure was made using EPG in order to minimize confusion between similar index values obtained from static palatographic data.

Median Anteriority Index (EMAI): calculated by counting the number of uncontacted midsagittal electrodes in front of the tongue blade closure, and then subtracting this number from the number of midsagittal electrodes in the FRONT region , i.e '8'. Again, as with the Anteriority Index, larger EMAI values represent more anterior tongue blade articulations.

EMAI= 8 – #uncontacted electrodes in median line of the FRONT REGION

Width index (EMAWI): measures the width of the anterior closure in the midsagittal plane. EMAWI was calculated by counting the number of activated electrodes along the median line in the region designated as FRONT. Larger index values represent broader tongue blade/tip contact.

Tongue Dorsum Measures

Given the difficulty in defining an adequate posterior region based on control utterances, and the inability to record the full extent of the tongue dorsum gesture on the pseudopalate, an alternative method to region definition was adopted in order to assess the tongue dorsum gesture. Qualitative analysis of EPG frames showed that the midsagittal electrodes alone gave a good indication of the tongue dorsum contact. Viewing the midsagittal electrodes then became a conservative way of looking at the tongue dorsum gesture.

Posteriority Index:(EPI): measures the position of the tongue dorsum by calculating the extent of contact in the back region of the palate along the midsagittal axis. The index is calculated by counting the number of activated electrodes in the posterior portion of the palate, along the median line. If three electrodes were activated then an index value of '3' was assigned. In most cases, if the third electrode was contacted it meant that the first and second electrodes were also activated. However, in a few cases the third electrode was activated but the first and second were not. For these cases, an index value of '3' was none-the-less assigned. A greater index value represents a more anterior tongue dorsum position. A second type of tongue dorsum analysis was also done on a subset of the data in the contexts of vowels /a/ and /e/. EPI was recorded and graphed, *frame-by-frame*, as a means of tracking the behavior of the tongue dorsum throughout the closure period. The graph was extended 15 frames prior to the tongue blade release and 2 frames after the release thereby depicting the progression of the articulation in a more detailed manner.

Table 7: Sample Index Calculations for the EPG frames in Figure 38

Timepoints⟹ Index Measure⇓	Closure	%Max	Release
Cavity Area (ECAI)	32	22	24
Absolute Asymmetry (ABASI)	2	1	2
%MAX	66%	72%	70%
Anteriority (EAI)	52	52	50
Median Anteriority (EMAI)	7	7	6
Median Width (EMAWI)	2	3	2
Posteriority (EPI)	1	1	1

Graphic display of Indices

Results of index calculations are typically depicted in line graphs. Figure 39 depicts a sample line graph of the Posteriority Index for the three click types, pooled across speakers and vowel contexts. It should be emphasized that the time course in these line graphs is crude in that the actual duration between any two points is not represented on the graph. We know that %MAX contact typically occurs between the closure and the release points, but the time-point at which maximum linguopalatal contact is achieved during the course of the articulation is not represented on the line graph. In some cases, %MAX contact coincided with either Closure or Release, but these events were rare.

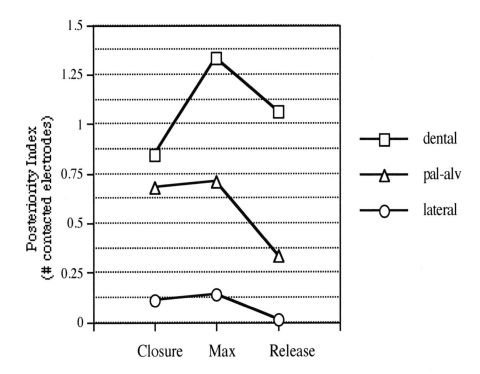

Figure 39: Sample line graph depicting the Posteriority Index results for the dental, palato-alveolar and lateral clicks at the time-points of initial tongue blade closure, maximum linguopalatal contact and the time-frame just prior to the tongue blade release, for data pooled across speakers and vowel contexts.

Duration Measurements

A series of specific time-points from which the durations of various articulatory phases could be calculated were marked in the palatographic and acoustic records. Figure 40 shows a waveform of the dental click in the /a/ vowel environment, as obtained from the phrase 'bathi bebacaba'. The waveform shows only the last three syllables of the test utterance.

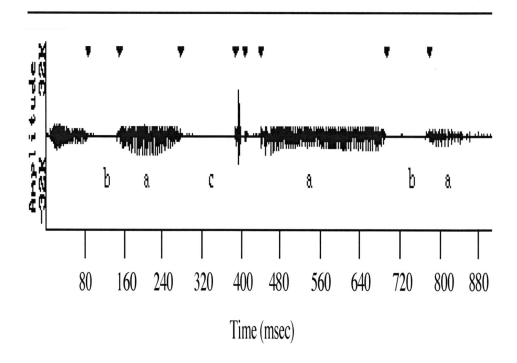

Figure 40: Acoustic waveform depicting the specific time-points from which the durations of various articulatory phases were calculated.

Seven time-points were demarcated from the acoustic waveform. (Recall that the acoustic data was simultaneously collected with EPG data.) The time-points from left to right are: 1. onset of the bilabial stop, 2. onset of the following vowel /a/, sometimes referred to as V1, 3. tongue dorsum closure for the click consonant, 4. onset of the click burst, 5. the velar burst, 6. onset of voicing for the penultimate vowel, or V2), 7. offset of the penultimate vowel, 8. onset of voicing for the utterance-final vowel /a/. Timepoint 5, the velar burst, was not always visible on the acoustic waveform. In many cases the velar burst was marked by the use of wide band spectrograms and expanded waveforms in combination.

Three articulatory timepoints were determined from the EPG data. They were the initial tongue blade closure, the time frame at which peak linguopalatal contact was reached, and the time at which the initial tongue blade seal was released. (These are the exact time-points at which the various index measures were calculated.) The following durational phases were calculated from a combination of these EPG and acoustic time-points.

<u>Onset Latency (ONL)</u>: defined as the duration from the tongue dorsum closure to the tongue blade closure. The tongue dorsum closure was determined from the acoustic closure for the click consonant while the tongue blade closure was based on EPG frames.

ONL (msec) = tongue blade closure (EPG) – tongue dorsum closure (Acoustic)

<u>Seal Duration (SD)</u>: defined as the duration during which there was complete tongue blade closure. The seal duration was demarcated at the EPG frame where the initial closure is formed, while the tongue blade release was determined from the acoustic onset of the click burst (timepoint 4, Figure 40).

SD (msec) = tongue blade release (Acoustic) – tongue blade closure (EPG)

<u>Offset latency</u> (OFL): defined as the acoustic duration from the tongue blade release (timepoint 4) to the tongue dorsum release (timepoint 5).

OFL (msec) = tongue dorsum release (Acoustic) – tongue blade release (Acoustic)

<u>Total Click Duration</u> (TCLD): measured from the tongue dorsum closure as measured from the acoustic waveform to the velar burst.

TCLD (msec) = tongue dorsum release (acoustic) – tongue dorsum closure (acoustic)

Statistical Analysis

Three factor Analysis of Variance tests, using Statview 4.5 for the Macintosh, were performed with CLICK, VOWEL and SPEAKER as the main independent variables on the seven indices, at the designated timepoints—CLOS, %MAX and REL. The statistical analysis focuses on results which characterize differences among click types and vowel environments. Only salient speaker differences are discussed, where clear differences in not just the magnitude of the difference is evident, but where a marked change in the rank order of vowels or click types is apparent. Three factor ANOVA's were also performed on the duration measurements using the same independent variables.

3.5 RESULTS

3.5.1 Qualitative Characterization of the Click Types

The purpose of this section is to qualitatively describe, both in words and with representative EPG time-series diagrams, specific aspects of click production for each of the three click types, as they are produced in IsiZulu.

General Comments on Click Production

One general aspect of click production that pertains to all click types is the order of closures of the tongue dorsum and tongue blade/tip. In principle, the order of these articulatory closures could freely vary given that there is no aerodynamic requirement in terms of producing the sounds that would regulate the order of these closures, as there is for the release gestures. While earlier work by Doke (1923) concluded that the tongue blade/tip closure preceded the velar closure, more recent work by Traill (1993), using acoustic data on IsiZulu, and Roux (1993), using EPG data, concluded the opposite—namely that the tongue dorsum closure precedes the tongue blade/tip closure. In this study, both EPG and pharyngeal pressure records, which are discussed in Chapter 5, show that the order of closures for every click type, regardless of vowel context or speaker, had the tongue dorsum closure preceding the tongue blade closure. In many repetitions, the tongue dorsum gesture is not visible on the pseudopalate. But it is none-the-less clear that the onset of the acoustic closure cannot be the result of tongue blade/tip closure, since no articulatory seal in the anterior region is present on the palatograms at the acoustic closure of the click (see Figure 35). It is possible that the initial consonantal closure could be glottal in nature given that no tongue dorsum or tongue blade closure is observed on the pseudopalate at this time. However, aerodynamic records from this study indicate that, at the acoustic closure, the pharyngeal pressure rises as it does in simple pulmonic velars produced by these same speakers. Since pressure in the pharynx would not rise if there was a closure at the glottis, we conclude that the closure, being neither coronal nor glottal, must be dorsal. The fact that no tongue dorsum seal is visible in the EPG record simply shows that the initial seal occurs further back, behind the back edge of the pseudopalate being worn by the speaker. In general, the tongue dorsum gesture was observable for the dental click for most speakers, while the palato-alveolar and lateral click types had tongue dorsum gestures that were much more posterior and therefore not visible on the palate. Based on the conclusions regarding the order of closures of the tongue dorsum and tongue blade/tip it makes sense to discuss the tongue dorsum lead i.e. the time period between these two closures as a positive duration value.

Characterizing the Click Types

Figure 41 depicts an acoustic waveform and an EPG time-series of palatograms for one token of the dental click, in the symmetrical vowel context of /a/, as uttered by Speaker NT. Recall that the acoustic and EPG data were simultaneously collected. EPG time-series frames begin approximately at the tongue dorsum closure, as determined from the acoustic waveform. In this particular token, frame 0.04 matches the acoustic closure of the consonant, which is marked by a circled tag on the waveform. The onset of the articulation begins in the posterior region of the palate and extends forward until the tongue blade/tip closure is made, at frame 0.07, making the lead phase approximately 3 frames long. During the overlap phase, which lasts for 10 frames, the anterior contact continues to form, increasing in width, especially along the median line. Once the tongue blade articulation is formed, it remains static until preparation for its release begins. Note that the location of the tongue blade articulation is fully dental. In frame 0.13 the tongue blade/tip articulation becomes thinner at the anterior edge of the closure, in preparation for its release. At frame 0.17 a narrow channel, created by the tongue blade, is observed. Ingressive airflow as a result of this opening into the cavity commences at this point, and given its narrowness, produces frication noise, which is also clearly observable on the acoustic waveform. In subsequent frames for this particular token, the opening continues to widen until full release of the tongue blade from the palate occurs in frame 0.20. The dental click for all speakers showed a narrow release channel in many repetitions and invariably some affrication of the release, although in some cases no frame depicting a narrow release channel was captured due to the sample rate. A thinning out of the anterior articulation in preparation for the release is clearly observable in nearly all tokens, indicating that the release develops rather gradually.

Full tongue dorsum closure becomes visible on the palate at frame 0.07, though the acoustic data indicates that a seal was present several frames earlier. At frame 0.14, the number of electrodes in the posterior region of the palate begins to diminish though a full dorsal seal remains visible until frame 0.17, after which the dorsum closure is no longer visible on the palate. The exact mechanism responsible for the diminution of contact in the posterior region is difficult to ascertain from EPG data alone.

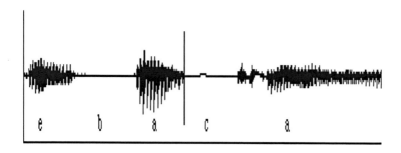

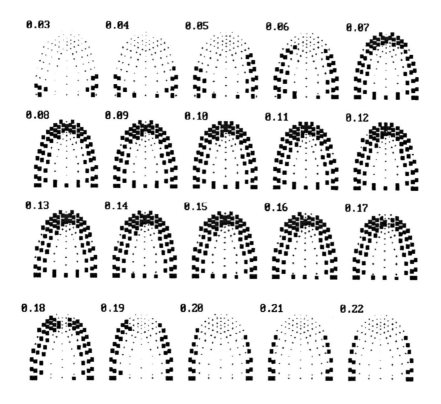

Figure 41: EPG time-series frames of one dental click with accompanying acoustic waveform. Mini-palates depict the onset of the tongue dorsum closure as determined from the acoustic waveform in frame 0.04. The figure also depicts the narrow release channel at 0.17

It is possible that the decrease in posterior electrodes contacted starting in frame 0.14 signals the onset of the tongue dorsum release gesture, where the actual movement would initially involve a lowering of both the anterior and posterior edges of the closure, leaving a thinner closure which would then be released. Another possibility is that there is active retraction of the tongue dorsum. Whether only one of these mechanisms or both lowering and retraction are involved in the dorsal release is hard to determine from EPG data alone. This point will be more fully considered later in this chapter. Another point to note has to do with the coordination of the tongue dorsum and tongue blade/tip. Note that the thinning out of contact in the anterior portion occurs at approximately the same time as the initial diminution of contacted electrodes in the area of the tongue dorsum closure. This observation highlights an important point about the coordination of the tongue dorsum and blade and is further discussed in the EPG data as well as in the aerodynamic data.

Figure 42 depicts a time-series of palatograms for the palato-alveolar click, in the symmetrical vowel context of /a/, as produced by Speaker GV. The initial frame in the series corresponds to the tongue dorsum closure, as determined from the acoustic waveform. The visible onset of the articulation on the pseudopalate begins along the lateral margins, at frame 0.03, and progresses forward systematically until the anterior closure is made, at frame 0.13. During the overlap phase, which occurs from frames 0.13-0.20, the anterior closure broadens. The position of the front edge of the anterior closure remains unchanged until frame 0.20, where a widening and retraction of the tongue blade/tip contact takes place, just prior to the release. The release for this click type, unlike the dental click type, is quite abrupt, going from maximum tongue tip contact to complete loss of linguopalatal contact from one frame to the next. Throughout the click, no tongue dorsum contact is visible across the central posterior region of the pseudopalate,

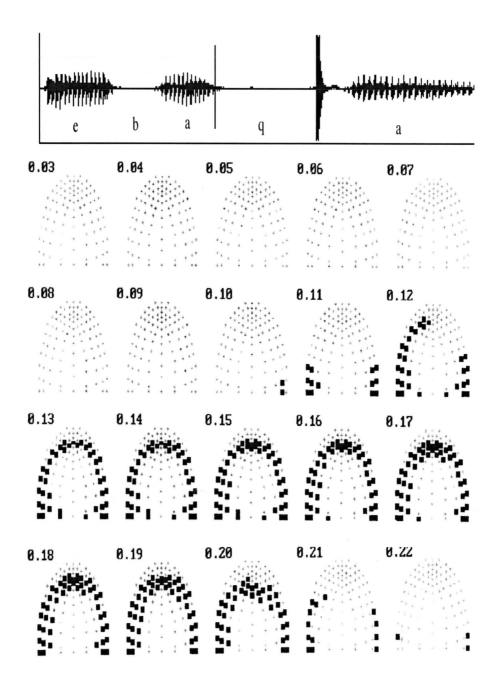

Figure 42: EPG frames and time-aligned waveform of the palato-alveolar click, from tongue dorsum closure to tongue blade release, of a male IsiZulu speaker, depicting a relatively long onset latency from 0.03-0.12 and tongue tip retraction during the closure at 0.20.

athough the front edge of the back contact is visible in the posterior electrodes adjacent to the midline, in frames 0.12. to 0.17. The acoustic record indicates that the tongue dorsum seal is formed at the time of frame 0.03 and presumably this contact broadens from its onset until it reaches a maximum around frame 0.13.

Figure 43 depicts EPG frames of the lateral click in the symmetrical vowel context of /a/, with the first frame beginning at the tongue dorsum closure—frame 0.06. The onset of the articulation proceeds from the posterior end of the pseudopalatepalate and progresses along the lateral margins in a continuous manner until the tongue blade seal is made, at frame 0.14. The width of the anterior closure, along the median line, is extensive, ranging from the dental to the post-alveolar region. During the lateral release, which begins on the right side at frame .23, the anterior closure begins to thin out along the median line at both the anterior and posterior edges of the closure. However, note that the anterior portion of the tongue remains elevated throughout the lateral release.

This click type has three release gestures, the lateral release, which is made along the posterior lateral edges of the palate, the anterior release, made by the tongue blade/tip, and the velar release of the tongue dorsum. The lateral release itself occurs in frame 0.23 on the right side of the palate.

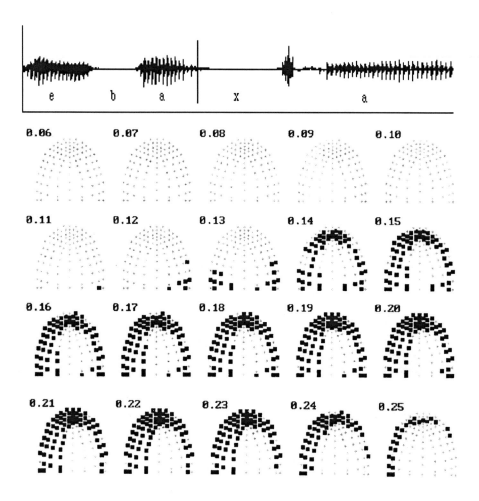

Figure 43: EPG frames of the lateral click from tongue dorsum closure to the lateral release, of a male IsiZulu speaker, depicting the relatively long onset latency from .06-0.13, the asymmetric nature of this click type and the narrow release channel in the velar region on the right side of the palate at .23.

The release channel is quite posterior, and this positioning of the lateral release channel is typical for all speakers. Also note that this particular token of the lateral click, which was produced by Speaker GV, is quite asymmetrical, with the left side of the palate having much more contact than the right side. In general, the lateral click for this speaker was more asymmetric than for the other three speakers. However, all speakers exhibited some degree of asymmetry for this click type.

Throughout the course of this click there is only a hint of the tongue dorsum gesture on the pseudopalate. Typically the tongue dorsum seal was quite posterior for all speakers for this click type. Typically the central release and the tongue dorsum release are simultaneous for all speakers in the majority of tokens, though in a few cases the tongue blade remains elevated after the dorsal release. In even fewer cases, the tongue blade release is made first, followed by the tongue dorsum release.

Summary of Qualitative Results

In general, this initial qualitative investigation of the EPG data shows all click types to be highly structured segments with complex internal phasing of their component gestures. All click types have a consistent onset, with the tongue dorsum closure occuring first, followed by a systematic anterior progression of the lateral edges until a full anterior seal is made. The onset latency times differed for the various click types, with the dental click having the shortest onset latency, the palato-alveolar the longest, and the lateral click intermediate between the two but with a value closer to that of the palato-alveolar click. In terms of overlap, the palato-alveolar click had the shortest overlap phase while the dental and lateral clicks had nearly equal overlap durations.

Tongue blade articulations showed that the palato-alveolar click had relatively thin contact, consistent with its apical nature as previously described in Chapter 2. EPG data also confirmed that this click is indeed post-alveolar throughout the course of its articulation. One surprising aspect that had not been previously noted was the retraction of the tongue tip that occurs during the closure phase of the articulation.

The dental click was quite static in its posture by comparison. The release gesture for this particular click type involved the formation of a narrow release channel, similar to that observed in pulmonic fricatives. Based on the EPG data observed here we can characterize the dental click as an affricate.

The lateral click showed quite a broad static anterior contact, much broader than the dental click. The observed release channel for this click type was quite posterior. The tongue blade/tip articulation thinned out during the lateral release and remained elevated throughout the lateral release gesture. The asymmetrical quality of this click type was also noted.

3.5.2 Quantitative Characterization of the Click Types

While it is useful to look at individual tokens of the three click types, in order to gain a better understanding of the sequence of articulatory events which combine to create a particular click type it is essential to analyze quantitative data from several speakers in order to differentiate idiosyncratic speaker differences, which might arise from genetically determined variations in palate morphology, from important facts about the general mechanism of click production common to all speakers. The following sections analyze pooled speaker data from duration measurements, contact profiles and index calculations. The point of these quantitative measures is to represent major aspects of the articulatory differences among the click types that were observed on the EPG time-series diagrams. Each duration measurement and index calculation was analyzed using a three-way analysis of variance with CLICK, VOWEL and SPEAKER as main effects, conducted at a confidence level of 99%. Post-hoc comparisons were conducted using Fisher's PLSD adjusted for unequal cell sizes. Significant main effects and their interactions are the primary focus of the discussion, however, marginal effects are discussed where deeemed appropriate. In order to facilitate the discussion involving comparisons of the click types with respect to any given measurement, the Zulu orthographic symbols, namely /c/, /q/ and /x/, respectively representing the dental click, the palato-alveolar click and the lateral click, are employed. In addition, the symbols '>' and '<', greater than and less than, are also used to show the relative order of the click types for the variable under consideration.

Articulatory Phase Durations

Figure 44 depicts the mean duration results of the three articulatory phases of click consonant production, pooled from the four speakers, across the vowels contexts of /a/, /e/ and /o/. Section 3.5.2 provides an in depth explanation on the measurement criteria used to characterize these various phases of click production.

We shall first consider the Tongue Dorsum Lead Phase for the three click types. The dental click type has the shortest lead phase, at 32 milliseconds. The palato-alveolar and lateral clicks have nearly equal durations, at 45 and 42 milliseconds, respectively. EPG time-series diagrams in the previous section clearly depicted this difference between the dental click and the other two click types. A three-factor ANOVA was conducted, with SPEAKER, CLICK and VOWEL as the main independent variables. There was a highly significant main effect of CLICK on the onset latency [$F(2,177) = 32$, $p<.0001$]. Post-hoc tests confirmed that the palato-alveolar and lateral click types were not significantly distinguished from each other. However, the dental click differed from both the palato-alveolar and lateral clicks at $p<.0001$. There was also a significant main effect of VOWEL on onset latency [$F(2,177)=32$, $p<.001$]. Post-hoc tests distinguished /o/ from both /a/ and /e/, at $p<.0001$, while the comparison of /a, e/ was not significant. The interaction between CLICK and VOWEL was not significant, suggesting that the lead phase is longest in the context of /o/ for all click types.

The Tongue Dorsum Lag phase, as measured by the offset latency, is now considered. Offset latency for the dental and palato-alveolar clicks have nearly equal values, at 26 and 23 milliseconds, respectively. The lateral click has a greater mean offset latency, at 44 milliseconds. A three-factor ANOVA with SPEAKER, CLICK and VOWEL as the main independent variables was conducted on offset latency. There was a significant main effect of CLICK on offset latency [$F(2,95) = 56$, $p<.0001$]. Post-hoc test results showed that the comparison of /c, q/ was not significant while the pair-wise comparsions with /x/ were significant at $p<.0001$. The main effect of SPEAKER was not significant, but the interaction between SPEAKER and CLICK was highly significant [$F(6, 95) = 6.2$, $p<.0001$].

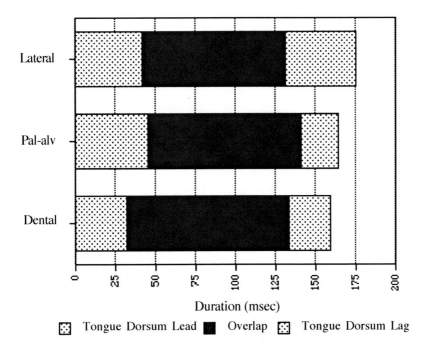

Figure 44: Duration measurements of the pooled data for the three phases of click consonant production. The phases are the Tongue Dorsum Lead, Overlap and Tongue Dorsum Lag.

All speakers exhibit the same click pattern, that is, the lateral click has a significantly longer lag than both the dental and the palato-alveolar clicks, except for Speaker NK, whose has equal offset latency values for the dental and the lateral clicks. The main effect of VOWEL was not at all significant. Only marginal significance was attained for the interaction between CLICK and VOWEL [$F(4, 95) = 2.9$, p<.03]. There was a highly significant 3-way interaction between SPEAKER, CLICK and VOWEL [$F(12, 95) = 5.8$, p<.0001]. No clear vowel pattern emerges with respect to the lag phase.

The Overlap phase was characterized by measuring the anterior seal duration. The means showed that the dental click had the longest overlap phase, at 102 milliseconds, the palato-alveolar had an intermediate phase duration, at 96 milliseconds, followed by the lateral click, at 89 milliseconds. A three-factor Analysis of Variance was performed on the anterior seal duration, with SPEAKER, CLICK and VOWEL as the main independent variables. There was a significant main effect of CLICK on the anterior seal duration [$F(2, 177) = 7.1$, p<.0001]. Post-hoc analysis showed that the comparison of /x, c/ was highly significant, at p<.001. The comparisons of /q, x/ and /c, q/ were only marginally significant at p<.04 and p<.07, respectively. There was a significant interaction of SPEAKER and CLICK [$F(6,177)$

= 7.5, p<.0001]. For example, for Speaker KK the mean anterior seal duration in the context of /e/ for /c/, /q/ and /x/ are 124 msec, 132 msec and 161 msec, respectively, whereas Speaker GV has the opposite ranking with 98, 63 and 61 msec. Three of the speakers follow the strong trend of CLICK, where c>x. The exception is for Speaker KK, who exhibits a reversal with x>c.

There was also a significant main effect of Vowel on seal duration [F(2, 177) = 10.2, p<.002]. Post-hoc comparisons showed that /e/ differed significantly from /a/ and /o/, at p<.001. But the comparison of /a, o/ was not at all significant. The interaction between CLICK and VOWEL was not significant. The pooled means for VOWEL show that *all* clicks are longer in the context of /e/ than in the other vowel contexts. There was a extremely marginally significant result for the 3-way interaction between SPEAKER, CLICK and VOWEL [F(12,177) = 1.58, p<.1]. Speaker GV had longer overlap durations in the context of /o/ than for /e/ for both /q/ and /x/. Speaker NK had a longer overlap duration in the context of /a/ than for /e/ for /c/ and /x/, while Speaker NT had a longer overlap duration in the context of /o/ for the lateral click.

The total click duration, i.e. the acoustic closure duration of the tongue dorsum gesture, is shown in Figure 44. The lateral click has the greatest mean closure duration, the dental click the shortest and the palato-alveolar click is intermediate between the two. Separate means for each vowel context are shown in Figure 45. For each click type, the mean closure duration is shortest in the context of /a/, with the /e/ and /o/ contexts having nearly equal durations. There was a significant main effect of CLICK on the total click duration [F(2, 95) = 4.2, p<.02]. Post hoc results showed that only the comparison of /c,x/ was marginally significant, at p<.03. There was also a significant main effect of vowel on the total click duration [F(2, 95) = 10.3, p<.0001]. Post-hoc comparisons showed that /a, o/ differed significantly, at p<.0001. The comparison of /a, e/ differed significantly at p<.01. The comparison of /e, o/ was less significant, at p<.03. The interaction between CLICK and VOWEL was not at all significant. However, the 3-way interaction between all independent variables was significant [F(12, 95) = 2.6, p<.01 indicating that there are some speaker differences in the way that vowel context affects the duration of the different clicks. The /a/ context does not always result in shortest closure duration, nor the /e/ context the longest. For the lateral click, Speakers GV, NK and NT pattern as o>a>e instead of o>e>a. Speaker GV also uses the same pattern—o>a>e—for the palato-alveolar click. In dental clicks Speaker NK has the longest dorsal closure in the /a/ context, with the ordering of a>o>e. For every click type, Speaker KK patterns with /e/ having the largest mean value for total click duration. Speaker NT shows this same order for the palato-alveolar click as well. Speaker KK has longer durations in general with both longer overlap duration and total click durations.

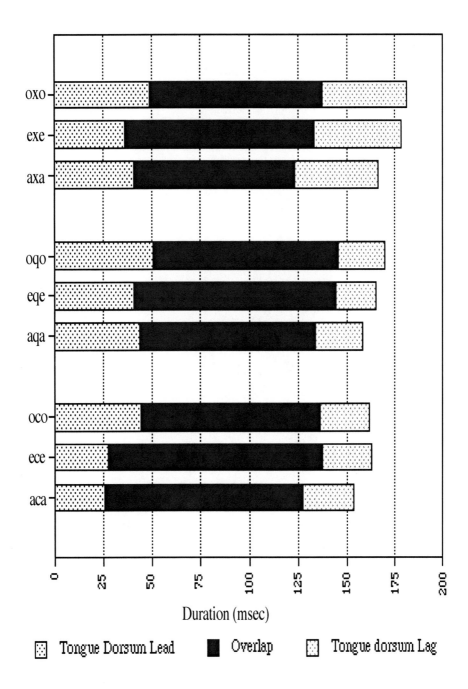

Figure 45: Duration measurements of the three phases of click consonant production for the dental, palato-alveolar and lateral clicks separated by vowel context. The phases are the Tongue Dorsum Lead, Overlap and Tongue Dorsum Lag.

Contact Profiles

Recall that contact profiles depict the percentage of contacted electrodes for a specifically defined region on a frame-by-frame basis, with frame intervals being 10 milliseconds apart. Figures 3.13, 3.14 and 3.15 depict the contact profiles for the dental, palato-alveolar and lateral click types, respectively, separated by speaker. These particular contact profiles represent the average of eighteen repetitions (in most instances), for each speaker and are based on percentages of all contacted electrodes. All graphs are aligned at the release burst, which is marked with a vertical line at time-zero on each graph.

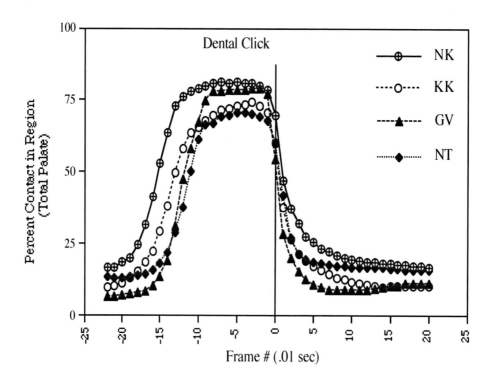

Figure 46: Contact profiles of the dental click, pooled across vowel contexts and aligned at click release, for Speakers NK, KK, GV and NT.

Figure 46 presents the contact profile of the dental click for each speaker. Each one shows a fairly symmetrical curve, consisting of a relatively gradual increase in contact from the onset-to-closure phase, a clear plateau representing the closure portion of the articulation, and a somewhat more rapid decrease of contact at the release.

All speakers follow a similar pattern, although clear magnitude differences in the extent of the gesture are readily observable from the profiles. Speakers NK and GV attain a similar peak magnitude while NT and KK have comparable magnitudes, but somewhat lower than NK and GV. Recall that individual differences of magnitude may reflect a variety of factors, including different sizes of the pseudopalates and placement of the electrodes, as well as the actual magnitude of articulatory gestures. However, the general articulatory pattern as well as the shape of the profile is quite similar for all speakers.

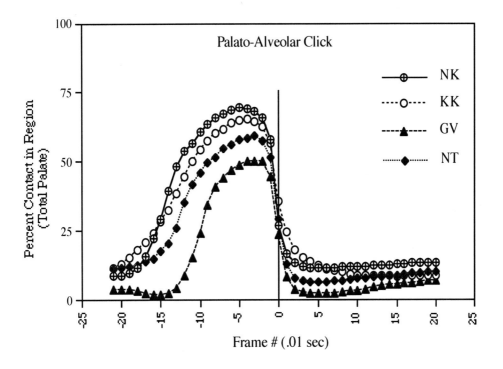

Figure 47: Contact profiles of the palato-alveolar click, pooled across vowel contexts, and aligned at click release, for Speakers NK, KK, GV and NT.

Figure 47 depicts the contact profiles for the palato-alveolar click type for each of four speakers, pooled across vowel contexts. The onset of the articulation gradually builds to maximum contact and then immediately declines, with little to no plateau, creating a more skewed distribution than is seen in the dental clicks. At the release, marked at time-zero, the percent of activated electrodes is markedly decreased when compared to the percentage of contacted electrodes in the frame just prior to release. For the dental click, a more gradual diminution of contacted electrodes occurs. Once again, clear magnitude differences emerge in maximum contact attained, with, in this case, the two male speakers having less contact than the female speakers. Percent of contacted electrodes correlates with the duration of the articulation in this case, but not in the case of the dental clicks. However, the basic progression of the articulation is similar for all speakers.

Figure 48 depicts contact profiles for the lateral click type for each speaker, pooled across vowel categories. Static palatographic and linguographic data from Chapter 2 showed that this click type was the most variable of the three, and the contact profiles in Figure 48 reinforce this point.

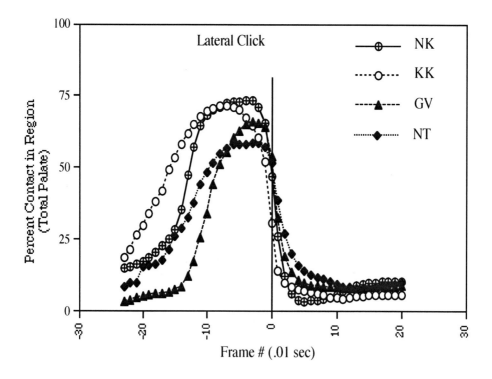

Figure 48: Contact profiles of the lateral click, pooled across vowel contexts, and aligned at click release, for Speakers NK, KK, GV and NT.

The figure depicts quite variable onsets, variations in the amount of peakedness for each speaker as well as differences in the timing of the release gesture. The curves for Speakers NK and NT are reminiscent of the shape of the curves for dental clicks, that for Speaker GV is reminiscent of the palato-alveolar clicks, and that for Speaker KK is unlike either of the other two click types. These speaker differences for lateral clicks reflect quite a different kind of speaker variation than the superficial differences seen in Figures 3.15 and 3.16.

Figure 49 depicts contact profiles comparing the dental, palato-alveolar and lateral click types pooled across vowel contexts and speakers. Given the similarities in the shape of the contact profiles for all speakers for their dental and palato-alveolar clicks, it is reasonable to pool the data across speakers in order to obtain an average contact profile for these click types. An average trace of the lateral click is included in this graph for comparison but in view of the speaker differences observed this cannot be regarded as representative, and subsequent discussion of lateral clicks will normally separate data from different speakers.

Direct comparison of the contact profiles for the various click types shows that the dental click is more symmetrical in shape than the palato-alveolar click, with a gradual onset-to-closure, a clear plateau during the closure, followed by a gradual offset. The palato-alveolar click shows a peaked, more asymmetrical distribution than the other two clicks. The EPG time-series display of the dental click showed that once the initial anterior seal was formed there was some additional increase in the width of the anterior articulation for several consecutive frames, after which, the articulation remained stable and unchanging, even along the lateral margins, until preparation for the release began. This relatively stable articulation of the dental click observed on one individual token is reflected in the pooled data as the plateau of the contact profile and appears to be a general feature of this click type. Recall that the palatograms in Figure 41 showed a narrow release channel such as that observed in canonical alveolar fricatives.

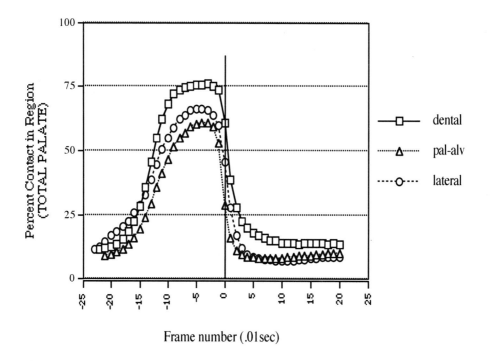

Figure 49: Contact profiles for the dental, palato-alveolar and lateral click types, pooled across speakers and vowel contexts.

This articulatory feature of the dental click is reflected in the contact profiles as a gradual decrease in the diminution of contacted electrodes just prior to and immediately following the tongue blade release.

        The palato-alveolar click has a more asymmetrical curve than the dental click type. The onset is gradual and the peak contact is late, but the offset is abrupt, creating a skewed distribution. The typically long tongue dorsum lead period contributes to the gradual onset phase apparent in the contact profile as well as the EPG time-series diagram for this click type. Once the initial seal is formed, time-series palatograms show that the articulation continues to form, particularly in the anterior portion of the palate. The rapid decline is most likely due, at least initially, to the decline of contacted electrodes in the velar region of the palate and then later, to a redistribution of contacted electrodes in the anterior region, directly related to the release gesture. Figure 42 showed that the anterior articulation for the palato-alveolar click undergoes a retraction just prior to the release. In the token illustrated, retraction occurred quite abruptly, with the tongue tip moving backwards several electrodes and simultaneously widening along the median line. The contact profiles show that the abrupt release gesture, also noted in the EPG frames, going from complete closure to a full release movement where little to no anterior contact remains on the palate, is typical for this type of click. At the moment of release electrode activation is at 25% for the palato-alveolar click and at approximately 60% for the dental click in the first frame after the initial tongue blade release. This difference in the amount of contact at the release is evidence that they have release gestures that are distinctly different in rate.

While the average contact profile for the lateral click is not totally reflective of individual idiosyncratic differences, it is none-the-less instructive to look at the average, and to draw generalizations from it, and then to discuss how speakers deviate from this average. The average lateral trace in Figure 49 depicts a symmetrical shape, much like the dental click type but without the extensive plateau. Only Speaker NT, shown in Figure 48, shows a plateau, though it is short in duration. The offset portion of the curve for the lateral click type is gradual, as observed in the dental click, once again reflecting the affricated nature of the release gesture.

Another important point is clearly depicted in the contact profiles in Figure 49. The profiles show that the dental click reaches close to its peak linguopalatal contact markedly earlier than the palato-alveolar and lateral click types, with the dental click being well into its plateau phase while the palato-alveolar and lateral click types have yet to reach maximum tongue-palate contact. In the following section this observation is statistically verified by measuring the duration to %MAX contact.

Index Calculations

In order to characterize the basic click types, measurements of the cavity area (ECAI), the absolute asymmetry index (ABASI) and the maximum percentage of linguopalatal contact attained across the total palate (%MAX) were made. Recall that the cavity area index was measured by counting the number of uncontacted electrodes in the cavity area. This index was taken at three time-points—Closure, %MAX and Release. The absolute asymmetry index was measured by subtracting the percentage of contacted electrodes on the right from the percentage on the left. Only the absolute value of this measure was considered. This index was also taken at the three designated timepoints.

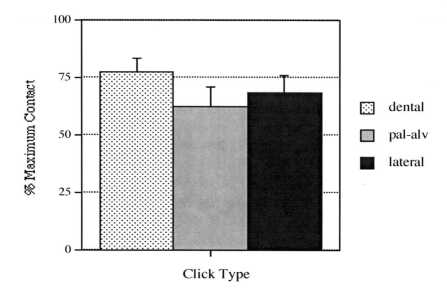

Figure 50: Graph depicting %MAX contact for the dental, palato-alveolar and lateral click types, pooled across speakers and vowel contexts.

Figure 50 depicts the mean values for %MAX, for the three click types, pooled across speakers and vowel contexts.

The dental click has the greatest amount of contact, followed by the lateral click and then the palato-alveolar click type. The rank order of click types for this variable is also evident in the contact profiles of the pooled data (see Figure 49). A three-factor ANOVA with the main independent variables of CLICK, SPEAKER and VOWEL was conducted. A highly significant main effect of CLICK on %MAX was observed [$F_{(2, 177)} = 269$, $p<.001$]. All speakers followed this basic pattern, though clear magnitude differences were evident.

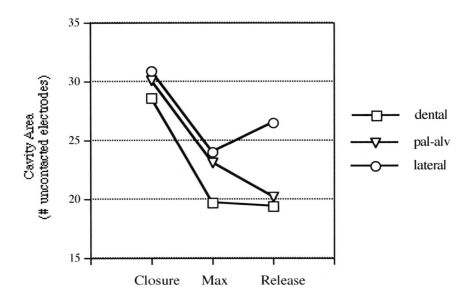

Figure 51: Mean results of the Cavity Area Index measure for the three click types at Closure, %MAX and Release.

Table 8: Mean Cavity Area Index values for the dental, palato-alveolar and lateral clicks, pooled across speakers and vowel contexts.

Timepoint⇒ Click Type⇓	Closure±SD	MAX±SD	REL±SD
Dental /c/	28.551± 8.19	19.609 ±6.472	19.391± 6.231
Pal-alv /q/	30.097 ±7.44	23.097± 7.202	20.194 ±6.106
Lateral /x/	30.819± 7.503	23.958 ±7.909	26.458 ± 7.662

The evolution of the cavity size during clicks as reflected in the EPG data is shown in Figure 51 which depicts the results of the ECAI measurements, pooled across speakers and vowel contexts, at the three designated time-points—Closure, %MAX and Release. Table 8 provides the raw mean values and standard deviations for these index calculations. At closure, the three click types have quite similar cavity areas. Although the initial cavity seal has been made, EPG time-series displays show that the tongue blade/tip articulation is still developing. While lateral contact for the palato-alveolar click is thinner than the lateral margins observed for the dental click, the anterior closure of the palato-alveolar click is more posterior than that of the dental click, which reduces the cavity area in the length dimension. At this particular timepoint, the lateral click is very similar to the dental click. From ONSET-to-MAX the articulations for all click types continue to strengthen.

At %MAX contact the cavity areas for all click types are, more-or-less, at their minimum. The dental click has a significantly smaller cavity area index value at this time-point than the palato-alveolar and lateral click types, while the latter two clicks have nearly equal index values. The small cavity area for the dental click results in part from broad contact along the lateral margins, a broad laminal anterior closure, and as shall be discussed in Section 3.6.4, a more forward tongue dorsum closure, at least in some vowel contexts, all of which combined result in a smaller cavity area.

From MAX-to-REL, the clicks behave radically different. The dental click remains static, the palato-alveolar click continues to contract, and the lateral click undergoes a marked expansion of the cavity area. Recall that the contact profile and the time-series palatograms showed that the dental click is static during the overlap phase, showing movement only during the closure in preparation for the tongue blade release. Note that this preparation for the tongue blade release, which involves the thinning out of the tongue blade contact, occurs at the anterior edge of the tongue blade closure, such that the cavity dimensions remain unaltered. We might expect to see an increase in the cavity area index as an indication of cavity expansion, which must occur if rarefaction of air inside the click cavity is to take place. The fact that an increase in this index is not observed raises questions regarding the mechanism of rarefaction for this click type.

The continued contraction of the palato-alveolar click from MAX-to-REL reflects the more dynamic nature of this click type. Time-series palatograms for this click type, shown in Figure 42, depicted tongue blade movement during the closure. For some speakers this movement occurs over several frames. The reduction of the cavity results from this retraction of the tongue blade. At the frame just prior to release, the cavity indices for the dental and palato-alveolar click types are nearly equivalent. As with dental clicks, the index does not reflect all the expansion of the cavity which must be occurring.

Expansion of the cavity area from time-points MAX-to-REL for the lateral click results for two reasons. First, the anterior coronal closure for this click type thins out along the back edge of the closure, which increases the cavity area. Secondly, some speakers narrow the lateral contact on the release side in preparation for the lateral release. These movements may well contribute to rarefaction in lateral clicks, suggesting that the mechanisms of rarefaction may differ in the different click types.

In lateral clicks there may be compensatory bracing on the opposite side but this does not totally offset the loss of contact on the opposing side, resulting still in a larger cavity area.

A three factor ANOVA with CLICK, VOWEL and SPEAKER as the main independent variables was performed on the cavity area index at time-points Closure, %MAX and Release. The ANOVA results are predictable based on the differences observed in Figure 51. At Closure, there was a significant main effect of CLICK on ECAI $[F(2, 177) = 7.0,$

p<.002]. Post-hoc analysis showed that comparisons of /c, q/ and /c, x/ were significantly different at p<.01, while the comparison of /q, x/ was not significant. At MAX there was also a highly significant main effect of CLICK on ECAI [F(2,177) = 30, p<. 001]. Post-hoc comparisons again showed that the dental click differed significantly from the palato-alveolar and lateral click types, at p< .001, while the comparison of the palato-alveolar and lateral click types was not at all significant. ANOVA tests showed a highly significant main effect of CLICK on ECAI at release as expected [F(2, 177) = 69.16, p<.001]. However, post-hoc comparisons showed that the comparison of /c, q/ is no longer significant, but that now the comparisons of /x, c/ and /x, q/ are highly significant, at p<.001.

Articulatory Asymmetry

Articulatory asymmetry has been shown to be a feature of normal speech (Farnetani 1988). Static palatographic data in Chapter 2 looked at the magnitude of asymmetry by measuring the difference between cavity widths, and found that all click types had a similar magnitude of asymmetry. Speaker differences showed idiosyncratic variation in the side and amount of contact as well. The index measurement discussed here addresses the magnitude of asymmetry, irrespective of whether the greater contact is on the left or right.

Figure 52 depicts the ABASI values for the dental, palato-alveolar and lateral click types, pooled across speakers and vowel contexts, at the timepoints closure, %MAX and Release. Greater index values indicate a greater magnitude of asymmetry. Three very different patterns emerge, reflective of the three click types. The lateral click begins quite asymmetric and remains quite asymmetric throughout the course of the articulation. The dental click begins as asymmetric as the lateral click, but by %MAX, it has become much less asymmetric and remains that way through the duration of the overlap phase. The palato-alveolar click, unlike the dental and lateral click types, begins more symmetric and becomes more asymmetric as the articulation progresses. From MAX-to-REL, the palato-alveolar click has become quite asymmetric. The difference between the dental click and the palato-alveolar click reflects the stable anterior articulation of the dental versus the dynamic pattern of the palato-alveolar.

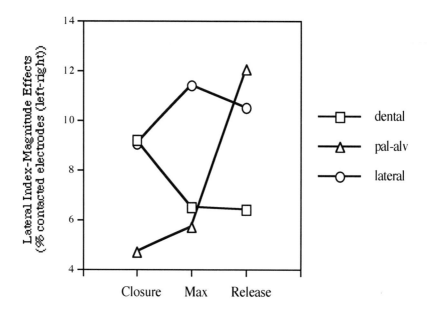

Figure 52: Mean results of the Absolute Asymmetry Index for the dental, palato-alveolar and lateral click types at the initial closure, maximum linguopalatal contact and the time-frame just prior to the tongue blade release.

Table 9: Mean Absolute Asymmetry Index Values (ABASI) for the dental, palato-alveolar and lateral clicks, for data pooled across speakers and vowel contexts.

Timepoint⇒ Click Type⇓	Closure±SD	MAX±SD	REL±SD
dental /c/	9.159 ±6.03	6.46 ±5.44	6.38 ±4.75
pal-alv /q/	4.68 ±4.19	5.67± 4.09	12.04 ±7.34
lateral /x/	9.04 ±8.02	11.38 ±10.68	10.46±11.18

Statistical analysis using a three-factor ANOVA test showed a significant main effect of CLICK on ABASI at all three designated timepoints. Post-hoc tests confirm the significance of comparisons that are clearly visible on the graph. At closure, the dental and lateral clicks were not significantly different from each other but each differed significantly from the palato-alveolar click, at p< .001.

At %MAX, the lateral click is significantly different from both the dental and palato-alveolar clicks, while the latter two clicks are not at all significantly different from each other.

At release, the dental click obviously differs from the palato-alveolar and lateral click types at p<.001 while the palato-alveolar and lateral click types are only marginally distinct, at p<.07.

Vowel effects

Different vowel contexts affect the cavity area index results for the dental and, to a lesser degree, palato-alveolar clicks but not the lateral click. Figure 53 depicts the ECAI means for the dental, palato-alveolar and lateral click types in the vowel contexts of /a/, /e/ and /o/. For each click type, regardless of vowel context, the changes in ECAI follow the same pattern as previously laid out in the pooled data in Figure 51. A three-factor Analysis of Variance was conducted on Cavity Area Index, with SPEAKER, CLICK and VOWEL as the main independent variables. There was a significant main effect of VOWEL on ECAI [F(2,177) = 11.3, p<.001]. Post-hoc comparisons resulted in all vowels being distinct from each other, but the comparisons of /o, a/ an /o, e/ were significant at p< .02 while the comparison of /e, a/ was significant at p< .0001. The main interaction between CLICK and VOWEL was significant [F (4,177) = 5.3, p< .001]. From the means presented on the graph, the significant vowel interactions between /e/ and the other two vowel contexts probably hinge on the behavior of the dental click. In order to unravel the vowel effects, six separate two-way ANOVA tests were conducted.

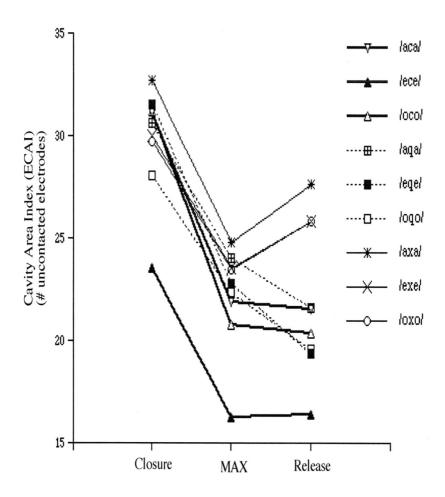

Figure 53: Line graph showing the Cavity Area Index results for the dental, palato-alveolar and lateral clicks in the symmetrical vowel contexts of /a/, /e/ and /o/, pooled across speakers.

Three tests considered each click separately, with SPEAKER and VOWEL as the main independent variables. The other three tests looked at a particular vowel context and considered the effects of SPEAKER and CLICK on ECAI. Table 10 presents the results of the first three tests, which determine VOWEL effects for any one click type, while Table 11 presents the results of the remaining three statistical tests, where the main effect of CLICK on ECAI is of interest. Results for the main effects are listed in the final column of each table while results of the post-hoc pair-wise comparisons are indicated in the middle columns. All significant p-values are explicitly stated; and shaded cells indicate non-significant comparisons.

Table 10: Vowel effects on the Cavity Area Index at % MAX, for speaker-pooled data

Vowel⇒ Comparsions Click type⇓	e/a	e/o	a/o	Statistics (Main effect of VOWEL on Cavity Area Index at %MAX contact)
c ⇒	*p<.0001	*p<.0001		F(2,57)= 33.7, p<.0001
q ⇒	p<.08		p<.02	F(2,60)= 3.3, p<.05
x ⇒				[F(2,60)=.643, p<0.6

Table 10 emphasizes the result that the traces in Figure 53 clearly depict, namely that the dental click in the /e/ vowel context is clearly distinguished from its production in the contexts of /o/ and /a/. Table 11 demonstrates that the dental click is significantly different from all other click types in any particular vowel context, but especially in the context of /e/. The palato-alveolar click, when considered on its own, shows that the mid vowels pattern together while the /a/ vowel context is at least marginally different for them. Table 3.7 shows that the palato-alveolar click is congruent with the lateral click in all vowel contexts. The lateral click has non-significant differences in mean ECAI values for all vowel contexts, as is predictable based on its overlapping traces in Figure 53.

Table 11: Click effects on the Cavity Area Index, for speaker-pooled data

Click⇒ Comparsions Vowel⇓	c/q	c/x	q/x	Statistics (Main effect of CLICK on Cavity area index at %MAX contact)
a	p<.03	p<.004		F(2,59)= 5.8, p<.006
e	*p<.0001	*p<.0001		F(2,60)= 4.2, p<.0001
o	p<.04	p<.001		[F(2,58)=4.8, p<.02

3.5.3 Characterizing the Anterior Articulation

Contact Profiles

Figure 54 depicts the contact profiles of the dental, palato-alveolar and lateral click types, for the region designated as FRONT. The profiles depict a more precise view of the tongue blade articulation from the previous profiles, which depicted linguopalatal contact across the TOTAL PALATE. The contact profiles in the following figure represent data averaged across speakers and vowel contexts. The palato-alveolar click has a skewed distribution, with a gradual onset and a rapid offset, while the dental and lateral clicks are more symmetrical in their contact distributions. The dental click shows a similar plateau as in the previous contact profiles, though it is not as steady as previously noted. Still, the dental click exhibits a marked difference in duration and peakedness from the palato-alveolar click. The trace for the lateral click mirrors that of the dental click. However, given the variability across speakers observed in the production of this click type, the average curve is not really representative. For this reason separate lateral click profiles for each speaker are shown in Figure 55.

The release gestures differ for the click types as previously described. That is, the release gesture for the palato-alveolar click is abrupt, as noted by the large decrease in contacted electrodes, at the line-up point as compared to the frame just prior to the tongue tip release. For the dental and lateral clicks, the diminution of contacted electrodes is more gradual, as might be expected for affricated release gestures. Also note that %MAX contact is nearly equal for the dental and lateral click types, both having greater linguopalatal contact than the palato-alveolar click.

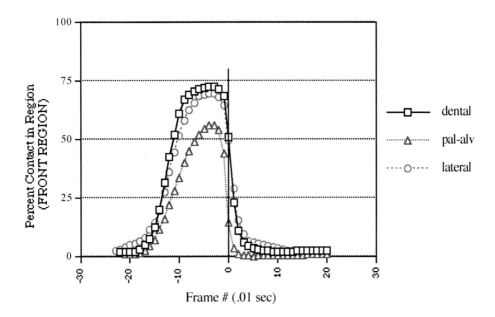

Figure 54: Contact profiles of the FRONT region for the dental, palato-alveolar and lateral clicks, pooled across speakers and vowel contexts, aligned at the release.

As noted earlier, the speakers vary a great deal in their production of the lateral click. The profiles in Figure 55 show variable onsets and different magnitudes of linguopalatal contact among the speakers. In addition, the duration of this click varies across speakers, as does the shape and peakedness of the contact distribution. The profiles for Speakers NT and GV are more peaked and asymmetrical in their contact distributions than Speakers NK and KK. Speakers NT and GV also show shorter duration and a lower peak magnitude of linguopalatal contact. The magnitude of contact at the line-up point for the release gesture for Speakers NT and GV is nearly identical. For these speakers the amount of contact at release is only slightly less than in the preceding frame. Speaker NK shows a marked decline in contacted electrodes at the release when compared to the frame just prior to its release.

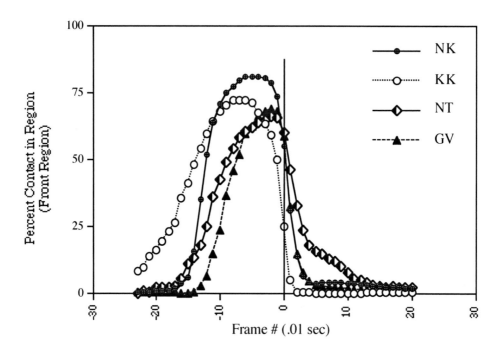

Figure 55: Contact profiles of the FRONT region for the lateral click, separated by speaker but pooled across vowel contexts.

Speaker KK shows much less linguopalatal contact at the release point but this could reflect an alignment error. In fact, if the curve for Speaker KK is shifted one frame to the right, the release gesture closely resembles the curves of the male speakers with respect to the release point. Criteria used to mark the lateral release were the same for all speakers but alignment errors may arise due to the extreme posteriority of the lateral release. For Speaker KK, it is possible that the onset of the lateral release occurred prior to its being recorded on the pseudopalate. In spite of the possible alignment error for Speaker KK, the shape of the curve is none-the-less accurate.

Indices characterizing the tongue blade/tip articulation

Clicks differ in the location and dynamics of the front closures involved. Some aspects of these differences are captured by the Anteriority Index results plotted in Figure 56. Recall that larger AI values indicate a more anterior position of the front edge of the articulations in the entire FRONT region. The dental click is the most anterior, followed by the lateral and then the palato-alveolar click. This is the expected rank order of the click types, based on the SPG data presented in Chapter 2, and this order is maintained at all three timepoints. A three-way ANOVA showed that there was a highly significant main effect of CLICK on Anteriority index at all articulatory stages—Closure [$F(2, 177) = 377.5$, $p<..001$], %MAX [$F(2, 177) = 363.7$, $p<.001$] and Release [$F(2, 177) = 402.8$, $p<.001$]. All post-hoc comparisons at all measured time-points were highly significant at $p< .001$.

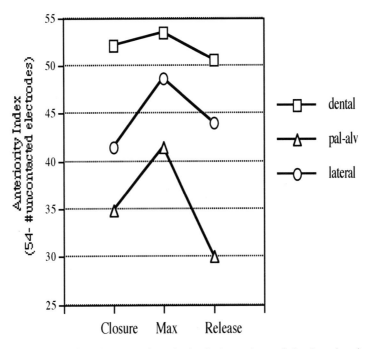

Figure 56: Line graph depicting the mean Anteriority Index values of the dental, palato-alveolar and lateral click types, pooled across speakers and vowel contexts.

Table 12: Mean Anteriority Index Values for the dental, palato-alveolar
and lateral clicks (AI), pooled across speakers and vowel contexts

Timepoint⇒ Click Type⇓	Closure±SD	MAX±SD	Release±SD
dental /c/	1.884±3.483	.565±1.28	3.435±1.989
pal-alv /q/	19.208±7.636	12.625±8.642	23.917±8.823
lateral /x/	12.625±7.141	5.375±3.77	10.069±7.629

Figure 56 also gives a good indication of the development of the anterior articulation for the various click types. For the dental click, at Closure, the tongue blade articulation is quite anterior, and becomes even more anterior at %MAX. But at the release, this click type becomes less anterior. This same general convex pattern is observed for the lateral and palato-alveolar clicks as well. For the lateral click type there is a pronounced increase in the Anteriority index from Closure-to-MAX. From MAX-to-Release, the index value decreases, but does not become as low as its Closure value. For the palato-alveolar click, the anteriority index shows a similar sharp increase from Closure-to-MAX, followed by a decrease from MAX-to Release. However, the difference between AI at MAX and AI at Release is much greater for the palato-alveolar click than that observed for either the dental or lateral clicks.

Figure 57 depicts the mean values for the Median Anteriority Index (EMAI) of the three click types at Closure, MAX and Release, pooled across speakers and vowel contexts. While the anteriority index depicts the overall posture of the anterior portion of the tongue, which includes the anterior lateral margins of the tongue as well, the Median Anteriority Index explores only midsagittal linguopalatal contact as produced by the tongue blade/tip. A greater median anterior index value denotes a more anterior front edge of the tongue blade/tip contact in the midline.

Median Anteriority Index curves from Closure-to-%MAX-to-Release for the three click types produced the same general convex patterns that were associated with the Anteriority Index results. For the dental click, there is a slight increase in EMAI from Closure-to-MAX. From MAX-to-Release there is a decrease in EMAI such that the tongue blade position is less anterior than at the Closure. The lateral click shows an increase in EMAI from Closure-to-MAX and a decline from MAX-to-Release, though this decline does not reach its Closure value. The palato-alveolar click shows an increase in EMAI from Closure-to-MAX and a decrease from MAX-to-Release, similar in magnitude to the dental click. At all timepoints the palato-alveolar click type is distinctly less anterior than the other click types. The dental and lateral clicks are more similar in their tongue blade/tip positions, though at Closure and MAX their articulations remain distinct, while at Release, the tongue blade/tip position for the lateral and the dental clicks converge. A three-factor ANOVA was done on the Median Anteriority Index for each of the three articulatory stages, with CLICK, SPEAKER and VOWEL as the main independent variables. There was a highly significant main effect of CLICK on MAI at Closure [$F(2, 177) = 291.7$, p<.001], MAX [$F(2,177) = 371.6$, p<.001] and Release [$F(2, 177) = 152$, p<.001]. Post-hoc results showed all comparisons to be significant at all timepoints except the comparison of /c, x/ at Release. As will be shown below, the changes over time in the anteriority measures observed in dental and lateral clicks are largely due to changes in the width of the contact in the sagittal plane. However, width changes cannot account for the results in palato-alveolar clicks.

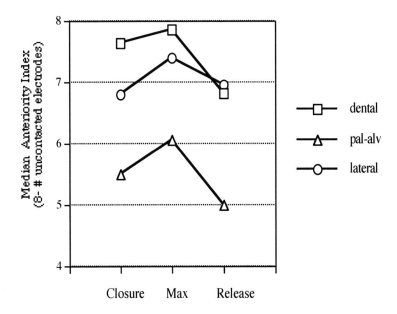

Figure 57: Mean results of the Median Anteriority Index measure for the dental, palato-alveolar and lateral click types at Closure, %MAX and Release for data pooled across speakers and vowels contexts.

Table 13: Mean Median Anteriority Index Values (AI) for the dental, palato- alveolar and lateral clicks, pooled across speakers and vowel contexts

Timepoint⇒ Click Type⇓	Closure±SD	%MAX±SD	Release±SD
dental /c/	0.362±.568	0.159± .369	1.188 ±.845
pal-alv /q/	2.5 ±.839	1.94 ± .991	3.01±.233
lateral /x/	1.21 ±.992	0.611± .742	1.06 ±1.21

Figure 58 depicts the width for the various click types (MAWI), pooled across speakers and vowel contexts, for timepoints Closure, %MAX and Release. A larger Median Anteriority Width Index value signifies greater tongue blade/tip contact. Note that while the dental and lateral clicks have clear convex patterns for this index, Median Anteriority Width Index for the palato-alveolar click type continues to increase from Closure-to-%MAX-to-Release, generating a nearly linear pattern.

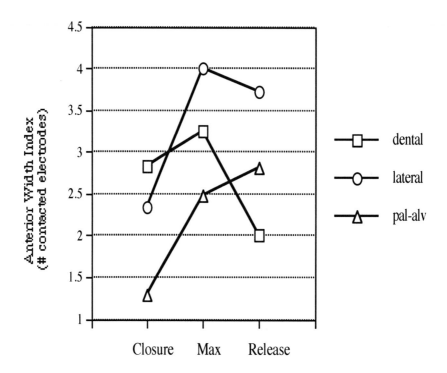

Figure 58: Mean results of the Median Anterior Width Index measure for the dental, palato-alveolar and lateral clicks at Closure, MAX and Release, for data pooled across speakers and vowel contexts.

Table 14: Mean Anteriority Width Index Values for the dental, palato-alveolarand lateral clicks, pooled across speakers and vowel contexts.

Timepoint⇒ Click Type⇓	Closure±SD	MAX±SD	Release±SD
dental /c/	2.826 ±1.084	3.246 ±.651	2.0± .748
pal-alv /q/	1.292 ±.458	2.486 ±.531	2.806± .705
lateral /x/	2.33 ±.628	4.0 ±1.008	3.722±1.078

Maximum width for the dental and lateral click types is achieved at %MAX while the greatest Median Anteriority Width Index value for the palato-alveolar click type is achieved at Release. The decrease in the width index observed at the release for the dental and lateral clicks is most likely tied to the release gesture. Recall that EPG frames of the dental click showed that there was a thinning out of contacted electrodes at the front edge of the tongue blade/tip closure in preparation for the release. This thinning out of electrodes at the anterior edge of the tongue blade closure effectively reduces the width of contact as well as the anteriority of the articulation. The palato-alveolar click type showed a large decrease in the median anteriority index value from MAX-to-Release but an increase in the tongue blade width during the same time period, demonstrating that there is a broader contact and an overall more retracted tongue tip position at release.

3.5.2   *Characterizing the tongue dorsum gesture*

Figure 59 depicts the mean results of the Posteriority Index for the dental, palato-alveolar and lateral click types at timepoints Closure, %MAX and Release. Recall that this index was calculated by counting the number of electrodes in the back area of the palate along the median line. Greater values for this index indicate more contact along the midsagittal line, that is, a more anterior position of the front edge of the tongue dorsum contact. The least linguopalatal contact is recorded on the pseudopalate in the case of the lateral click. In some tokens, the tongue dorsum was visible on the palate at Closure and at %MAX but by the Release in nearly all instances, no tongue dorsum contact was recorded on the pseudopalate. The palato-alveolar click has tongue dorsum contact, which extends further forward than the lateral click. From Closure-to-MAX, the index value remains nearly constant, showing only a slight increase. From %MAX-to-Release a significant decrease in contacted electrodes has occured. The dental click shows more tongue dorsum contact on the pseudopalate than the other two click types.

A three-factor ANOVA with SPEAKER, CLICK and VOWEL as the main independent variables was conducted. There was a highly significant main effect of CLICK on EPI at all three designated timepoints. At Closure [$F_{(2,177)} = 73.9$, $p<.001$], at %MAX [$F_{(2, 177)}=138.7$, $p<.001$] and at Release [$F_{(2, 177)} = 151.4$, $p<.001$]. All post-hoc comparisons were highly significant other than the comparison of /c, q/ at Closure, which was only marginally significant at $p< .02$.

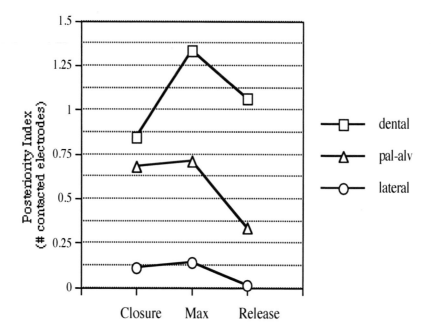

Figure 59: Posteriority Index results for the dental, palato-alveolar and lateral clicks at time-points Closure. %MAX and Release, for data pooled across speakers and vowel contexts.

Table 15: Mean Posteriority Index Values for the dental, palato-alveolarand lateral clicks, pooled across speakers and vowel contexts.

Timepoint⟹ Click Type⇓	Closure±SD	MAX±SD	Release±SD
dental /c/	0.841± .885	1.33 ±.816	1.058± .765
pal-alv /q/	0.681 ±.784	0.708± .759	0.333± .671
lateral /x/	0.111± .316	0.139 ±.348	0.014 ±.118

The nature and timing of the tongue dorsum movement bears strongly on the issues of multigestural coordination, so it is important to pursue this issue further. The best opportunity to extract more information from the EPG data is provided by speakers NK and KK who tend to show more contacted electrodes in the posterior region than the other two speakers, perhaps because their pseudopalates extend to a relatively further back location in the mouth. EPI was calculated for the dental and the palato-alveolar clicks in the symmetrical vowel contexts of /a/ and /e/, for these speakers, on a *frame-by-frame* basis. Since the lateral click shows the least contact among the click types, and the /o/ vowel context shows the least contact among the vowel contexts, these tokens were omitted from the analysis because they provide little information. Figure 60 presents the results of EPI, frame-by-frame. Each trace represents 12 repetitions of the test sequence, six for each speaker. The graphs were aligned at the tongue blade release. The graph records index values 15 frames prior to the release and 3 frames after the release. The results suggest that changes in the position of the front edge of the tongue dorsum contact for the two click types should be attibuted to two different effects. For the dental click, the tongue dorsum contact shows an early increase and then remains relatively stable throughout the remainder of the overlap phase, until shortly before the release. This pattern suggests that there is no movement in the front-back plane but rather the dorsum flattens out as it is pressed against the palate and extends the width of the contact.

On the other hand, for the palato-alveolar click, the posteriority index declines fairly steadily over the 10 frames prior to tongue tip release. The early occurence of the peak and subsequent decline suggest that for this click type the tongue dorsum position retracts a little during the overlap phase. Backward movement of the tongue dorsum may be connected with the backward movement of the tongue tip, as measured by the Anteriority and Median Anteriority indices as shown in Figures 56 and 57. Or it may be a supplementary mechanism used for rarefaction in just this click type. There is an initial increase that occurs prior to MAX, which probably represents the compression and flattening of the tongue dorsum toward the beginning of the closure. This early increase was not captured when data from all the speakers was pooled. As a result, the posteriority index curves appear linear from Closure-to-Max in Figure 59.

Tongue dorsum: Vowel effects

Figure 60 also highlights the effect of vowel context on the tongue dorsum position. For both clicks, the tongue dorsum position is more forward in the front vowel context of /e/ than in the context of the cental low vowel /a/.

Figure 61 depicts the posteriority index for the dental, palato-alveolar and lateral clicks at timepoint MAX, separated by vowel contexts. Note that the dental click has the highest value of this index for any particular vowel context as previously noted.

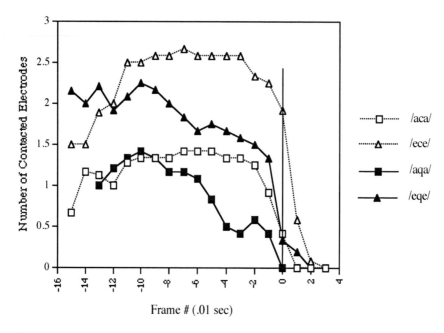

Figure 60: Mean results of the Posteriority Index, calculated on a frame-by-frame basis, for the dental and the palato-alveolar clicks in the vowel contexts of /a/ and /e/, for the female speakers, NK and KK. Time 0 represents the click burst.

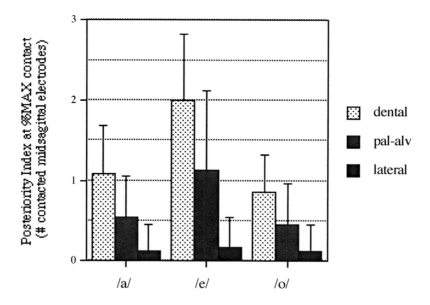

Figure 61: Mean results of the Posteriorty Index measure at %Max contact for the vowel contexts of /a/, /e/ and /o/, for data pooled across speakers.

The context of /e/ has the greatest posteriority index values for both the palato-alveolar and dental clicks, while the vowel means of /a/ and /o/ for any one click type are nearly equal. A three-factor ANOVA test with CLICK, VOWEL and SPEAKER was performed. A highly significant main effect of VOWEL on EPI at MAX was observed [F(2,177) = 45.6, p<.001]. Post-hoc comparisons showed that /e/ differed significantly from both /a/ and /o/ at p<.001, while the comparison of /a, o/ was not even marginally significant. The lateral click shows nearly equal means in all three vowel contexts so the vowel results discussed here derive from the dental and palato-alveolar clicks. Recall that dorsal contact for the lateral click in any vowel context is rarely visible on the pseudopalate. There was also a highly significant main effect of SPEAKER on the posteriority index [F(3, 177) = 44.4, p<.001]. Post hoc comparisons showed that the comparison of /NK, KK/ was not significant, while all other speaker comparisons were. These speaker differences are probably the results of different effective areas covered by the individual pseudopalates.

Summary of the Quantitative Results

The quantitative results presented in the previous sections mathematically characterized some important aspects about the nature of the anterior and posterior gestures of the click types, as previously observed in the qualitative descriptions of these click types. Chapter 4 compares the dental, palato-alveolar and lateral clicks to the simplex non-click alveolar and velar gestures using both qualitative and quantitative approaches as previously applied in earlier sections of this chapter.

CHAPTER 4.0 CONSONANT COMPARISONS

Maddieson (1996) takes the view that complex segments are more likely than not to be composed from simple gestures. For example, Maddieson (1993) explored the articulatory gestures of labio-velar stops in Ewe and compared them to plain bilabial and velar stops using EMMA technology. He concluded that the bilabial and velar gestures which make up the complex segment were similar in amplitude, duration and shape to the gestural movement trajectories of simply-articulated bilabial and velar stops as produced in the same language. Re-use of gestures in this way has been referred to as "gestural economy." Given that clicks are complex segments composed of overlapping tongue dorsum and tongue blade/tip gestures, we would like to know to what extent these individual gestures that comprise the complex segment mirror the gestures found in simply-articulated tongue blade and tongue dorsum articulations. This section compares the singly-articulated alveolar and velar gestures to the component tongue blade/tip and tongue dorsum gestures of clicks.

4.1 Methodology

4.1.1 Corpus and Data collection

Table 16 lists the pulmonic and ejective comparison utterances used in this study. The test sequence is underlined. The simple alveolar segments are aspirated ones in the contexts of /a/ and /o/ and an unaspirated one in the context of /e/. The simple velar stops are of mixed VOT quality as well. In the context of /a/, the simple velar segment is a voiceless unaspirated one but a voiced one in the contexts of /e/ and /o/.

Data for the alveolar and velar plosives were collected with the clicks while the lateral segments were collected in a separate data collection session six months later. The recording set-up for the lateral consonants was identical to the set-up used for collecting the bulk of the data, as described in Section 3.4. Only three subjects—NT, GV and NK—were still available to participate in the study when the lateral segments were recorded.

4.1.2 Data Analysis Procedure

In order to examine the similarities between the tongue blade/tip articulations of the pulmonic and velaric consonants, the index measurements used to characterize the tongue blade/tip position and width—namely the Median Anteriority Index and the Median Anterior Width Index—previously used to analyze clicks are again put to use here. The asymmetry of the different consonant types are also compared using the Absolute Asymmetry Index. Temporal analysis once again makes use of contact profiles and acoustic closure durations. Closure durations of the velar and alveolar pulmonic consonants were measured from the cessation of voicing from the previous vowel to the acoustic release burst of the stop consonant. In the case of the lateral fricative, the acoustic duration of frication was measured from a wide band spectrogram. In addition, the duration of the tongue blade closure was also measured for this consonant type. In comparing the velar gesture of pulmonics and clicks, the posteriority index, taken at the time of peak linguopalatal contact, was used in addition to closure duration data. Discussions of the data in this section focus only on non-click/click comparisons. Statistical tests using two- or three-factor ANOVAs are employed in the same manner as before.

Table 16: Pulmonic and Ejective Consonant Utterances

Click type⇒ Vowel⇓	Alveolar plosive	Velar plosive	Lateral fricative	Velar Lateral Ejective Affricate
/a/	beb<u>ath</u>aba	beb<u>ak</u>abha	beb<u>ahl</u>aba	bebakl'aya
/e/	bab<u>et</u>efa	bab<u>eg</u>eba	bab<u>ehl</u>eba	bebakl'eba
/o/	bab<u>oth</u>oba	bab<u>og</u>oba	bab<u>ohl</u>oba	bebakl'oza

4.2 Qualitative Analysis

4.2.1 Plosives

Figure 62 depicts an example of the simple alveolar plosive [t^h], in the symmetrical vowel context of /a/, as produced by Speaker NT. Onset of the articulatory closure for this consonant occurs in frame 0.09, and is consistent with the acoustic closure as marked in the accompanying waveform. The articulation appears relatively static, with little movement of the tongue blade/tip during the closure. The tongue blade/tip articulation remains relatively thin throughout the closure[9].

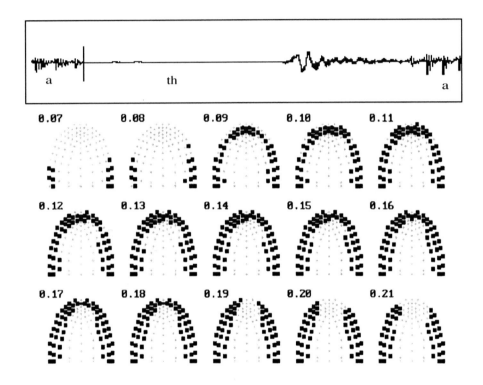

Figure 62: EPG time-series of the voiceless aspirated alveolar plosive in the symmetrical vowel context of /a/, as uttered by Speaker NT.

---

[9] The aspirated alveolar stop in the context of /e/ has broader tongue blade contact. Given the differences in VOT among the alveolars, coarticulation as a function of vowel environment is not analyzed.

Preparation for the tongue blade/tip release begins two to three frames prior to the actual release gesture, where thinning out of contacted electrodes occurs at the posterior edge of the tongue blade/tip closure, in frame 0.17, though in some instances the diminution of contact occurs at the anterior edge of the closure similar to the dental click. Frame 0.19 depicts the actual release gesture, which is quite an abrupt opening. In some instances a narrow channel is observed prior to the acoustic release burst, but this channel usually persists for just one frame; and there is no acoustic evidence of sustained frication during the release of these pulmonic alveolars as there is for the dental click.

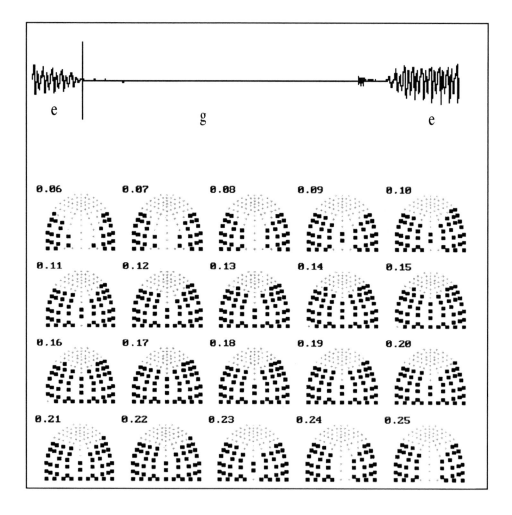

Figure 63: Simple velar plosive in the symmetrical vowel context of /e/, as spoken by Speaker KK

Figure 63 depicts EPG time-series palatograms and accompanying waveform of the simple velar plosive in the symmetrical vowel context of /e/, produced by Speaker KK. The front vowel context was chosen for this figure in order to illustrate a more anterior contact whose articulation could be recorded on the pseudopalate. A full velar closure is evident at time-frame 0.09, and coincides with the acoustic closure as marked in the waveform. Note that the velar closure is initially formed anterior to the backmost row of electrodes in this particular utterance, indicating that the tongue body is pulled forward due to the front vowel context. At frame 0.12 the backmost midsagittal electrodes become fully contacted. There is no obvious evidence of forward displacment or retraction of the dorsal articulation once the initial closure has been formed, but the closure extends from two electrodes in the midline in 0.09 to three in 0.12 and four in 0.14, indicative of a widening contact, before reducing to three again in 0.19, and two in 0.23, in preparation for the release. The acoustic release occurs at about the time of the seal break in frame 0.24.   There is a large amount of lateral contact that encroaches slightly in the defined FRONT region. This extensive lateral and midsagittal contact is the result of the front vowel context, as this segment in the context of /a/ and /o/ is not nearly as fronted. It should also be mentioned that two speakers, NK and KK, show this type of extensive contact for the velar plosive while Speakers NT and GV, although they exhibit vowel effects, do not show nearly the amount of overall contact on the pseudopalate. This same speaker difference with respect to magnitude of contact in the velar area was also noted for clicks and probably results from differences between speakers in the coverage of the pseudopalates, rather than real articulatory differences.

4.2.2 Laterals

IsiZulu has three types of lateral segments in addition to the lateral clicks—an alveolar lateral approximant, alveolar lateral fricatives (voiced and voiceless) and a velar lateral ejective affricate. Given that the lateral click has a fricated release, only the lateral fricative and the velar lateral ejective affricate were considered. We consider first the velar lateral ejective affricate. This segment has been obscurely described. It has previously been reported as alveolar or palatal (Ladefoged 1971), velar (Doke 1924, Ladefoged and Maddieson 1996) as well as a complex segment involving both velar and alveolar contact (Maddieson 1984). Figure 64 depicts the lateral ejective affricate in the symmetrical vowel context of /e/, as produced by Speaker GV. EPG time-series diagrams clearly show that there is no tongue blade/tip contact whatsoever for this segment, and as such, it is purely velar, as initially noted by Doke, though his conclusion was based on phonological information rather than articulatory data. Observations made during the production of this segment revealed that all speakers place the tongue blade behind the bottom incisors. The acoustic closure as marked in the waveform coincides with the epg time-frame at 0.05 though a complete seal is not visible in the velar region until time-frame 0.07. The velar articulation continues to broaden, reaching its maximum contact in the midsagittal region at time frame 0.18. The diminution of contacted electrodes begins in frame 0.22 and continues to decline in contact until time frame 0.26, where the full release is made. There is extensive lateral contact, though not as anterior as observed for the simple velar plosive in Figure 63.

Figure 65 depicts a wide band spectrogram and the corresponding EPG frames for the voiceless lateral fricative in the symmetrical vowel context of /a/. Time frame 1.59 marks the acoustic onset of frication as marked in the corresponding wide-band spectrogram. Note that the tongue blade/tip closure has not yet formed even though acoustic frication has begun. The frication channel is located in the posterior region of the palate, on the right side. And, for all speakers, the channel is quite posterior. For some speakers, the frication channel is not observable on the palate, indicating that it has an even more posterior position than indicated in Figure 65. A complete tongue blade seal in the front region has been made by time-frame 1.62. The tongue blade/tip contact appears to be quite broad throughout much of the closure, but does thin out towards the end of the acoustic frication period. The end of the acoustic frication is nearly always simultaneous with the central front tongue blade release, which in this case occurs at frame 1.81. From this example we expect the acoustic frication duration to be longer than the tongue blade closure duration as a result of the difference in the timing of the onset of frication and the tongue blade closure. Finally, note that the articulation is asymmetrical, with greater contact on the same side as the release channel.

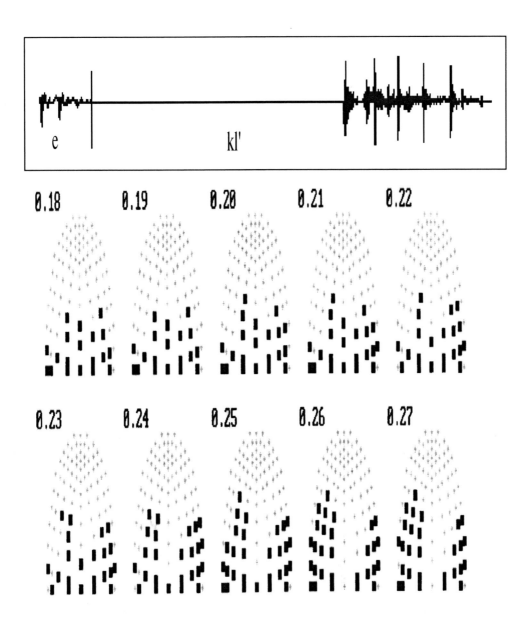

Figure 64: EPG time-series and time-aligned waveform of the velar lateral ejective affricate, in the symmetrical vowel context of /e/, uttered by Speaker GV

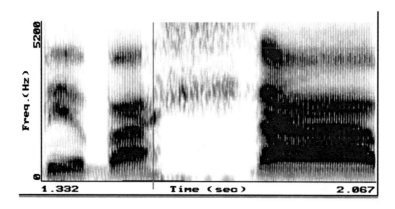

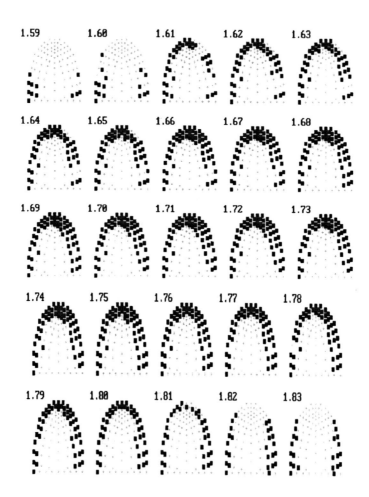

Figure 65: EPG time-series and corresponding wide band spectrogram of the voiceless lateral fricative in the symmetrical vowel context of /a/, for Speaker NK.

4.2.3   Summary of the Qualitative Data

The alveolar plosive showed a consistent gradual onset. It maintained a thin apical-like contact with an abrupt release, much like the palato-alveolar click, but without the dynamic movement observed for this click type. The velar articulation showed not just a broadening of contact in the posterior area but a tongue dorsum closure that was, at onset, formed more anterior than previously seen for clicks in the same vowel context, with the *back* edge of the velar contact being observable on the pseudopalate. Overall, the extent of dorsal contact was much greater than the back contact seen in the velaric segments.

Both the lateral fricative and the velar lateral ejective affricate may be compared to the alveolar and velar gestures that comprise the lateral click. The velar lateral ejective had a large amount of dorsal contact that was clearly observable on the pseudopalate. Recall that there was rarely visible dorsal contact for the lateral click, even in the front vowel context, showing that the velar gestures of the two lateral segments are quite different. The lateral fricative forms a posterior release channel, such as that observed for the lateral click. The tongue blade articulation for the lateral fricative has a similar position to the lateral click, but with a narrower contact. There is some indication that the function of the asymmetry differs for the two lateral segments. In the representative token shown for the lateral click, the side with the greater amount of contact is opposite the release channel. For the lateral fricative, the greater contact is on the same side as the release channel.

4.3   Quantitative Results: The Anterior Articulation

The following section attempts to capture some of the salient similarities and differences among the simplex and complex alveolar and velar gestures among the different segment types. Results focus on comparisons of the blade/tip articulations of the alveolar plosive and the dental and palato-alveolar clicks, while the tongue blade articulation of the lateral click is compared to that of the lateral fricative. The comparison for the velar gesture of the lateral click and the velar lateral ejective affricate is not considered here, given that the qualitative data makes their comparison obvious, rendering continued quantitative analysis uninformative.

4.3.1 Duration Measurements

Figure 66 depicts the front closure durations for the various click types and the simple alveolar stop. For the click types the seal duration of the tongue blade/tip is considered here, except in the case of the lateral click, where the seal duration is terminated by the lateral release, though the tongue blade is still making palate contact. In other words, for all clicks, the articulatory phase being measured here is Overlap.

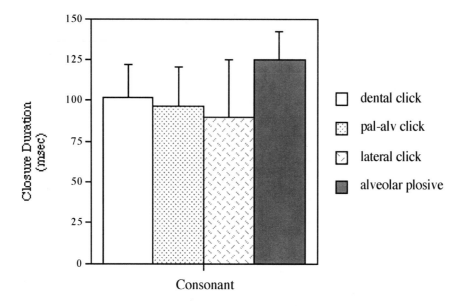

Figure 66: Mean closure durations for the three click types and the alveolar stop.

The alveolar plosive has the longest closure duration among the segments compared, with a mean duration value of approximately 125 milliseconds. The dental click has a mean duration value just over 100 milliseconds, followed by the palato-alveolar click, at 96 milliseconds. The lateral click has the shortest mean duration value, at 89 milliseconds. A three-way ANOVA with CONS, VOWEL and SPEAKER as the main independent variables showed a significant main effect of CONS on closure duration [$F(3, 236) = 63.5$, $p<.001$]. Post-hoc analyis showed that comparisons of the alveolar plosive with all click types yielded highly significant results, at $p< .001$. All speakers showed this same trend though magnitude differences among speakers were evident.

4.3.2 Contact Profiles

Figure 67 shows contact profiles for the FRONT region, for the simple alveolar stop, the dental click and the palato-alveolar click. The lateral click is compared to the lateral fricative in a separate analysis. The maximum linguopalatal contact for the alveolar stop is nearly equal to both the dental and lateral clicks, all of which reach approximately 75% contact. The palato-alveolar click has the smallest peak contact, at slightly greater than 50%. With respect to the peakedness of the contact distribution, the simple alveolar plosive patterns more like the palato-alveolar click type, with contact rising and then immediately tapering off in preparation for the release. However, the contact profile for the simple alveolar is more symmetrical than the palato-alveolar click profile. The onset portion of the profile for the alveolar plosive is more like that of the dental clicks (for 2 of the 4 speakers only). The offset portion of the profile is not as gradual as in the dental and lateral clicks, and there is no acoustic evidence of frication at the release of this segment. As is shown in Figure 67 at the release, the decrease in the percentage of contacted electrodes compared to the frame just prior to release is nearly as great as it is for the palato-alveolar click, confirming that the alveolar stop has an abrupt, non-fricated release.

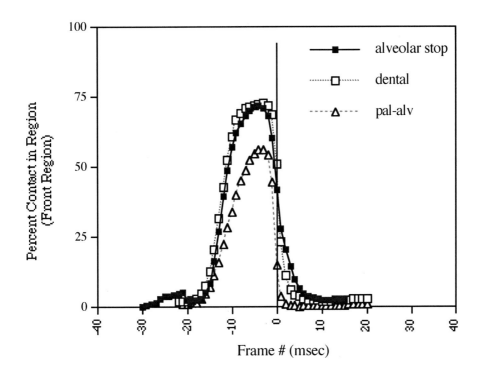

Figure 67: Contact profiles comparing the tongue blade/tip articulations of the simple alveolar stop and the dental and palato-alveolar clicks.

4.3.3 Laterals

Recall that the lateral clicks showed the greatest amount of variation in the magnitude and shape of the contact profiles across speakers. For this reason, the comparison between the lateral click and the lateral fricative is made separately for each speaker. Figures 68, 69 and 70 depict contact profiles for the TOTALPAL region, for the lateral click and the lateral fricative, for Speakers GV, NK and NT, respectively. The lateral segments are aligned at time-zero, which represents the lateral release for the click and the offset of the acoustic frication for the fricative. The contact profile of the lateral fricative ranges from frames -25 to +20 and the lateral click from -23 to +20.

Clearly observable from the contact profiles is the stable, long plateau for the lateral fricative, as compared to the shorter plateaus for the lateral clicks. Particularly noticeable is the extremely long, stable peak for the lateral fricative of Speaker NT. More importantly, note that the lateral fricative is much longer in duration than the lateral click for all speakers. Speakers GV and NK show a slight decline from the plateau towards the end of the steady state portion of the fricative, around frame # -7 for both speakers. This decline likely reflects the preparation for the release, which must obviously involve a decrease in linguopalatal contact. Speaker NT shows only a slight decline of contacted electrodes in preparation for the release. At any rate, the contact profiles for the lateral fricatives are very similar for all speakers. Finally, note that for all speakers, the lateral click has greater peak contact than the lateral fricative as expected, given that /hl/ is a fricative, whereas /x/ is a stop, and moreover has some contacted electrodes in the back area due to raising of the back of the tongue. This difference in peak contact is especially great for Speaker NK, probably again due to the fact that the pseudopalate extends to a relatively further back position in her mouth than it does for the males.

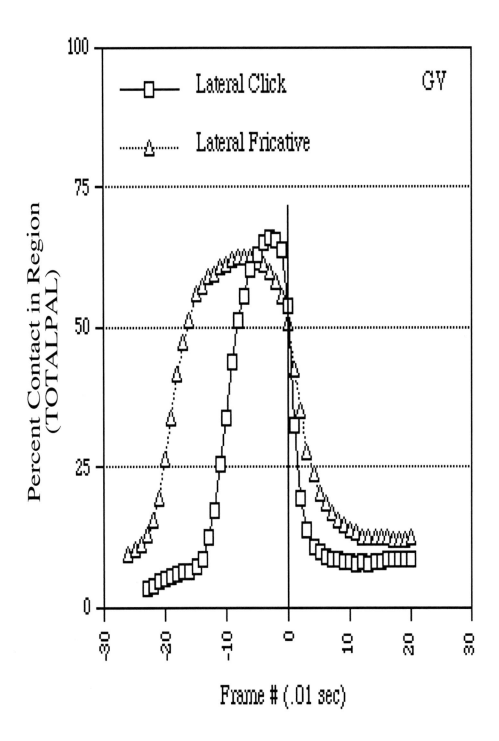

Figure 68: Contact profiles comparing the lateral click and the lateral fricative, calculated for the total palate, for Speaker GV.

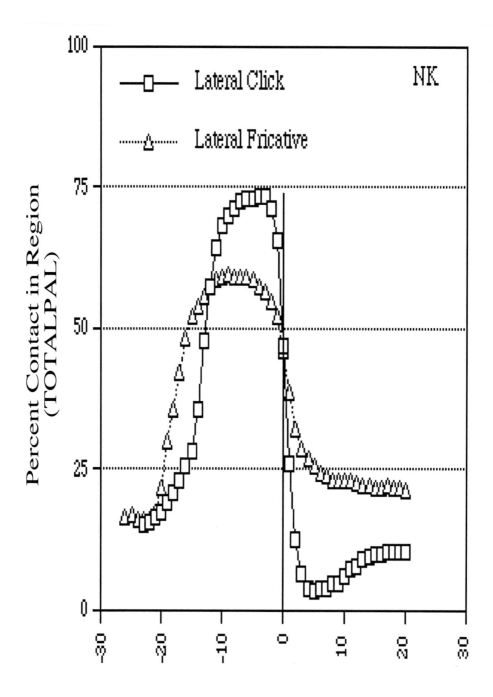

Figure 69: Contact profiles comparing the lateral click and the lateral fricative, calculated for the total palate, for Speaker NK.

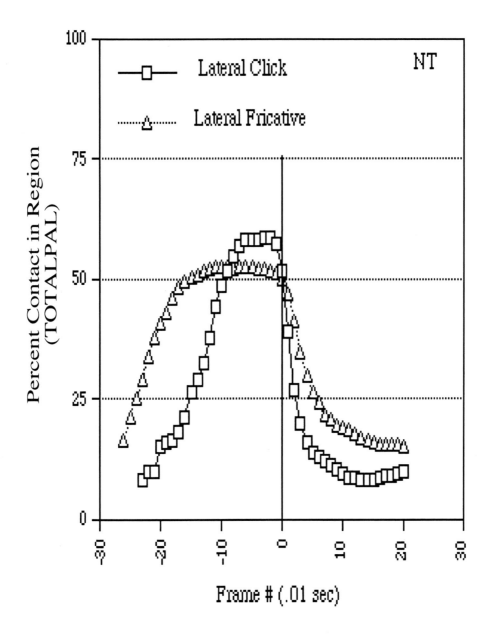

Figure 70: Contact profiles comparing the lateral click and the lateral fricative, calculated for the total palate, for Speaker NT.

Figure 71 depicts the means of the various closure durations for the lateral segments. For the lateral fricative, both the duration of frication is reported as well as the closure duration of the tongue blade/tip. For the lateral click, the seal duration is measured as well as the duration of the tongue blade /tip closure. As was seen in the contact profiles, the duration of the lateral fricative is considerably longer than the front articulation of the lateral click. However, for the lateral fricative, the tongue blade closure is shorter in duration than the frication duration, which continues for 13 milliseconds once the tongue blade begins its initial release. Qualitative analysis (see Figure 65) of the lateral fricative showed that acoustic frication begins before the tongue blade/tip closure makes a complete seal on the palate and, the initial release of the tongue blade occurs some 20 milliseconds prior to the cessation of frication. For the lateral click, the tongue blade remains in a raised posture for several frames after the lateral release begins. In all respects considered here, the lateral fricative is longer in duration than the lateral click.

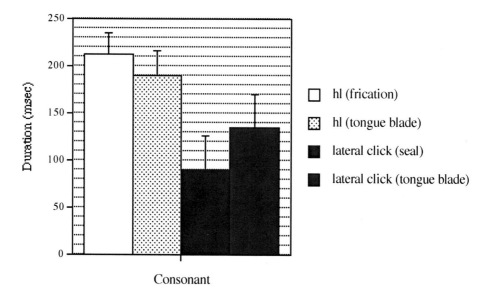

Figure 71: Assorted mean closure durations comparing the lateral fricative and the lateral click, pooled across speakers and vowel contexts.

Analysis of Variance was performed on these assorted closure durations, with CONSONANT, VOWEL and SPEAKER as the main independent variables. There was a highly significant main effect of consonant on closure duration [$F(3, 240) = 197$, $p<.001$]. Post-hoc analysis showed that pair-wise comparisons of the means for the duration of frication of the lateral fricative, the duration of the tongue blade closure for the lateral fricative and the lateral click and the seal duration for the lateral click all differed significantly from each other at p< .001. The main effect of VOWEL was not significant, nor were any post-hoc comparisons of that variable. The interaction between CONS and VOWEL was not significant either. There was a significant main effect of SPEAKER [$F(2,180)$ = 21.1, p<.001], but this result represents magnitude differences among the speakers, as the rank order of the categories shown in Figure 71 is consistent for all subjects.

4.3.4 Indices

This particular section compares the tongue blade articulations of the three click types, the lateral fricative and the plain alveolar stop using three index measurements—Median Anteriority Index, Median Anterior Width Index and Absolute Asymmetry Index. Recall that the Median Anteriority Index assesses place of articulation while the Median Width Index measures the width of the articulation. The Absolute Asymmetry Index determines the overall magnitude of asymmetry for a particular articulation, without indicating which side had the greater contact.

Figure 72 depicts the Median Anterior Index for the three click types, the lateral fricative and the simple alveolar stop at Closure, %MAX and Release. Recall that a more anterior articulation has a greater index value. Figure 72 shows that all consonants, at Closure and %MAX, pattern in the expected manner with respect to place of articulation, with the dental click having the greatest MAI value, the palato-alveolar click having the smallest EMAI value and the alveolars, namely the lateral fricative, simple alveolar plosive and the lateral click, having intermediate index values.

The results of a two-factor ANOVA, with CONSONANT and VOWEL as the main independent variables showed that at Closure there was a highly significant main effect of CONS on the Median Anteriority Index [$F(4, 323)$ = 53.3, p<.001]. Post-hoc analysis showed that the lateral fricative, the lateral click and the simple alveolar stop all differed significantly from both the dental click and the palato-alveolar click at p<.001. In addition, the simple alveolar plosive differed significantly from the lateral click, (p<.002) and marginally from the lateral fricative (p<.06). The comparison between the lateral click and the lateral fricative was not at all significant at this particular time-point.

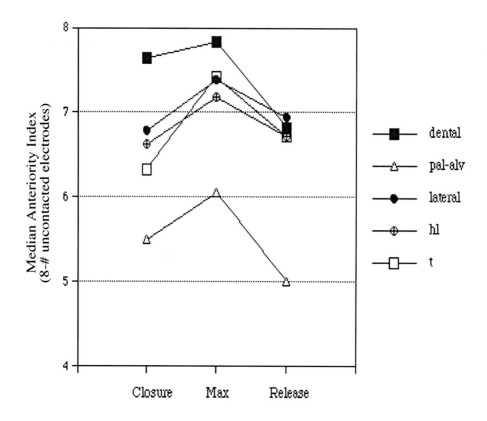

Figure 72: Mean results of the Median Anteriority Index measure for the three click types, the lateral fricative and the alveolar plosive, at Closure, %MAX contact, and the frame just prior to the tongue blade release.

At %MAX, the dental click remains distinct from all other consonants, as does the palato-alveolar click. However, the alveolars converge at this time-point such that comparisons of /hl, t/ becomes slightly less significant, at p< .07, and the comparison of /t, x/ are no longer distinguished at all, with p< .8. The difference between /hl, x/ remains insignificant, at p< .11. Thus, at this time-point, where the maximum extent of the gesture has been reached, a clear place distinction is made between alveolars (regardless of manner), dentals and palato-alveolars.

At Release, the dental and alveolars converge, and together remain distinct from the palato-alveolar click. This result for the dental click was attributed to the specific type of release movement where tongue blade contact diminishes at the anterior edge of the constriction. The same type of preparation is apparent for the alveolar segments as /hl/, /x/ and /t/ all become slightly more posterior at Release, though not to the same degree as observed for the dental click. A two-way ANOVA with CONS and VOWEL as the main independent variables confirm a significant main effect of CONS on EMAI [$F_{(4,323)}$ = 49.4, $p<.001$]. The only significant post-hoc comparisons at Release are those comparisons involving the palato-alveolar click.

Figure 73 depicts the mean values of the Median Anterior Width Index for the three click types and the pulmonic consonants /hl/ and /t/ at Closure, %MAX and Release. The lateral fricative and the simple alveolar plosive use a convex pattern, and in this sense pattern very much like the dental click. At Closure the dental click is wider than both /hl/ and /t/ but by %MAX contact these three consonants converge, having nearly equal EMAWI values. From MAX-to-Release, there is a marked decrease in width for /c/, /hl/ and /t/. Taken together with the results shown in Figure 72 the patterns here indicate that these three consonant types have a stable place of articulation throughout their duration, with the front edge reaching a little further forward at the time of maximum contact because the tongue has flattened and broadened its contact at the peak.

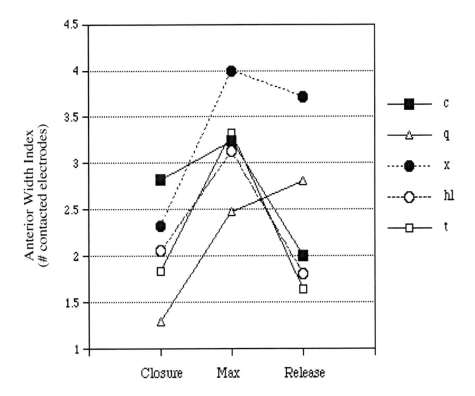

Figure 73: Line graph comparing the Median Anterior Width Index for the comparisons of the three click types and the pulmonic consonants /hl/ and /t/, pooled across speakers and vowel contexts.

The lateral click patterns differently from the lateral fricative. While a clear nearly symmetrical convex pattern is observed for the lateral fricative, a sharp rising pattern from Closure-to-%MAX, followed by only a small decline from %MAX-to-Release, is observed for the lateral click. Recall that the EMAI values for these consonants were nearly equivalent at all three timepoints. For the lateral click, the tongue blade/tip closure is maintained even though the lateral channel has already formed in the velar region. For the lateral fricative, the diminution of contacted electrodes begins much earlier during the course of the articulation, so that by the time the offset of frication for the consonant is reached, the tongue blade/tip closure is nearly non-existent.

Figure 74 depicts the differences in the width of the lateral segments at or near the release. The lateral click is shown at the initial frame depicting the lateral release while the lateral fricative is shown at the frame just prior to cessation of frication.

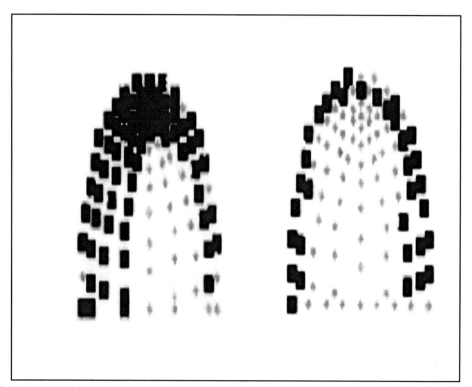

Figure 74: EPG frames for the lateral click and the lateral fricative at the release, depicting the difference in the tongue blade/tip articulation, as produced by Speaker NK.

A two-factor ANOVA with CONS and VOWEL as the main independent variables was conducted on the Median Width Index at Closure, %MAX and Release. There was a highly significant main effect of CONS on the width index at all three timepoints. At Closure $[F(4, 323) = 44.6, p<.001]$, post-hoc comparisons showed all pair-wise comparisons to be significant at p<.001, except for /hl, x/ which was only marginally significant at p<.04, and /hl, t/, which was not at all significant. At %MAX, [F(4,323)=28.1, p<.001], post-hoc analysis showed that the palato-alveolar click remained significantly distinct from all other segments, at p<.001. The lateral click also remained distinct from all other segments, at p<.001. The remaining pair-wise comparisons of /c, t/ and /hl, t/ were not at all significant. At Release [F(4,323)=82.9, p<.001], post-hoc comparisons maintained the distinctiveness of the palato-alveolar and lateral clicks, at p<.001. The comparison of /c, hl/ was significant at p<.01, while the comparisons of /c, hl/ and /hl, t/ were not even marginally significant.

Figure 75 depicts the results of the Asymmetry Index for the three click types, the lateral fricative and the plain alveolar stop. The results of this index measure show important similarities among the pulmonic consonants and the click types. For the lateral click type, we previously noted that this particular click, at onset, had a high degree of asymmetry and, more importantly, remained highly asymmetric throughout the course of its articulation. The same is true for the lateral fricative. At Closure the lateral fricative has the greatest mean ABASI value. From Closure-to-%MAX, asymmetry increases as it does for the lateral click. From %MAX-to-Release there is just a slight decline in asymmetry. The lateral fricative, at all three time points, has a greater magnitude of asymmetry than the lateral click.

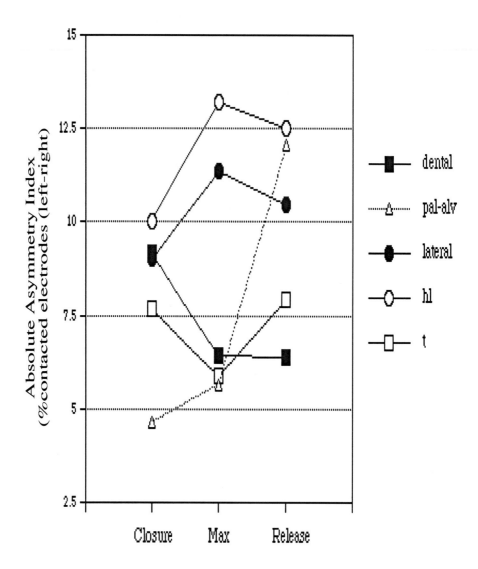

Figure 75: Mean results of the Absolute Asymmetry Index measure for the three click types, the lateral fricative and the plain alveolar stop.

Though the lateral fricative and the lateral click yielded non-significant results with respect to the magnitude of asymmetry, Figure 74 points to a difference in the function of the asymmetry. For the lateral click, the asymmetry seems to result from the need to brace one portion of the tongue along the surface of the pseudopalate in order to facilitate the lowering of the opposite side away from the palate surface to create the release channel. This type of bracing creates more linguopalatal contact on the opposite side of where the release channel is located. In the case of the lateral fricative, it is the side where the frication channel is created which has the greater linguopalatal contact. The frication channel observed in the lateral fricative is created from the onset of the articulation and does not result from lowering of one side of the tongue dorsum. The greater magnitude on the side of the release channel for this segment aids in forming and maintaining a stable frication channel.

ABASI means indicate that the simple alveolar plosive behaves mainly like the dental click. At Closure, the dental click has a greater magnitude of asymmetry than the alveolar plosive, though not significantly so. At %MAX contact the means for the simple alveolar and the dental click converge, along with the palato-alveolar click, while the lateral segments remain apart. From %MAX-to-Release, the alveolar plosive achieves a greater magnitude of asymmetry than the dental click, although the difference is not significantly different.

In order to confirm the observations apparent in Figure 75 regarding the asymmetry index values, a two-factor ANOVA test was conducted with CONS and VOWEL as the main independent variables. The results indicate a significant main effect of CONS on ABASI at Closure [$F(4, 323) = 7.4$, $p<.001$], %MAX [$F(4,323)=14.4$, $p<.001$] and Release [$F(4,323) = 6.95$, $p<.001$]. Post-hoc comparisons showed that at Closure the comparison of /c, q/ was significant at $p<.001$, while all other pair-wise comparisons with the dental click were not significant. The palato-alveolar click was significantly different from all other segments. The comparison of /hl, t/ was only significant at $p< .05$, while the comparison of /hl, x/ was not at all significant, as expected. The comparison of /t, x/ was not significant either.

At %MAX, post-hoc comparisons showed that the pair-wise comparisons of /c, t, q/ are not significantly different from each other, but each is significantly different when compared to /hl/ or /x/, at $p< .001$. Once again the comparison of /hl, x/ was not significant either. At Release, post-hoc comparisons yielded two groups whose pair-wise comparisons yielded non-significant results. They are /hl, x, q/ and /c, t/. All pair-wise cross comparisons among the two groups were significant at $p< .004$. The comparison of /t, x/ yielded only marginal results, at $p< .07$.

4.4 The Dorsal Articulation

Recall that in Section 3.5 the tongue dorsum gesture for the click types was analyzed using the Posteriority Index, which measured the number of contacted electrodes along the median line in the posterior region of the palate. The Posteriority Index was also calculated for singleton pulmonic velar plosives in the same manner in order to compare the dorsal gesture of the simplex and complex consonants.

Figure 76 depicts the results of the mean posteriority index values for the three click types as well as the simple velar plosive, pooled across speakers and vowel contexts. The simple velar plosive had the greatest overall Posteriority Index (EPI) value, indicating that this articulation has the most anterior position of the front edge of the tongue dorsum gesture for the consonants being compared. A three-way Analysis of Variance, using SPEAKER,

CONS, and VOWEL as the main independent variables, was performed on EPI in order to determine if the positional differences between the tongue dorsum gesture of the click types and the simple velar plosive were significant. The results yielded a highly significant main effect of CONS on EPI [F(3, 237) = 162.5, p<.001. Post-hoc analysis showed that all consonants were significantly different from each other. In addition, it should be noted that all speakers follow this pattern except GV, whose velar plosive has a lower mean index value than that of the dental click. For Speaker GV, the tongue dorsum gesture was not visible on the pseudopalate in the case of the palato-alveolar and lateral clicks.

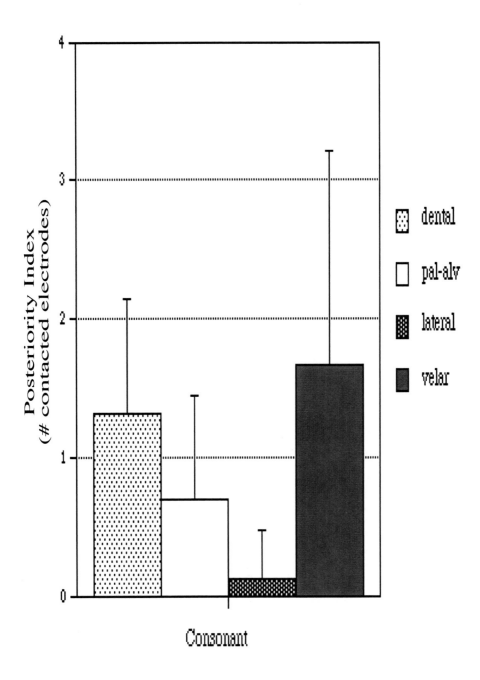

Figure 76: Mean results of the Posteriority Index values at %MAX contact for the tongue dorsum gesture of the various clicks types as compared with the simple velar plosive.

Figure 77 depicts the acoustic closure durations for the tongue dorsum articulation for the three click types and the simple pulmonic velar stop. The results indicate that the simple velar stop is a little shorter in duration than the tongue dorsum durations of the three click types. A three-factor Analysis of Variance test was conducted on the acoustic closure durations of the tongue dorsum, with the main independent variables of SPEAKER, CONS and VOWEL. There was a significant main effect of CONS on the tongue dorsum closure duration [$F(3, 155) = 25.7$, $p<.001$]. Post-hoc comparisons showed that the pair-wise comparisons of the simple velar stop significantly differed from the mean tongue dorsum closure durations of /c/, /q/ and /x/ at $p< .001$. The only other marginally significant comparison was /c, x/, with $p< .03$. All other comparisons were not significant.

There was a main effect of SPEAKER [$F(3,155) = 40$, $p<.001$]. All post-hoc comparisons of subjects were significant at $p< .001$, other than /GV, KK/, which was not significant. However, the SPEAKER effects reflect magnitude differences among subjects. For all speakers the duration of the tongue dorsum movement made in the simple velar stop was shorter than the tongue dorsum gesture made in the clicks.

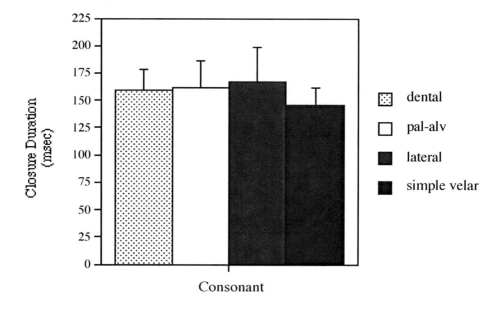

Figure 77: Mean results comparing the tongue dorsum closure durations of the click consonants and the simple velar stop, pooled across speakers and vowel contexts.

4.4.1 Vowel effects

Figure 77 showed that across vowel contexts, the tongue dorsum gesture of the simple velar, when compared to the tongue dorsum closure durations of the three click types, had the shortest closure duration. We would like to know if this is also the case in every vowel context. Three separate two-way ANOVA's were conducted, one for each vowel context, with SPEAKER and CONS as the main independent variables. The results are listed in Table 17. Main effects of the independent variable are listed in the final column. Post-hoc results of pair-wise comparisons of /k/ and each of three clicks are given in the middle three columns. Shaded cells indicate non-significant comparisons.

The results indicate that the tongue dorsum duration for the simple velar stop does not differ from the tongue dorsum closure duration as produced in clicks in the /a/ context. However, in the contexts of both /e/ and /o/, the simple velar has a significantly shorter mean closure duration when compared to the tongue dorsum duration of the dental, palato-alveolar and lateral clicks.

Table 17: Statistics showing the effect of CONS on Closure duration, comparing the dorsal articulation of the simple alveolar plosive and the three click types.

Cons ⇒ Comparsions Vowel ⇓	k/c	k/q	k/x	Statistics (Main effect of CONS on Closure duration)
a ⇒				$F(3,50)= .89$, p<.453
e ⇒	p<.0001	p<.0001	p<.001	$F(3,60)= 11.8$, p<.0001
o ⇒	p<.001	p<.0001	p<.0001	$F(3,45)= 4.8$, p<.0001

Three separate three-factor ANOVA's were performed on the closure durations for the pair-wise comparisons of the simple velar with each of the click types. The independent variables were SPEAKER, CONS and VOWEL. This analysis was done in order to exclude the comparisons of /c, q/, /c, x/ and /q, x/, namely the click-click comparisons, so as not to confound the vowel results. Each ANOVA resulted in non-significant main effects of VOWEL on the closure durations for the particular consonant comparison being made, except in the case of /k, x/. For this comparison, there was a marginally significant main effect of VOWEL on closure duration [$F(2,79) = 2.7$, p<.08]. Post-hoc tests showed that the comparison of /e, o/ was marginally significant for the /k, x/, at p< .07. For each comparison, there was a significant interaction between CONS and VOWEL, confirming the results noted in Table 17, that the pair-wise comparisons of /k/ with any click type are not significantly different in the context of /a/, while highly significant results were observed in the contexts of /e/ and /o/.

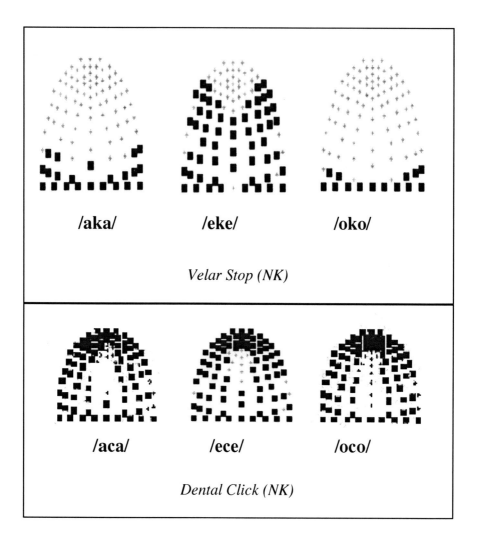

Figure 78: EPG palatograms, at %MAX contact, of the simple velar stop and the dental click in the symmetrical vowelcontexts of /a/, /e/ and /o/, depicting the tongue dorsum positions between the two segment types, as produced for Speaker NK.

Figure 78 depicts "snapshots" of the simple velar plosive and the dental click at %MAX contact, in the vowel contexts of /a/, /e/ and /o/, as produced by Speaker NK. We focus only on palatograms of the dental click, where the tongue dorsum contact is partially visible on the pseudopalate (the *back* edge of the dorsal contact is rarely visible on the pseudopalate for the dental clicks).

Tongue dorsum contact is, in many instances, not visible at all on the palate for the palato-alveolar and lateral clicks. The EPG contact patterns in the posterior region show *very similar* variations in tongue dorsum position across these vowel contexts for the velar plosive and the dental click. Both segments show greater anterior contact in the context of /e/ when compared to their contact in /a/ and /o/. Also, the contact in /a/ extends further forward than the contact in /o/, for both segments. Figure 78 depicts the difference in the extent of contact between these segments in the context of /e/. The tongue dorsum gesture for the dental click is less anterior than it is for the simple velar plosive in this vowel context. For the velar segment, the back edge of the tongue dorsum is visible in the /e/ context, indicating that the tongue dorsum is indeed pulled forward, as opposed to being simply a broader contact. In the vowel contexts of /a/ and /o/, the two segments have congruent tongue dorsum positions.

Figure 79 depicts the mean EPI values for the dental click and the pulmonic velar plosive. The figure confirms what the EPG frames show in Figure 78, namely that in the context of /e/, the velar plosive has a more forward contact. However, in the contexts of /a/ and /o/, the mean EPI values for the /c/ and /k/ are analogous. A three-factor Analysis of Variance, with SPEAKER, CLICK and VOWEL as the main independent variables was conducted on EPI, as measured at %MAX contact. There was a significant main effect of CONS on EPI [$F(1,117) = 19$, $p<.0001$], indicating that /k/ has a significantly greater EPI.

There was also a significant main effect of VOWEL on EPI [$F(2,117) = 158$, $p<.0001$]. Post-hoc comparisons indicate that pair-wise comparisons with the vowel /e/, namely /a, e/ and /o, e/—are highly significant, with $p< .0001$, while the comparison of /a, o/ is not at all significant. There was also a significant main effect of SPEAKER [$F(3,117) = 69$, $p<.001$], but these results reflect the magnitude differences between the male and female speakers, with the female speakers having more overall contact on the pseudopalate than the male speakers. All speakers follow the general pattern laid out in Figure 79 except in the case of Speaker GV, who has equal mean EPI values for /c/ and /k/ in the vowel context of /e/.

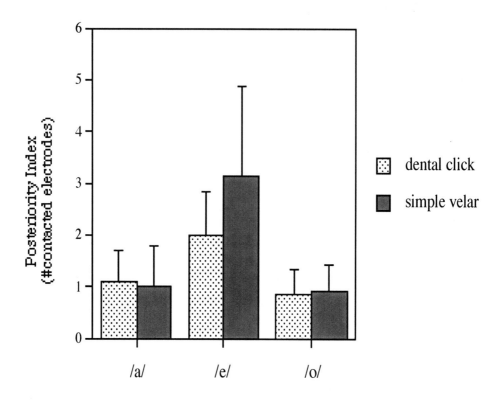

Figure 79: Mean results of the Posteriority Index values at %Max Contact comparing the simple velar plosive and the tongue dorsum closure of the dental click in the vowel contexts of /a/, /e/ and /o/, for speaker-pooled data.

4.5 Discussion

Duration results for the consonant comparisons show that the mean duration of the front gesture for any particular click type is shorter than the mean duration of the simple alveolar stops. Mean duration values for the simple velar gesture are only 20-25 milliseconds shorter than the velar gesture as measured for clicks. In this respect, click consonants have a similar segment duration to simple velars. Maddieson (1993) showed the same magnitude of difference between the labio-velar and simple velar gestures of Ewe.

The dorsal component of the dental click was spatially very similar to the simple velar gesture across the various vowel contexts, though the position of the dorsal closure of the clicks was not as forward in the context of /e/, presumably because such a fronted contact would encroach into the cavity area.

Tongue blade/tip articulations of the non-click consonants were similar in some respects to the click types, in particular the dental click and the alveolar plosive have notable similarities. However, click articulations are not identical to other consonants in their spatial or temporal organization. The fact that the tongue blade/tip gestures are shorter in clicks than in pulmonic coronal consonants may be important in keeping the total segment duration of the clicks similar to the duration of simple plosives.

Rarefaction must occur in order to produce a click sound. Active rarefaction does not occur in pulmonic consonants, so there is no parallel to be made with click consonants here. The following chapter on the aerodynamics of clicks considers this very important process of rarefaction as it occurs in IsiZulu click production. As shall become apparent, an in-depth examination of the rarefaction process yields a wealth of information on the nature of the gestures invloved in click production.

CHAPTER 5: AERODYNAMICS OF CLICK CONSONANTS

5.0 Introduction

Previous chapters investigated various aspects of the nature and coproduction of click gestures using both static and dynamic palatography. This chapter uses pressure and airflow measurements to explore the coordination of click gestures as well as the coarticulatory effects associated with click production.

5.1 Methodology

5.1.1 Data Collection

Multichannel simultaneous recordings of the audio, intraoral pressure, ingressive oral airflow and pharyngeal pressure records were obtained using the Computer Speech Laboratory (CSL). CSL is a data analysis package that allows for data collection and analysis of aerodynamic and acoustic data (as well as other types of data). A sample of the aerodynamic data is depicted in Figure 80. The audio signal is depicted in channel 1, the intraoral pressure signal in channel 2, ingressive oral flow in channel 3, and pharyngeal pressure in channel 4. The audio channel was recorded at a sample rate of 5000 Hz using a free-standing microphone. Ingressive oral airflow was collected by means of a modified Rothenberg mask. Intraoral pressure was recorded as described below. Pharyngeal pressure data, used to assess tongue dorsum movement, was collected by inserting a small diameter polyethylene tube into the pharynx by way of the nostril. Aerodynamic data collection methods for oral flow and pharyngeal pressure data have been described in detail by Ladefoged in various publications (Ladefoged 2003, 1997, 1993b). While pharyngeal pressure, oral flow and nasal flow have been measured before for click consonants, empirical

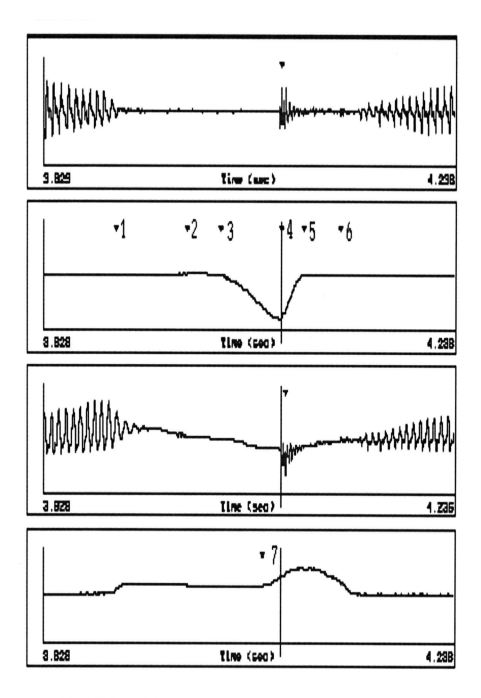

Figure 80: Multichannel simultaneous recording of audio, intraoral pressure, oral flow and pharyngeal pressure,

data on intraoral pressure had not previously been obtained; only estimates of intraoral pressure exist (Kagaya 1978), which are based on Traill's (1985) x-ray cineradiology data of ! Xo͂o clicks.

Intraoral pressure of the click cavity was measured by means of a custom-fitted acrylic pseudopalate approximately .2mm thick, depicted in Figure 81. A small polyethylene tube was fixed to this pseudopalate at the highest point of the hard palate with dental adhesive. The tube was threaded from the palate leftward at a 45 degree angle, looped around the back-most molar and then threaded out of the mouth along the outer gumline. Positioning of the tube in this manner was particularly important to assure that it did not interfere with the articulation of the consonant.

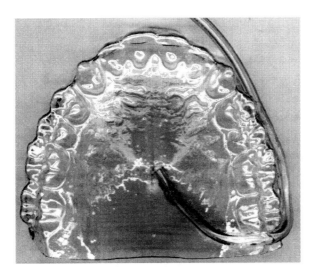

Figure 81: Custom-fitted acrylic pseudopalate with attached tubing, used to measure the intraoral pressure in clicks.

Methods for calibrating pressure transducers used for collecting oral airflow and pharyngeal pressure data have been described in detail by Ladefoged (1997, 2003). Briefly, oral airflow was calibrated using a standard flow meter, while both pharygeal pressure and intraoral pressure were calibrated using a water manometer. In calibrating the intraoral pressure data, the probable range of pressure values was determined to be between -100 to -200 cm H_2O. Calibration was accomplished by sucking water up a tube. Other than this minor difference, the basic calibration procedure for the intraoral data was similar to the calibration procedure previously described in Ladefoged (1980, 1997).

5.1.2 Recording set-up

Each subject inserted their own nasal catheter about 15 centimeters into the pharyngeal cavity, just below the uvula. The tubing outside of the mouth was fixed to the cheek using adhesive tape and then the endpoint was attached to the pressure transducer. The position of the tube was tested by having the subject speak, and then checking the resulting data.

Once the nasal catheter was properly situated in the throat cavity, the acrylic pseudopalate for measuring intraoral pressure was then put in the mouth. All subjects had been wearing this pseudopalate for at least one hour before data collection in order to get accustomed to the palate. It was removed from the mouth prior to inserting the nasal catheter.

In order to collect airflow data, a rubber mixing bowl outfitted with the proper wire mesh resistance, as described in (Ladefoged 1997, 1993b), was placed tightly around the speaker's mouth. Tubes from the pseudopalate and the nasal catheter were adjusted and the system was tested to make sure that all channels were properly recording data.

Audio data was collected using a free-standing microphone. Given the presence of the oral flow mask, the recorded audio signal sounds muffled and as such, is not a high quality signal to be used for any serious acoustic analysis. This signal does provide reference points for locating vowel onsets and offsets as well as consonantal releases, and in this respect, is valuable data.

Test utterances consisted of the dental, palato-alveolar and lateral click types in three vowel environments—/a/, /e/, and /o/— uttered in the carrier phrase *bathi* _____ 'they say _____.' These were the same test utterances used in Chapter 3 for Electropalatography, and are repeated in Table 18 for convenience. A description of the morphology of these words may be found in Appendix A.

Each test utterance was read in series three times. All three tokens on each channel were checked to determine if the data had been properly recorded. Unacceptable data usually resulted from the intraoral pressure tube and/or the pharyngeal pressure tube being blocked with mucus. When irregular traces were observed, the tubes were cleared out using a rubber bulb, and the tokens were re-recorded. In general, the subjects were able to produce natural sounding speech and tolerated the tubes long enough to collect the entire corpus of words in one sitting.

Three of the four speakers—GV, NT and NK—participated in aerodynamic data collection. Speaker KK was not available for this portion of the study.

5.2 DATA MEASURMENT

5.2.1 Timing measurements

Figure 80 provides a sample of the overall data as obtained from these four channels. The tag in channel 1, as well as the time-aligned cursors in channels 2, 3 and 4, mark the burst. Various time points were marked in order to calculate the duration of various stages of click production. The tags are numbered from 1-6, where 1 represents the tongue dorsum closure, 2 the tongue blade seal, 3 the onset of rarefaction, 4 the onset of the click burst, 5 the offset of the click burst and 6 the velar burst. Timepoint 7, located on the pharyngeal pressure trace, represents the point at which there is a large increase in the pharyngeal pressure. The initial

Table 18: Test utterances used in aerodynamic data collection.
(*Test utterances consisted of the three click types—dental, palato-alveolar and lateral—in symmetrical vowel contexts of /a/, /e/ and /o/, said in a carrier phrase.*)

Click type⇒ Vowel ⇓	Dental	Palato-alveolar	Lateral
/a/	bathi beb<u>ac</u>aba	bathi beb<u>aq</u>apha	bathi beb<u>ax</u>aba
/e/	bathi bab<u>ec</u>eba	bathi bab<u>eq</u>eba	bathi bab<u>ex</u>eba
/o/	bathi bab<u>oc</u>oba	bathi bab<u>oq</u>oba	bathi bab<u>ox</u>ova

rise in pharyngeal pressure near time-point 1 signals the onset of the dorsal closure. However, a further rise in pharyngeal pressure during this closure may not necessarily be caused solely by dorsal activity. It is difficult to determine the cause of this large rise in pharyngeal pressure, but there are several obvious possibilities, which will be discussed in Section 5.3.5. For now, we simply note the presence of this large pharyngeal pressure increase. The following measurement criteria for marking the seven timepoints are discussed below.

Tongue dorsum closure, marked at timepoint 1, was demarcated at the offset of the vowel, as seen from the audio channel. The tongue blade seal, at timepoint 2, was demarcated by the initial perturbations seen in the intraoral pressure channel. The onset of rarefaction, at timepoint 3, and the offset of the click burst, at timepoint 5, were determined from the intraoral pressure curve. Onset of rarefaction was marked from the first decreased value from the baseline number as obtained from the maximally expanded intraoral trace while the offset of the click burst was marked at the first increased value from the baseline number. The click burst itself, at timepoint 4, was determined from the audio channel. The velar burst, at timepoint 6, was usually determined by simultaneously analyzing the acoustic waveform, the airflow trace and the pharyngeal pressure trace, but for many tokens it was still difficult to ascertain. In Figure 80, the velar burst can be seen on the audio channel. Perturbation of the oral flow seems to confirm the burst noted in the audio signal. A steady decline of the pharyngeal pressure trace at the same timepoint coincides with the audio and airflow traces, providing some reassurance that the timepoint being noted is indeed the velar burst. Even still, the velar burst for some tokens could not be reliably noted, perhaps due to its proximity to the tongue blade/tip release. In these cases, rather than risk an erroneous measurement, no timepoint was noted at all.

From these 7 timepoints, the following durations, in milliseconds, were calculated:

Onset latency (ONL): the time between the onset of the tongue dorsum closure and the tongue blade closure, from timepoints 1-2.

Seal Duration (SD): the time during which there was simultaneous tongue blade and tongue dorsum closures, from timepoints 2-5.

Offset latency (OFL): measured the duration from the tongue blade release to the tongue dorsum release, timepoints 4-6.

Tongue blade/tongue dorsum latency (BDL): This duration was obtained by subtracting timepoint 4, the tongue blade release, from timepoint 7, large rise in pharyngeal pressure. Though it is not clear what articulatory event is being measured here, the change in pharyngeal pressure is drastic and may be important in understanding how the tongue dorsum and the tongue blade/tip are coordinated. The latency values should be recorded in the following manner: If the latency value is negative, the pharyngeal pressure rise preceeds the click burst. Positive latency values indicate that the click burst precedes the pharyngeal pressure rise.

Peak intraoral pressure/burst latency (IOBRL): the duration of time from the peak intraoral pressure to the click burst, as measured from the audio channel. The click burst did not always occur when the negative intraoral pressure was at its peak. That is, maximal cavity expansion and the click burst were not always simultaneous. The change in amplitude, termed IOBRA, of these two timepoints will also be calculated. Negative latency values as well as amplitude values indicate that the click burst preceded the peak intraoral pressure while positive amplitude values indicate that the click burst occurred after maximal cavity expansion.

5.2.2 *Average Velocity Measurements*

Two velocity measurements were made from the intraoral pressure trace. They were the Average Offset Velocity (OFVEL) and the Average Rarefaction Velocity (ARVEL). It should be noted that these velocity measurements represent an indirect measure of articulator movement. That is, the technique involved does not directly track the articulatory movement but the air pressure changes which result from the articulatory movements themselves. In the case of OFVEL, it can be easily ascertained from EPG contact data that the measured velocity is the direct result of the tongue blade pulling away from the palate. However, for ARVEL, it is difficult to determine which articulator movements are coordinated with the rarefaction event. None-the-less, ARVEL is a particularly important measurement in the attempt to unravel articulatory strategies of intergestural timing for this segment type.

Average Offset Velocity (OFVEL): Calculates the average speed it takes for the pressure in the click cavity, once the tongue blade begins to pull away from palate, at timepoint 4, to reach atmospheric pressure, at timepoint 5. The following calculation was used, where $AMPL^{t\#}$ refers to the amplitude of the intraoral pressure at a particular timepoint, 't'.

$$OFVEL = \frac{(millivolts)}{(msecs)} = \frac{\Delta A}{\Delta t} = \frac{AMPL^{t4} - AMPL^{t5}}{t^4 - t^5}$$

Average Rarefaction Velocity (ARVEL): Calculates the average rate of rarefaction, from timepoint 3 to the peak negative intraoral pressure, near timepoint 4. The following equation was used to calculate ARVEL. Note once again that $AMPL^{\#}$ refers to the amplitude of the intraoral pressure at a particular timepoint, 't'.

$$ARVEL = \frac{(millivolts)}{(msecs)} = \frac{\Delta A}{\Delta t} = \frac{AMPL^{t4} - AMPL^{t3}}{t^4 - t^3}$$

Both OFVEL and ARVEL calculations have idealized the intraoral pressure trace to be a combination of linear movements, which is not entirely accurate. However, this standard linear rate calculation probably gives the best approximation of the average velocities for this trace.

5.2.3 Magnitude Measurements

In addition to the duration and velocity calculations, magnitude measures of peak negative intraoral pressure (PNEG), maximum ingressive airflow ($INGAF_{max}$) and peak pharyngeal pressure ($PHPR_{max}$) were noted. These values were obtained by scrolling through the expanded waveforms of each trace in order to locate the maximum amplitude value, expressed in millivolts, but converted to standard aerodynamic measures by the calibration techniques employed.

5.2.4 Statistical Analysis

A three-factor ANOVA was performed with the main independent variables of CLICK, SPEAKER and VOWEL on the following dependent variables: onset latency, overlap, offset latency, blade/dorsum latency, intraoral peak/burst latency and intraoral peak/burst amplitude difference, average rarefaction velocity, offset velocity, peak intraoral pressure, maximum oral ingressive airflow and peak pharyngeal pressure. Post-hoc comparisons were made using Fisher's PLSD at a 95% confidence level. This analysis mainly focuses on describing main effects of CLICK, VOWEL and their significant interactions.

5.3 RESULTS

In this section we first characterize the lead, overlap and lag phases of the three click types using duration measurements. We then independently characterize the tongue blade/tip articulation, assessing the rate of the tongue blade/tip release as well as the resulting ingressive oral airflow. The overlap phase is characterized by considering in tandem the intraoral rarefaction velocity and peak intraoral pressure. Pharyngeal pressure data is employed in order to assess tongue dorsum behavior. Various aspects of the coordination of the tongue blade/tip release and the tongue body are considered as well as the effects of vowel context on the production of the various click types.

5.3.1 Phase Duration Results

Order of the closures

Results from the EPG data indicated that, for all three click types, the tongue dorsum preceded the tongue blade/tip closure. Recall that this conclusion was based on the fact that there was an acoustic closure but no tongue blade contact in the anterior region of the palate. We concluded that the initial acoustic closure in clicks must be dorsal in nature and alluded to the fact that the aerodynamic records show that the pharyngeal pressure rises at the onset of the click closure just as it does in simple pulmonic velars. If this were the case, it would prove that the acoustic closure did not result from a glottal closure, but instead resulted from a dorsal closure that was simply not visible on the pseudopalate. Figure 82 presents the aerodynamic records comparing the initial pharyngeal pressure rise in pulmonic and velaric segments.

The audio signal for the simple velar along with its time-aligned pharyngeal pressure trace is shown in the first two panels. The final three panels depict the pharyngeal pressure traces of the dental, lateral and palato-alveolar clicks, respectively. The vertical lines mark the acoustic closure of the consonant, based on their corresponding acoustic channels (the audio channels are not shown for the clicks). Note that for all four segments the pharyngeal pressure rises steadily at the same time as the acoustic closure is made, leaving little doubt that the initial closure in clicks is the result of a dorsal closure.

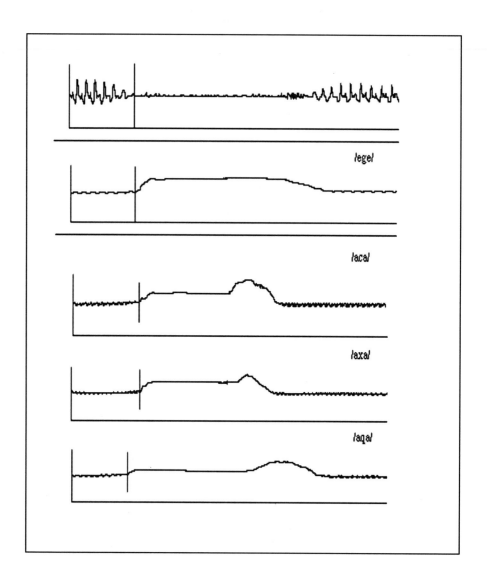

Figure 82: Pharyngeal pressure traces comparing the rise in pharyngeal pressure at the initial tongue dorsum closure, as produced by simple pulmonic velars and velaric segments, produced by Speaker GV. The first two panels depict the audio signal and the pharyng pressure trace of the pulmonic velar. The last three panels depict the pharyngeal pressure trace for the dental, lateral and palato-alveolar clicks.

Click Effects

In this section the lead, overlap and lag phases of the three click types are analyzed. Figure 83 depicts the mean durations for the three articulatory phases for the dental, palato-alveolar and lateral click types, pooled across vowel contexts. Section 5.2 provides an in-depth explanation of the measurements used to characterize these three phases. In comparing the lead phase for the three click types, the dental click has a much smaller mean duration value than the palato-alveolar and lateral clicks, while the latter two click types have nearly equal durations.

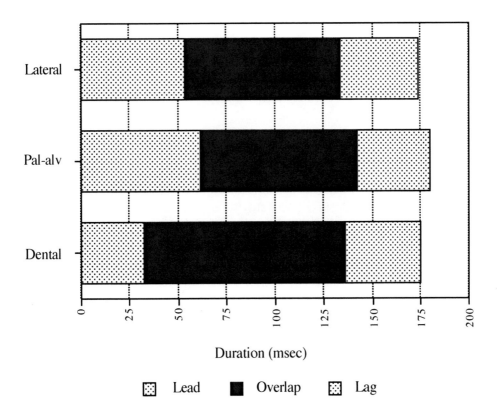

Duration (msec)

▨ Lead   ■ Overlap   ▨ Lag

Figure 83: Mean durations of the three articulatory phases for the dental, palato-alveolar and lateral clicks, pooled across speakers and vowel contexts.

Mean duration values of the overlap phase show that the dental click type has the greatest mean duration, at 104 msec. The palato-alveolar and lateral clicks have nearly equal durations, at 81 and 80 milliseconds, respectively. With respect to the lag phase, all three click types show similar mean durations.

A three-factor ANOVA was performed with the main independent variables of CLICK, SPEAKER and VOWEL on the following dependent variables, which were used to characterize the lead, overlap and lag phases, respectively termed Onset Latency, Seal Duration and Offset Latency, respectively. The ANOVA results yielded the expected results based on the aforementioned mean duration comparisons. Specifically, there was a significant main effect of CLICK on onset latency [(F(2, 43)=10.006, p<.001]. Post-hoc comparisons showed that the dental click differed significantly from the palato-alveolar and lateral click types, at p< .0001, while the palato-alveolar and lateral click types did not differ.

The clicks also differed significantly with respect to their mean seal duration values (F(2, 43)=6.38, p<.004). Post-hoc comparisons showed that the dental click differed significantly from the palato-alveolar and lateral click types, at p<.0001. The palato-alveolar and lateral clicks were not significantly different.

No significant differences were found for OFL. The relative mean durations of the articulatory phases for the various click types, as presented in the aerodynamic data, are in general agreement with the patterns in the EPG results presented in Chapter 3.

Vowel Effects

All click types had the greater mean onset latency values in the context of /o/ than in the contexts of /a/ and /e/. Mean seal duration values were greater in the context of /e/ than in the contexts of /a/ and /o/. While the EPG results showed strong vowel effects, statistical analysis on the phase durations using aerodynamic data did not yield significant main effects of VOWEL on either the onset latency or the seal duration but the general trend in the rank order of vowels, as observed from the mean durations are consistent with the results found in the EPG data. The weaker vowel effects obtained in the aerodynamic data for these phase durations are probably due to the difference in the volume of data. It is likely that, given more aerodynamic data, stronger vowel effects would emerge such as those observed in the EPG data. None-the-less, the agreement across the two types of data provides strong evidence that the observed variations in the tongue dorsum lead and overlap phases for the various click types is stable and systematic.

5.3.2 Characterizing the tongue blade/tip articulation

The release phase for the various click types has been previously characterized using acoustic methods of data analysis (e.g. Sands 1991). Recall that aerodynamic data may also be used to characterize the release burst of click consonants by measuring the rate at which pressure in the intraoral cavity equalizes with the atmospheric pressure, referred to here as the offset velocity. In short, this measure characterizes the rate of the tongue blade/tip release movement. Maximum ingressive oral airflow is also considered. Discussion focuses on the three click types, pooled across speakers and vowel contexts.

Offset Velocity

Recall that the EPG data in Chapter 3 described the dental click as having a narrow release channel resembling a canonical pulmonic alveolar fricative. A narrow channel was also noted in the case of the lateral click, though the channel is typically quite posterior such that the observed narrowness may arise from our limited visibility at the posterior end of the palate. EPG frames of the palato-alveolar click showed a quite abrupt release of the tongue tip from the palate, going from full contact in one frame to little or no contact in the front region of the palate in the next frame. Contact profiles of the time-series data also depicted these differences in the release gestures for the various click types. Figure 84 depicts the mean results of the offset velocity for the dental, palato-alveolar and lateral clicks, pooled across speakers and vowel contexts. The expectation is that the abruptly released palato-alveolar click should equalize air pressure more rapidly than the affricated clicks, which, by their very nature, have more gradual release gestures. Indeed, the results show that the offset velocity was greatest for the palato-alveolar click at 14.4 cm H_2O/msec, followed by the dental click at 7.9 and the lateral click at 4.2 cm

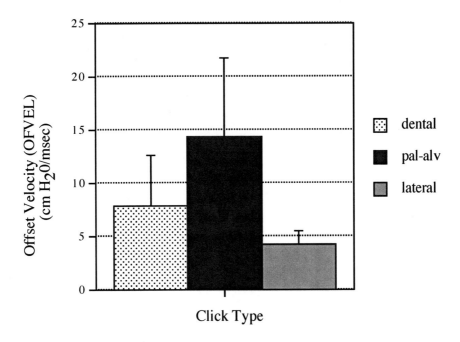

Figure 84: Mean results of the Offset Velocity for the dental, palato-alveolar and lateral clicks, for data pooled across speakers and vowel contexts

H_2O/msec. Anova tests produced a significant main effect of CLICK [$F(2,43)=98.3$, $p<.05$]. All post-hoc pair-wise comparisons were significantly different at $p<.0001$. These results follow the expected pattern, with the abruptly released click having the greatest offset velocity while the affricated clicks equalize air pressure more slowly, indicative of a constricted release channel being maintained after the initial breaking of linguopalatal contact.

Among the affricated clicks, the lateral click has a significantly slower offset velocity than the dental click. This may in part be attributed to differences in the part of the tongue being used to create the release. In the lateral click, the release gesture involves a gradual pulling away of the lateral margins of the tongue body which proceeds from the posterior lateral edges and progresses forward. The lateral release gesture might also involve jaw lowering, given that the contact is quite posterior. The lateral release gesture is perhaps slower due to the use of inherently slower articulators—the tongue body and the lower jaw. The dental click uses the tongue blade to effect its release, which is capable of more rapid movements, which do not require jaw lowering. Given that the bulky tongue body and, to a certain extent, the jaw, are involved in the lateral release, we might expect a slower offset velocity when compared to the inherently faster tongue blade/tip movement involved in the dental release. Also, as we shall see, the dental click has a greater negative intraoral pressure, which would generate greater offset velocity.

Maximum Ingressive Oral Airflow (INGAF$_{max}$)

Maximum ingressive oral airflow of the release bursts was also measured. Figure 85 depicts the mean results for INGAF$_{max}$ measured in ml/sec, for the dental, palato-alveolar and lateral click types, pooled across speakers and vowel contexts. The results indicate that the palato-alveolar click has the greatest rate of ingressive oral airflow at 6,527 ml/sec, followed by the lateral click at 1,775 ml/sec and then the dental click at 734 ml/sec. Anova tests produced a significant main effect of CLICK on INGAF$_{max}$ [$F(2,42)=235$, $p<.0001$]. In post-hoc tests, pair-wise comparisons were highly significant at $p< .0001$ for all comparisons involving the palato-alveolar click. The comparison /c, x/ was significant at $p< .001$. Among the affricated clicks, the lateral click has a greater peak ingressive oral airflow when compared to the dental click.

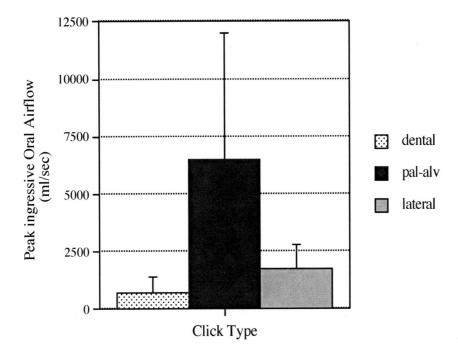

Figure 85: Mean results of the ingressive oral airflow for the dental, palato-alveolar and lateral clicks, for data pooled across speakers and vowel contexts.

The greater peak ingressive oral airflow for the lateral clicks might suggest that the lateral click has a shorter frication duration. However, our auditory impression of the frication duration for the lataral click, as produced in IsiZulu, is that the frication duration is at least equal to, if not longer than the frication duration of the dental click. The slower offset velocity seen with the lateral click is consistent with this observation. Sustained frication in the case of the lateral click might be the result of the continued rarefaction of air inside the click cavity. As previously observed in the EPG and SPG data, the lateral click is asymmetric. One side of the tongue is braced up against the palate. As the release channel is formed and frication begins, the opposite side of the tongue continues to lower, continually increasing the negative pressure inside the cavity, thereby sustaining frication.

As previously noted, peak negative intraoral pressure influences both the offset velocity and the ingressive oral airflow such that a greater negative intraoral pressure would increase the offset velocity and would generate a greater ingressive flow given the larger pressure differential between the oral and atmospheric pressures. The specific type of release gesture also plays a role in determining the offset velocity and the ingressive oral flow as the release gesture determines how the build-up of intraoral pressure in the cavity is vented. The interrelationship between the offset velocity and ingressive oral flow and their relationship to the peak negative intraoral pressure are fully considered in Section 5.3.5.

5.3.3 Characterizing the Overlap Phase

Two measures—Average Rarefaction Velocity (ARVEL) and Peak Negative Intraoral Pressure (PNEG)—are used to characterize Overlap, the phase during which rarefaction occurs. Recall that the average rate of rarefaction was measured from the intraoral pressure curve as the change in magnitude across a defined time interval, namely the time of onset of rarefaction to the peak intraoral pressure. It is important to remember that the intraoral velocity values reported here depict the change in intraoral pressue inside the cavity and as such provide only an indirect measure of tongue body movement. That is, rarefaction velocity data does not provide any information about the specific articulator used in cavity expansion. Along the same lines, obtained PNEG values from the data represent relative changes in volume only and provide little direct information about tongue body position during rarefaction. Tongue body positions must be inferred from looking at PNEG and ARVEL results in tandem.

Rarefaction Veloctiy

Figure 86 depicts the mean rarefaction velocity values for the dental, palato-alveolar and lateral click types, pooled across speakers and vowel contexts. The palato-alveolar click had the greatest intraoral velocity at 3.37 cm H_2O/msec while the dental and lateral click types had much lower values, at 2.59 and 2.35 cm H_2O/msec, respectively. ANOVA tests confirmed that the clicks differed significantly in their mean rarefaction rates [$F_{(2, 43)}=33.8$, $p < .0001$.] All post-hoc comparisons involving the palato-alveolar click were highly significant, at $p < .0001$. The comparison of /c, x/ was significant at $p < .05$. There was a significant interaction between SPEAKER and CLICK [$F_{(4,43)}=11.3$, $p<.0001$]. Mean ARVEL values for Speakers NT and NK follow the expected rank order of q>c>x, while GV has the rank order of c>q>x, where c and q have nearly identical ARVEL values.

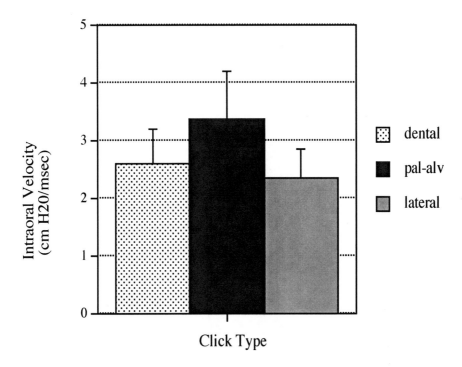

Figure 86: Mean durations of the average intraoral rarefaction velocity airflow for the dental, palato-alveolar and lateral clicks, for data pooled across speakers and vowel contexts.

Peak Negative Intraoral Pressure

Figure 87 depicts the mean PNEG values for the dental, palato-alveolar and lateral clicks, pooled across speakers and vowel contexts. The palato-alveolar click has the greatest negative intraoral peak pressure at -202 cm H20, followed by the dental and then the lateral click, at -179 and -141 cm H20, respectively.

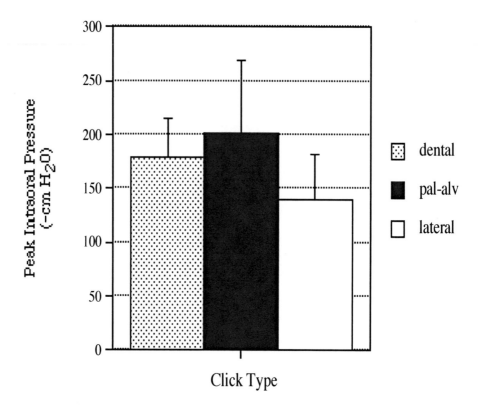

Figure 87: Mean results of the peak negative intraoral pressure for the dental, palato-alveolar and lateral clicks, for data pooled across speakers and vowel contexts.

A significant main effect of CLICK was observed on PNEG ($F(2,43)= 34.4$, $p<.001$). All post-hoc comparisons were significantly different, at $p< .0001$ for pair-wise comparisons involving the lateral click and $p<.003$ for the comparison /c, q/. There was a significant interaction of SPEAKER and CLICK on PNEG [$F(4,43)=33.9$, $p<.0001$]. Speaker NK follows the expected order of q>c>x. However, Speakers NT and GV show nearly equal PNEG values for all click types.

Mean PNEG measurements are positively correlated with the means for the average rarefaction results. The palato-alveolar click, which has the greatest intraoral velocity, also has the greatest peak negative intraoral pressure. PNEG and ARVEL means patterned similarly for the dental and lateral clicks, with the lateral click having lower PNEG and ARVEL values than the dental click. Table 19 provides a summary of the means for the peak negative intraoral pressure, the average rarefaction velocity as well as peak ingressive oral airflow and offset velocity, for data pooled across speakers and vowel contexts.

Table 19: Mean Results for the Intraoral Velocity, Peak Negative Intraoral Pressure, Peak Ingressive Oral Airflow and the Offset Velocity, for data pooled across speakers and vowel contexts.

Measured Variable⇒ (units)⇒ Click type⇓	Rarefaction Velocity (cm H_2O/msec)	Peak Intraoral Pressure (cm H_2O)	Peak Ingressive Oral Airflow (ml/sec)	Offset Velocity (cm H_2O/msec)
Dental	-2.59	-179	-734	7.9
Palato-alveolar	-3.37	-202	-6527	14.4
Lateral	-2.35	-141	-1775	4.2

The means for PNEG and ARVEL results, when compared, show that a faster rarefaction rate produces greater peak intraoral pressure i.e. greater cavity expansion. The indication from this data implies that the tongue center has a lower position for the palato-alveolar click than for the dental click. The lateral click only lowers partially due to the need for bracing, and probably has a relatively high tongue body position compared to the palato-alveolar click as well. However, a note of caution is in order here. It should be emphasized that the exact mechanism by which cavity expansion occurs for any particular click type has yet to be delineated, but based on Traill's (1985) x-ray study on !Xóõ. clicks, and from the EPG data in this study, we assume that there is a certain amount of lowering of the tongue center for all clicks. Rarefaction strategies for the various click types are discussed in greater detail in Chapter 6, where the confluence of all data types is brought to bear on this issue.

5.3.4 Relationship Among the Variables

Simple linear regression was done to determine the strength of the correlations between the peak negative intraoral pressure and the average rarefaction rate, the peak ingressive oral flow, and the offset velocity. The correlation between the offset velocity and peak ingressive oral flow was also tested. Raw values for each of the variables were converted to percentage values by taking the average of the test utterances for each speaker and then expressing the raw values as a percentage of this mean. Conversion of raw values to percentages preserves the relationship between the variables but abstracts away from differences in magnitude of the measures that might result from differences in overall palate size and shape.

Figure 88 depicts the results of the correlation between peak negative intraoral pressure and rarefaction velocity. Strong positive correlations were obtained for all click types. The dental click had the strongest correlation, with an R^2 value of .584. The palato-alveolar and lateral clicks had slightly weaker correlations, with respective R^2 values of .433 and .325. All correlations were significant at $p < .01$.

Simple linear regression showed that maximum ingressive oral flow and offset velocity yielded weak non-significant correlations for all click types, as depicted in Figure 89. These results indicate that the rate of release and the ingressive oral airflow are largely independent of each other. We now assess the correlations of ingressive oral flow and offset velocity to PNEG.

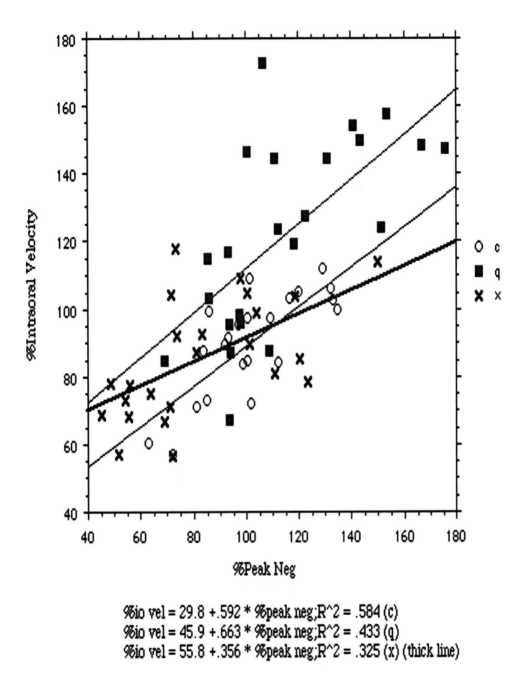

%io vel = 29.8 + .592 * %peak neg;R^2 = .584 (c)
%io vel = 45.9 + .663 * %peak neg;R^2 = .433 (q)
%io vel = 55.8 + .356 * %peak neg;R^2 = .325 (x) (thick line)

Figure 88: Linear regression correlations between peak negative intraoral pressure and intraoral velocity, for the dental, palato-alveolar and lateral clicks, for normalized data, pooled across speakers and vowel contexts.

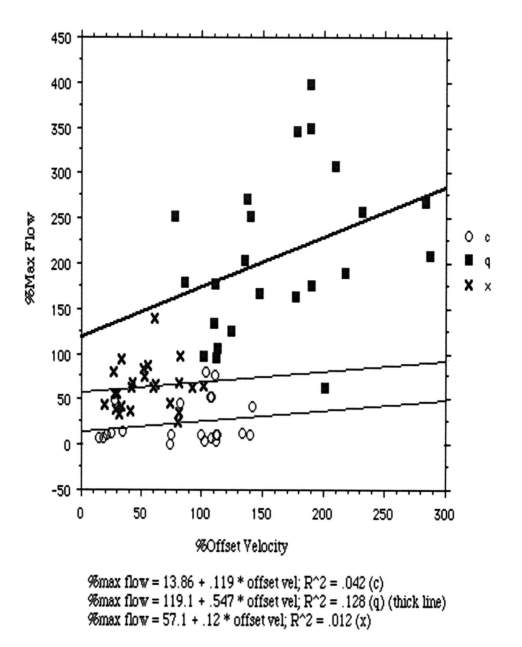

%max flow = 13.86 + .119 * offset vel; R^2 = .042 (c)
%max flow = 119.1 + .547 * offset vel; R^2 = .128 (q) (thick line)
%max flow = 57.1 + .12 * offset vel; R^2 = .012 (x)

Figure 89: Linear regression correlations between maximum ingressive oral airflow and offset velocity, for the dental, palato-alveolar and lateral clicks, for normalized data, pooled across speakers and vowel contexts.

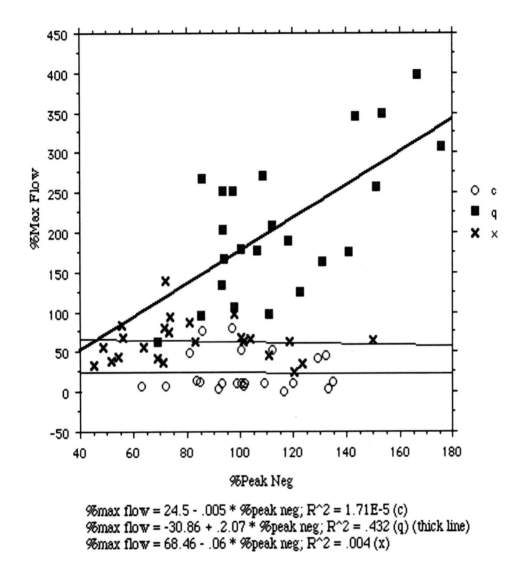

%max flow = 24.5 - .005 * %peak neg; R^2 = 1.71E-5 (c)
%max flow = -30.86 + .2.07 * %peak neg; R^2 = .432 (q) (thick line)
%max flow = 68.46 - .06 * %peak neg; R^2 = .004 (x)

Figure 90: Linear regression correlations between peak negative intraoral pressure and peak ingressive oral airflow, for the dental, palato-alveolar and lateral clicks, for normalized data, pooled across speakers and vowel contexts.

Figure 90 depicts the results of the correlation between PNEG and Max Flow. The results indicate a fairly strong significant relationship between these variables for the palato-alveolar click, with an R^2 value of .432. The correlation was significant at p< .001. These variables were not correlated at all for the affricated clicks.

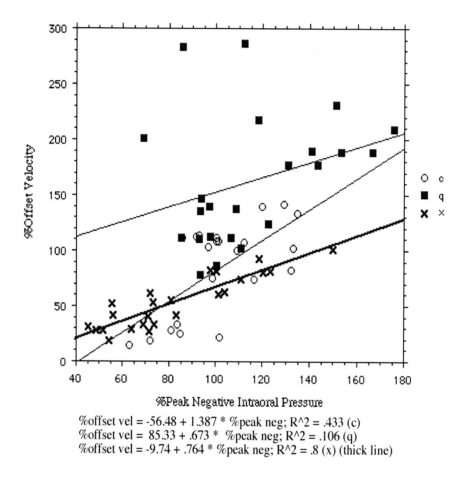

%offset vel = -56.48 + 1.387 * %peak neg; R^2 = .433 (c)
%offset vel = 85.33 + .673 * %peak neg; R^2 = .106 (q)
%offset vel = -9.74 + .764 * %peak neg; R^2 = .8 (x) (thick line)

Figure 91: Linear regression correlations between peak negative intraoral pressure and offset velocity, for the dental, palato-alveolar and lateral clicks, for normalized data, pooled across speakers and vowel contexts.

However, the correlation between PNEG and the offset velocity was strong for the affricated clicks, while the palato-alveolar click showed only a weak correlation between these same two variables. The correlations for the dental click were highly significant, at p<.001. Overall, the results of the correlations between PNEG with the offset velocity and the peak ingressive oral flow showed a division between the affricated and the unaffricated clicks. The affricated clicks, which have more controlled release gestures, show a strong relationship between the peak negative pressure and the offset velocity. The palato-alveolar click, which has an instantaneous release, shows that maximum ingressive airflow is directly affected by the amount of negative pressure generated. Greater PNEG values should generate increased ingressive airflow as more air is drawn in due to the greater pressure differential between the oral cavity and the atmosphere. The direct correlation between PNEG and ingressive airflow does not exist for the affricated clicks because the release gesture for these clicks vents the intraoral pressure more slowly through a narrow release channel. Table 20 provides a summary table of the correlations between the variables, their R^2 values and significance levels.

Table 20: Summary Table of the R2 and p-values for the correlations among the variables Peak Negative Intraoral Pressure (PNEG), Average Intraoral Velocity (IO VEL), Maximum Ingressive Oral Airflow (Flow) and the Offset Velocity (Ofset Vel)

Click type⇒ Correlation⇓	Dental $(R^2$; p-value)	Palato-alveolar $(R^2$; p-value)	Lateral $(R^2$; p-value)
PNEG vs. IO Vel	**.378; p<.003**	**.43; p<.001**	**.325; p<.004**
PNEG vs. Flow	.004; p<.79	**.432; p<.008**	.004; p<.77
PNEG vs. Ofset Vel	**.46; p<.001**	.106; p<.13	**.80; p<.0001**
Ofset Vel vs. Flow	.04; p<.38	.128; p<..10	.012; p<.61

5.3.5 Late Pharyngeal Pressure Rise

Peak Pharyngeal Pressure

Peak pharyngeal pressure was also measured, although the interpretation of this data is problematical. Figure 92 depicts time-aligned audio and pharyngeal pressure channels for the palato-alveolar click, in the symmetrical vowel context of /a/, uttered by Speaker GV. Note the large increase in the pharyngeal pressure near the click burst release.

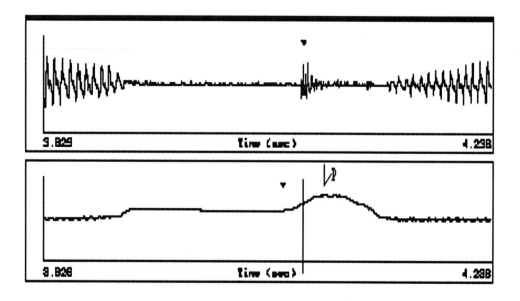

Figure 92: Time-aligned audio and pharyngeal pressure traces depicting the large increase in pharyngeal pressure near the click burst for one token of the palato-alveolar click in the symmetrical vowel context of /a/, as produced by Speaker GV.

Similar increases in pharyngeal pressure were also observed for the dental and lateral clicks as well. Peak pharyngeal pressure, denoted by the arrow labeled 'p' in the figure, was taken at the peak of this rise for all speakers[10]. We will describe the results obtained before discussing possible interpretations of the height of the peak and the timing of the rise.

Figure 93 depicts the mean peak pharyngeal pressure values for the dental, palato-alveolar and lateral click types, pooled across speakers and vowel contexts. The results indicate that the palato-alveolar click has the greatest peak pharyngeal pressure at 22 cm H_2O, followed by the dental and lateral clicks, at 18 and 16 cm H_2O, respectively. A three-factor ANOVA showed a significant main effect of CLICK on $PHPR_{max}$ [$F(2,39)=16.9$, $p<.0001$]. Comparisons of /q/ with /x/ and /c/ in post-hoc tests yielded significance levels of $p<.0001$ and $p<.0003$, respectively. The comparison of /c/ to /x/ was not at all significant. No main effect of VOWEL was observed but there was a SPEAKER*CLICK interaction [$F(4, 39)=2.8$, $p<.04$], which resulted from the different rank order of the dental and lateral clicks for different speakers. For all speakers, the palato-alveolar click has the greatest peak pharyngeal pressure. Because there are consistent effects in this data some explanation is called for.

---

[10]Speaker NT had a much less drastic rise in pharyngeal pressure near the release burst than Speakers NK and GV.

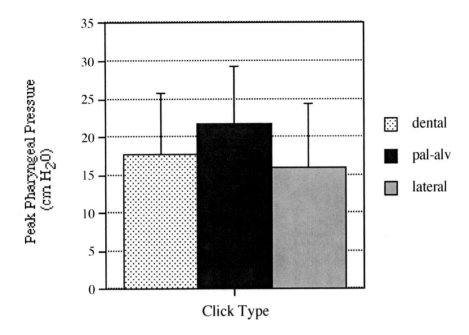

Figure 93: Mean results of the peak pharyngeal pressure for the dental, palato-alveolar and lateral clicks, for data pooled across speakers and vowel contexts

Pharyngeal Pressure Rise

Recall that there is a large increase in the pharyngeal pressure which occurs very near to the click burst, as noted in Figure 92. The following section analyzes the timing of this rise in relation to the click burst. Figure 94 aligns pharyngeal pressure traces for the dental, palato-alveolar and lateral clicks in the symmetrical vowel context of /a/, as uttered by Speaker GV. The tracings show the timing of the rise in pharyngeal pressure relative to the click burst. The vertical line marks the onset of acoustic energy for the click burst. Figure 94 shows that the pharyngeal pressure rise is timed differently to the click burst for each click type.

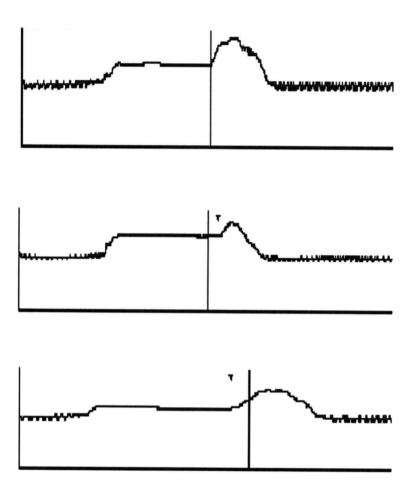

Figure 94: Comparison of the pharyngeal pressure rise relative to the click burst for the dental, palato-alveolar and lateral clicks in the /a/ vowel context, as produced by Speaker GV. The pharyngeal pressure rise is marked by an arrow, and the acoustic burst is marked by the vertical line.

For the dental click, the pharyngeal pressure rise is simultaneous to the acoustic onset of the click burst. The pharyngeal pressure rise precedes the click burst in the palato-alveolar click, while the pharyngeal pressure rise occurs after the onset of the lateral release in the lateral click. The timing of the late pharyngeal pressure rise close to or after the click burst makes clear that whatever causes the rise is not related to rarefaction. EPG data, which charted the midsagittal posterior electrodes on a frame-by-frame basis for the dental and palato-alveolar clicks for Speakers NK and KK, showed that the palato-alveolar click showed dorsal retraction very early during the overlap period. The pharyngeal pressure does not increase during this retraction gesture. The late pharyngeal pressure increase is therefore due to some event that is taking place at or near the click burst. It is possible that it is related to the release gesture of the dorsal closure. There are at least several probable causes for the increase in pharyngeal pressure. Firstly, we might consider dorsal movement to be the cause of the pressure increase. If the location of the dorsal closure shifts backwards, this would compress the air inside the pharyngeal cavity, causing the increase in pressure. Given the large change in pharyngeal pressure, we must assume that the glottis is at least partially closed. Otherwise, given the volume in the chest cavity compared to the change in volume created by the backward movement of the tongue dorsum, the change in the pharyngeal cavity volume would be negligible and the rise in pressure hardly detectable.

Speakers GV and NK both exhibit this large increase in pharyngeal pressure while Speaker NT shows only a small rise in pressure. We could attribute this difference in pharyngeal pressure rise to a difference in glottal setting. On this account, Speaker NT would be hypothesized to have a greater glottal aperture. In some instances glottalization was auditorily present, though no physical evidence is available to confirm this impression.

The large rise could also be caused by the pharyngeal pressure tube being squeezed by the tongue dorsum, or by the velum becoming more firmly raised. On this account, there would still be dorsal retraction but the pressure being measured is not exactly in the pharynx.

Another possible scenario is that the entire tongue root is pulled back in conjunction with the central release, thereby constricting the entire pharyngeal cavity. This would also cause a large rise in pharyngeal pressure, provided that the glottis is at least partially closed. In the affricated clicks, which have slow release movements, constriction of the pharyngeal cavity would occur simultaneous to the release. For the palato-alveolar click, anticipation of the release is necessary given the abrupt nature of this click type. Before we can adequately determine whether tongue dorsum retraction or constriction lower in the pharynx is occuring, more data must be analyzed. For example, learning more about the glottal configurations of the click types, including the voiceless aspirated accompaniment, will provide more clues to the cause of the rise in pharyngeal pressure. For the moment, we must conclude that there is some articulatory activity, perhaps dorsal retraction or constriction of the pharyngeal cavity, (or both together and with a partially closed glottis) that is somehow related to the release burst. We can only present the results of the pooled data on this issue and leave the remaining questions on the exact nature of this articulatory movement to future research.

Figure 95 depicts the mean results for the blade/dorsum latency measure, pooled across speakers and vowel categories.

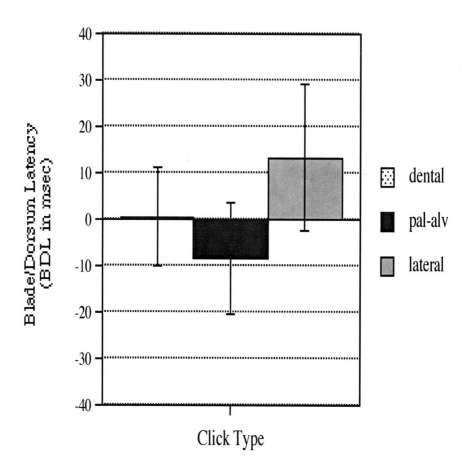

Figure 95: Mean duration results of the latency between the initial tongue blade/tip release and the tongue dorsum retraction for the dental, palato-alveolar and lateral clicks, for data pooled across speakers and vowel contexts.

Negative values indicate that the rise in pharyngeal pressure occurs before the click burst, while positive values indicate a pharyngeal pressure rise after the click burst. The dental click shows that the pharyngeal pressure rise is simultaneous to the acoustic click burst. For the lateral click, the pharyngeal rise occurs after the onset of acoustic energy, which corresponds to the lateral release. The palato-alveolar click shows an early pharyngeal pressure rise relative to the click burst. ANOVA results indicate a significant main effect of CLICK on BDL [$F_{(2, 39)}=34$, $p<.0001$]. Post-hoc comparisons of /x, c/ and /x, q/ are significant at $p<.0001$ while the comparison /c, q/ is significant at $p<.002$.

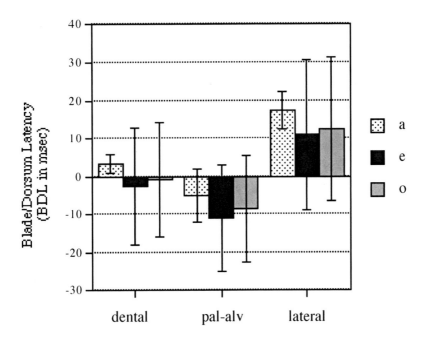

Figure 96: Mean blade/dorsum latency results for the dental, palato-alveolar and lateral clicks in the symmetrical vowel contexts of /a/, /e/ and /o/, pooled across speakers.

Figure 96 depicts the mean blade/dorsum latency results for the dental, palato-alveolar and lateral clicks in the vowel contexts of /a/, /e/ and /o/, pooled across speakers. For each click type, the context of /a/ shows greater mean blade/dorsum latency values than the mid vowels. The standard deviations are quite large for all click types in all the vowel contexts, but for /axa/ and /aca/ the values ranged in the positive domain only. Anova statistics confirmed that there was a significant main effect of VOWEL on BDL [F(2,39)=4.0, p<.03. Post-hoc comparisons showed that the only significant result achieved from the pair-wise comparisons was /a, e/, which yielded p< .05. The interactions of CLICK and VOWEL, as well as SPEAKER, CLICK and VOWEL were not at all significant, indicating a very consistent click/vowel pattern across subjects.

5.3.6 Coordination of the Tongue Center to the Click Burst (IOBRL)

This section focuses on the latency between the peak negative intraoral pressure and the acoustic onset of the click burst, termed intraoral burst latency, or IOBRL. It is important to note that the initial onset of the tongue blade release does not always occur at the same time as the peak negative intraoral pressure. The burst may either preceed or occur later than the peak intraoral pressure. Figure 97 depicts the mean duration values of the intraoral burst latency for the dental, palato-alveolar and lateral click types, pooled across speakers and vowel contexts. Recall that positive values for the timing measurement means that the click burst occured after the peak negative pressure, while negative values represent an earlier click burst relative to the peak intraoral pressure. There is a corresponding decrease in amplitude of the intraoral pressure when the burst occurs after the peak intraoral pressure, as the intraoral pressure curves are quite peaked, with no plateau. The decrease in negative intraoral pressure while there is a complete seal signals that a contraction of the click cavity is taking place. The corresponding change in amplitude when the burst occurs after the peak intraoral pressure is much greater for the palato-alveolar click than for the dental and lateral clicks, as the figure clearly shows.

IOBRL values are always positive for the palato-alveolar click type, while the dental and lateral clicks are more variable, with means clustering around point zero and large standard deviations. ANOVA statistics confirmed that there was a significant main effect of CLICK on IOBRL [$F(2,43)=18$, $p<.0001$]. Post-hoc results showed that pairwise comparisons of the palato-alveolar click with either the dental or the lateral click were highly significant, at $p<.0001$. Comparison of the latter two clicks yielded non-significant results.

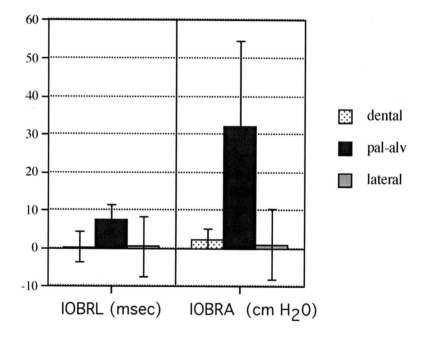

Figure 97: Mean duration results of the latency between the time peak negative intraoral pressure is reached and the initial tongue blade/tip release, for the dental, palato-alveolar and lateral clicks, for data pooled across speakers and vowel contexts. The change in amplitude

of the negative intraoral pressure between these two time-points is also depicted in the right-most panel.

Figure 98 depicts the IOBRL results for the dental, palato-alveolar and lateral click types in the contexts of /a/, /e/ and /o/, pooled across speakers. Negative values indicate that the burst occurs before the peak intraoral pressure is reached. Positive values indicate that the burst occurs after the intraoral peak has been reached. The click types pattern similarly, each having the lowest IOBRL values in the context of /a/. Anova tests produced a significant main effect of VOWEL on IOBRL, $[F(2,43)=4.3, p<.03]$. Post-hoc tests differentiated /a/ from the mid vowels, at $p<.002$ for its pair-wise comparison with /e/, and $p<.02$ for the pairwise comparison of /a/ to /o/. The comparison of /e, o/ was not signifcant. Thus in the context of the mid-vowels, a contraction of the intraoral cavity seems to occur; and this is especially notable for the palato-alveolar click. The fricated clicks pattern similarly to each other. For them, cavity expansion may continue to occur even after the onset of the click burst, particularly in the /a/ context. The lateral click shows a great deal of variabilty, but EPG data has shown this click to be the most variable of the three click types. The dental click is more variable in this measure than in others, though much less than the lateral click.

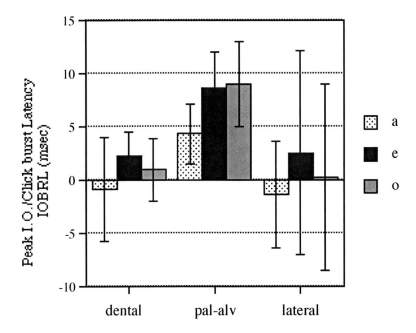

Figure 98: Mean peak intra-oral burst latency results for the dental, palato-alveolar and lateral clicks in the symmetrical vowel contexts of /a/, /e/ and /o/, pooled across speakers.

The results obtained for BDL and IOBRL show marked similarities in their vowel patterns. Positive IOBRL values are reflected as negative BDL values and vice versa. The overriding generalization that may be drawn here is that an earlier pharyngeal pressure rise (based on BDL results) goes hand-in-hand with click bursts that occur *after* the peak intraoral pressure has been reached. This situation arises in the context of the midvowels. Contraction of the click cavity in the context of the higher vowels likely reflects the need for the tongue center to move from a lower target position required for click production to a tongue center position more suitable for the upcoming vowel. The magnitude and duration of this movement is greater for the palato-alveolar click because the tongue center reaches a lower position than it does in the dental and lateral clicks, though some adjustment in tongue body position is necessary for the affricated clicks in the mid-vowel contexts as well, even though their tongue body position is higher than that of the palato-alveolar click.

The following section looks at vowel effects on rarefaction velocity and the peak negative intraoral pressure.

5.3.7 Vowel Effects: Rarefaction Velocity and PNEG

This section analyzes vowel effects on the average intraoral velocity and peak negative intraoral pressure. There is no uniform pattern of vowel differences for these aerodynamic measures. Rather, vowels have different effects on different clicks.

Previous analysis of the rarefaction velocity and peak negative intraoral pressure on data pooled across speakers and vowel contexts allowed some inferences to be made about relative tongue body position for the three click types. We now consider the average intraoral velocity and the peak intraoral pressure for the three click types, split by vowel.

Figure 99 depicts the mean intraoral velocity values for the dental, palato-alveolar and lateral clicks in the vowel contexts of /a/, /e/ and /o/. Two distinct patterns emerge, one for the dental click and a similar pattern for the palato-alveolar and lateral clicks. The dental click has the smallest mean velocity value in the context of /a/ and the largest in the context of /o/, with the mean for /e/ falling intermediate between the two. The palato-alveolar and lateral clicks display the same pattern, though the overall magnitude for the lateral click is smaller than the palato-alveolar click, as previously noted. For both of these clicks, the mean velocity is greatest in the context of /a/, smallest in the context of /o/, while the means for /e/ lie intermediate between /a/ and /o/.

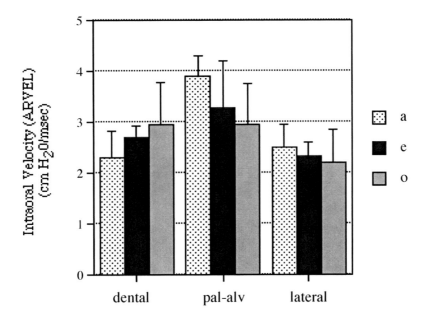

Figure 99: Mean results of the average intraoral velocity measure for the dental, palato-alveolar and lateral clicks in the symmetrical vowel contexts of /a/, /e/ and /o/, pooled across speakers.

Given that the dental click patterns differently from the other click types, it is appropriate to do a separate two-factor ANOVA for *each* click type, with SPEAKER and VOWEL as the main independent variables. ANOVA results showed that, for the dental click, there was a highly significant main effect of VOWEL on Intraoral Velocity $[F (2, 14) = 9.88,$ $p< .003]$. Post-hoc comparisons showed that the mid vowels were not distinguished from each other but the pair-wise comparisons of /a/ to /e/ and /a/ to /o/ were significant at $p< .05$ and $p< .004$, respectively. There was also a significant main effect of the interaction between SPEAKER and VOWEL on Intraoral Velocity $[F(4, 14) = 5.37, p<.008]$. Speakers NK and NT display a similar pattern, with /e/ having the greatest mean velocity value and /a/ the lowest, while Speaker GV has the greatest velocity for /o/ and the lowest in the context of /e/.

The palato-alveolar click distinguishes the mid vowels from the low vowel as does the dental click, though the magnitude of the distinction for the palato-alveolar click is the opposite of that observed for the dental click, with the /a/ vowel for the palato-alveolar click having the greatest intraoral velocity. There was a significant main effect of VOWEL on Intraoral Velocity $[F(2,14) = 2.79, p<.001]$. Post-hoc comparisons yielded significant results for the pair-wise comparisons of /a/ to /e/ and /a/ to /o/, at $p< .007$ and $p<.0004$, respectively. The comparison of the mid-vowels /e/ and /o/ was not significant. There was only a marginally significant interaction between SPEAKER and VOWEL on Intraoral Velocity for this click type [F(4, 14) = 2.79, p<.07]. Speakers GV and NT patterned similarly with /a/ having the greatest average velocity while /e/ and /o/ had more similar mean values. Speaker NK had similar mean values for /e/ and /a/, with /e/ having the greatest value at -4.36, /a/ at -4.28, and /o/ the lowest, at -3.74 cm H2O/msec.

The lateral click had the greatest intraoral velocity in the context of /a/, followed by /e/ and then /o/ at -2.51, -2.33 and -2.22 cm H2O/msec, respectively. The main effect of VOWEL was not significant, nor was the interaction between SPEAKER and VOWEL.

We now consider the peak intraoral pressure. Figure 100 illustrates the mean peak negative intraoral pressure for speaker-pooled data for each of the click types in the vowel contexts of /a/, /e/ and /o/. For the palato-alveolar click type, the peak negative pressure values are equivalent in all three vowel contexts. ANOVA results confirm a non-significant main effect of VOWEL on the intraoral pressure for this click type.

For the lateral click, peak intraoral pressure is greatest in the context of /e/ while the mean peak intraoral pressure values in the contexts of /a/ and /o/ are equal. Anova results confirmed that there was a significant main effect of VOWEL on intraoral pressure for the lateral click [F(2,15) = 5.42, p<.02]. Post-hoc tests yielded significant results for the pair-wise comparisons of /e/ with /a/ and /o/, at p< .02 and p<.01, respectively. The comparison of /a/ to /o/ was not significant. The interaction between SPEAKER and VOWEL on intraoral pressure for the lateral click was significant [F(4,15) = 8.03, p<.01]. Speaker NK had the greatest intraoral pressure in the context of /a/, followed by /e/ and then /o/. Speaker NT had the pattern, from greatest to lowest, of /e/> /a/ > /o/, while Speaker GV had the greatest intraoral pressure in the /e/ context, followed by /o/ and then /a/. These varying vowel patterns for speakers likely reflect individual patterns in lateral contact and magnitude of asymmetry in the varying vowel contexts for the various speakers, as the intraoral velocity was not significantly different for the three vowel contexts.

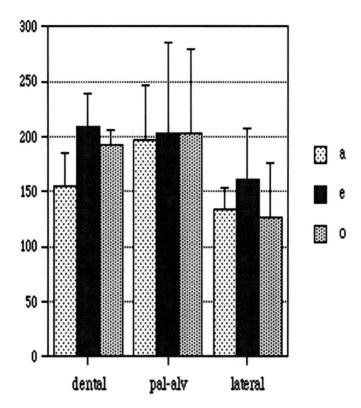

Figure 100: Mean results of the peak intraoral pressure measure for the dental, palato-alveolar and lateral clicks in the symmetrical vowel contexts of /a/, /e/ and /o/, pooled across speakers.

For the dental click type, the smallest mean intraoral pressure value is obtained in the context of /a/, the greatest in the context of /e/ while /o/ has an intermediate mean pressure value. There was a significant main effect of VOWEL on intraoral pressure [F(2,14) = 15.14, p<.001] for the dental click. Post-hoc comparisons showed that the pairwise comparisons of /e/ and /o/ with /a/ differed significantly at p< .001 and p<.003, respectively. The mid vowels did not differ significantly from each other. All speakers followed this same trend of having lower peak intraoral values in the context of /a/ for this click type. The interaction between SPEAKER and VOWEL was not at all significant.

Table 21 presents the speaker-pooled mean values for the intraoral velocity and the peak negative intraoral pressure for the dental, palato-alveolar and lateral clicks in the vowel contexts of /a/, /e/ and /o/.

Table 21: Mean results of Intraoral Velocity and Peak Negative Intraoral Pressure measures for the dental, palato-alveolar and lateral clicks in the vowel contexts of /a/, /e/ and /o/, for data pooled across speakers

Measures⇒ Vowel-Click-Vowel ⇓	Intraoral Velocity (cm H_2O/msec)	Peak Intraoral Pressure (cm H_2O)
/aca/	-2.30	-155
/ece/	-2.72	-210
/oco/	-2.96	-193
/aqa/	-3.92	-197
/eqe/	-3.29	-204
/oqo/	-2.97	-203
/axa/	-2.51	-134
/exe/	-2.33	-161
/oxo/	-2.22	-127

Table 22 presents the statistical results of the comparisons vowel comparisons for each of the three click types; non-significant comparisons are shaded. Table 21 compares the intraoral velocity and the peak intraoral pressure. For the dental click, the mid vowels are distinguished from the low vowel, for both intraoral velocity and peak intraoral pressure, with the mid-vowels having both greater velocity and greater peak intraoral pressure. For the palato-alveolar click, the mid vowels are distinct from the low vowel with respect to the intraoral velocity, but all vowels have equivalent peak negative intraoral pressures. For the lateral click, intraoral velocity does not significantly differ across vowel category. Yet, intraoral pressure for the mid vowel /e/ is distinguished from /a/ and /o/.

By considering the intraoral velocity and the peak intraoral pressure together, certain inferences may be made about the rarefaction strategies used for the various click types. An important inference is that the different vowel patterns for the various click types lead to the conclusion that the rarefaction strategies involved are adaptable. Slightly different articulator movements may be a function of the particular vowel environment for any given click type. Another important inference from looking at the bulk of the data is that typically a greater intraoral velocity implies more rarefaction, resulting in a greater peak intraoral pressure. Simple regression shows that this correlation is strong but does not account for the entire story. Tongue dorsum retraction for the palato-alveolar click may be involved in the rarefaction process. For the dental click, tongue dorsum retraction is simultaneous with the blade release, and early dorsum retraction is typically not a strategy used in rarefaction for the dental click. (Early tongue dorsum retraction for the dental click was noted in one instance of the aerodynamic data. Speaker GV had earlier tongue dorsum movement for the dental click in the context of /o/. This speaker also showed much higher peak pharyngeal pressure, greater intraoral velocity and greater peak negative intraoral pressure for the same click in the same vowel context, deviating from the other two speakers in this respect. The implication here is that the early tongue dorsum retraction played at least a partial role in rarefaction for this particular token. There was only one token for this Speaker's dental click in this vowel context, so there is no way of knowing if this production is fairly typical for this speaker.)

Table 22: Statistical Table listing the results for the vowel comparisons for each click type for the measures of Intraoral Velocity and Peak Negative Intraoral Pressure

Dependent Variables⇒ Vowel Comparisons⇓	Intraoral Velocity	Peak Negative Pressure
aca/ece	p<.05	p<.001
aca/oco	p<.004	p<.003
ece/oco		
aqa/eqe	p<.007	
aqa/oqo	p<.001	
eqe/oqo		
axa/exe		p<.02
axa/oxo		
exe/oxo		p<.005

In dental clicks the lateral margins seem to play an important role in delimiting the cavity area. Notably, the dental click in the /e/ vowel context has the smallest cavity area, as measured from the SPG and EPG data, the smallest cavity width, and produced the greatest peak negative pressure when looking at all tokens individually. The slow intraoral velocity, along with the consistent vowel pattern for the lateral click, points to the constrained nature of the tongue center for this click type.

In Section 5.3.3 we concluded, based on the overall patterning of the click types for pooled data for the measures of intraoral velocity and peak negative intraoral pressure that the palato-alveolar click reaches a lower tongue body position than the dental and lateral clicks. The vowel data shows that the click with the low tongue body position has the greatest rarefaction velocity in the context of the low vowel. The dental click, hypothesized to have a higher tongue body position, has a greater intraoral velocity in the context of the high vowels rather than the low vowel. The vowel patterns suggest that we must consider that the various click types have different target heights for the tongue center—an important determining factor in how a specific click in a particular vowel context is articulated.

5.4 CONCLUSION

This aerodynamic investigation differs from previous aerodynamic studies on clicks in two important respects. Firstly, it used aerodynamic data to focus on the details of the timing of the component gestures involved in click production, namely the tongue blade, tongue body and tongue dorsum rather than examining click accompaniments. Secondly, it provides empirical data on the intraoral pressure inside the click cavity, which has never before been reliably obtained. The intraoral pressure data alone provides a wealth of new information on the nature and timing of the articulatory gestures involved in click production.

Aerodynamic data presented in this chapter provides good evidence of temporal coarticulation. Results showed that rarefaction results mainly from tongue center lowering, especially given the very high negative intraoral pressures generated, which are much higher than previous estimates (Kagaya 1978, see also Stevens 1998 pp.121-124). We inferred from rarefaction velocities that the palato-alveolar click undergoes the greatest amount of tongue center lowering while the affricated clicks have higher tongue center positions overall. Competing demands between the tongue center "target" required for click production and the optimal target position for the upcoming vowel were resolved by early anticipation of the tongue center prior to the click burst in the context of the midvowels. The magnitude of this preparatory movement was greatest for the palato-alveolar click, an expected result if indeed our inference regarding its low tongue center position (at maximal cavity expansion) is correct. For those clicks that are thought to have higher tongue center positions—the affricated clicks—the cavity continued, in some cases, to expand after the click burst. That is, the tongue center continued to move downward, most obviously interpreted as a preparatory movement for the upcoming low vowel. We consider these preparatory movements of the tongue center to be essential in facilitating the production of clicks in connected speech.

Ultimately, it is the goal of this research to integrate the information on the aerodynamics of click consonants with palatographic knowledge in order to provide a comprehensive perspective on the articulatory dynamics of this complex segment and its production in various vowel contexts. The following chapter draws together SPG, EPG and Aerodynamic data in an attempt to provide a better understanding of the coproduction of clicks and the various coarticulatory strategies used in the production of this complex segment.

CHAPTER 6: TOWARDS A UNIFIED ACCOUNT OF CLICK CONSONANT PRODUCTION

6.0 Introduction

The previous chapters have provided a detailed picture of click production, which confirms what was generally known or believed about clicks and, in addition, provided substantial new information on the three IsiZulu clicks with respect to their compensatory nature. This chapter provides a qualitative review of these results and suggests a model of organization from which to view click production.

6.1 Summary of the Articulatory Aspects of IsiZulu clicks

6.1.1 Dental click

In order to produce a dental click, the tongue blade is typically in a laminal posture, and is placed along the back of the upper teeth. Cavity formation for the dental click takes a relatively short time compared to the other click types, and the back closure is more forward than it is in the palato-alveolar and lateral clicks. Once the initial seal has formed, rarefaction does not begin immediately. Instead, both the back closure and the front closure continue to strengthen. The back closure either broadens or moves further forward (our data cannot distinguish between these two possibilities), and the front articulation broadens as well. The lateral margins are broadest for this click type, and play an important role in determining the initial cavity size, and ultimately the amount of negative pressure generated during rarefaction. Minimal cavity size is attained very early during the overlap period. Due to the large lateral contact on the palate and the more anterior dorsal position, dental clicks have the smallest cavity area at the onset of the overlap phase (and most likely the smallest cavity volume as well). During the closure phase, the dorsal and coronal closures are static in place. Rarefaction is accomplished solely by lowering the tongue center. Though lowering of the tongue center occurs, we presume, based on comparing rarefaction velocities and the resulting intraoral pressure generated, that tongue center lowering is not as extensive for the dental click as it is for the palato-alveolar click. Tongue lowering also results in a decrease in the lateral margins, creating a larger proportional change in cavity volume, resulting in greater negative pressure. Dorsal retraction does not play a role in rarefaction for the dental click.

During the overlap phase, the tongue blade is static in place. However, just prior to the click burst, the anterior closure starts to separate from the palate, usually at the anterior edge of the tongue blade closure. A narrow fricative channel is held for about 20-40 milliseconds before a fuller release movement occurs. The position of the front edge of the dorsal closure does not move during the overlap phase but, from EPG data, we know that as the tongue blade begins its initial release, dorsal movement also becomes evident. Based on EPG data, it cannot be determined whether dorsal movement involves lowering of the contact edges, without a change in the location of contact, or if there is actual tongue dorsum retraction resulting in an actual shift in position of the dorsal closure.

6.1.2 Palato-Alveolar Click

In order to produce a palato-alveolar click, an apical tongue posture is typically used. The tongue tip is initially positioned at the base of the upper front teeth, and during the course of the closure, it slides back along the palate, beyond the alveolar ridge. The lateral margins of the click cavity are thinner and the position of the dorsal closure is more posterior compared to the dental click. Both of these differences result in a larger cavity area than was observed for the dental click. The formation of the cavity takes longest for this click type and it has the shortest overlap phase. Rarefaction is achieved mainly by lowering the center of the tongue as evidenced by intraoral pressure data. Rarefaction velocity and peak negative intraoral pressure data suggest that the greatest proportional change in cavity volume occurs for this click type, and the resulting tongue center position prior to release is lowest compared to the affricated clicks. In addition to lowering of the tongue center, EPG data provided good evidence that, for this click type, dorsal retraction occurs during the rarefaction stage, and as such, contributes to the overall proportional change in cavity volume. Typically, dorsal retraction begins early during the overlap phase and tongue tip retraction occurs more towards the end of the articulation, and are therefore assumed to be independent of each other. However, the relationship between these two movements is not clear; but it is possible that early dorsal retraction is a preparatory movement for the upcoming tongue tip retraction. It is also plausible that tongue tip retraction is essential in creating an abrupt non-affricated release. The dorsal release occurs shortly after the anterior release and is uvular in nature due to retraction during the rarefaction process.

6.1.3 Lateral Click

Cavity formation proceeds for the lateral click as it does for the dental and palato-alveolar clicks, except that placement and posture of the tongue blade/tip are variable. Tongue blade/tip posture was observed to be either laminal or apico-laminal, but never apical. Place of articulation of the tongue blade ranged from fully dental to post-dental. Cavity formation for this click type was similar in duration to that observed for palato-alveolar clicks but the initial dorsal position was further back than for the dental and palato-alveolar clicks, and was rarely visible on the pseudopalate, even at the onset of the overlap phase. The release of lateral clicks is through a narrow channel whose position is also held for some time. This channel is located far back, typically on the right side, and the releasing motion involves a slow reduction of the extent of contact in front of this location, often matched by an increase in contact on the opposite side. Increased contact on the non-releasing side constrains the tongue center from fully lowering during the rarefaction process. The constrained nature of the tongue is reflected in the extremely low rarefaction velocities and their corresponding low negative intraoral pressures. Rarefaction occurs from lowering one part of the tongue center. Once the lateral release begins, continued lowering of one side of the tongue aides in sustained frication and, in some cases, continued rarefaction. In most cases, the dorsal release and the central coronal release are simultaneous.

6.1.4 Vowel Effects

Both spatial and temporal coarticulation were observed for the three click types. In the case of the dental and palato-alveolar clicks, the dorsal closure was more fronted in the context of /e/. Vowel effects on the dorsal articulation of lateral clicks could not be assessed in this respect because the dorsal closure was rarely visible on the pseudopalate. SPG data indicated that dental clicks in the context of /e/ were broader in contact width and more-anterior as well. Dental clicks in the /e/ vowel context had the broadest lateral contact and, as a result, produced the greatest proportional change in cavity volume in this vowel context.

Contraction of the click cavity from its maximal cavity expansion occurs prior to the click burst in the contexts of the mid vowels, suggesting that the tongue center rises before the burst occurs in order to prepare for the following vowel position, which has a higher target position than that of the click. This occurs for all click types but the effect was greatest for the palato-alveolar click, which we inferred had the lowest tongue center position at peak cavity expansion. In the case of the dental and lateral clicks, which were inferred to have a higher tongue center position, the click cavity continued to expand even after the onset of the click burst, but only in the low vowel context, indicating continued lowering of the tongue center. Given the high position of the tongue center and the low target position of the vowel, the tongue center likely continues to lower in preparation for the upcoming low vowel. In the context of the mid vowels, the same pattern was observed for the dental click as for the palato-alveolar click, but the magnitude of the effect was smaller. Table 23 summarizes in tabular form the important articulatory characteristics of IsiZulu clicks.

Table 23: Articulatory Characteristics of IsiZulu clicks

Click Type⇒ Summary Results⇓	Dental	Palato-Alveolar	Lateral
Release	affricated	abrupt	affricated
Tongue Center Target	high	low	high and asymmetric
Tongue blade/tip posture	laminal	apical	apico-laminal
Rarefaction	lowering of the tongue center, lateral edges crucial	lowering of tongue center, tongue dorsum retraction	lowering of one side of the tongue

6.2 Phase Relationships

Thus far we have been discussing click production as a series of discrete closure and release gestures consisting of asynchronous onsets and offsets with overlapping closure durations. For descriptive purposes we have been referring to these gestures in terms of articulatory phases—namely the Lead, Overlap and Lag phases. However, the serial ordering of these phases has been an unchallenged assumption, made only for the sake of descriptive convenience. There are at least several possible ways in which the tongue blade/tip and the tongue dorsum gestures could be organized. We consider only two possibilities here, the impetus of which is derived from studies on the organization of consonants and vowels.

Some examples of experimental work that investigated the phasing of vowels and consonants are, Öhman (1967), Fowler (1983), Smith (1995) and Browman and Goldstein

(1990). One view (Browman and Goldstein 1990) supposes that vowels and consonants are organized in serial fashion, with each segment coordinated to adjacent segments. Another view (Öhman 1967, Fowler 1983 and Smith 1995) suggests that consonants and vowels are organized in parallel fashion, that is, vowels are produced independently of consonants. We will compare 'independent' and 'dependent' duration models.

Figures 6.1 and 6.2 schematize these two different ways of conceptualizing the organization of the tongue blade/tip and tongue dorsum gestures. Figure 101A depicts the gestures in the way we have been describing them throughout this dissertation, that is, in terms of three serial phases—the Tongue Dorsum Lead, Overlap and Tongue Dorsum Lag phases—whose durations are independent of each other. This model may be referred to as the 'independent' model of click production. This model assumes that the various phases can vary in duration independently with the total click duration such that an increase in one phase would be compensated for by a decrease in some other phase. Figure 101B shows that an increase in the duration of the overlap phase, shown in black, results in a decrease in the lead and/or lag phases. That is, we expect to see strong negative correlations between the phases if clicks are organized in this independent manner.

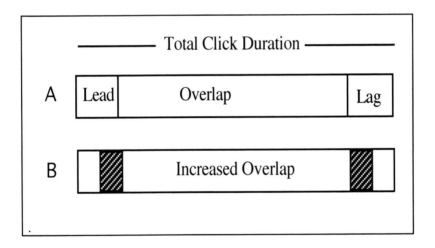

Figure 101: Mean results of the peak intraoral pressure measure for the dental, palato-alveolar and lateral clicks in the symmetrical vowel contexts of /a/, /e/ and /o/, pooled across speakers

Figure 102 presents the 'dependent' model of click production. In this model, the dorsal and coronal gestures have their own intrinsic timing, but are lexically specified to have a certain degree of overlap. This suggests that their phasing must somehow be fixed at either the onset of the gestures, or their offsets, (or both). We must at least assume that the order of the closures is fixed, as a click would not be produced if the dorsal release were to occur first.

Empirical evidence from this study also indicates that the order of the onsets is fixed as well, as the tongue dorsum closure was made before the tongue blade/tip closure in every token. Thus, in this model, a substantial increase in the tongue blade articulation would necessarily entail an increase in the dorsal component if the mandatory order of closures and releases is to be maintained. Figure 102B depicts an increase in the tongue blade/tip gesture and the concomitant durational increase in the dorsal gesture. Thus, we would expect the seal duration to be positively correlated to the total click duration if this model is in operation.

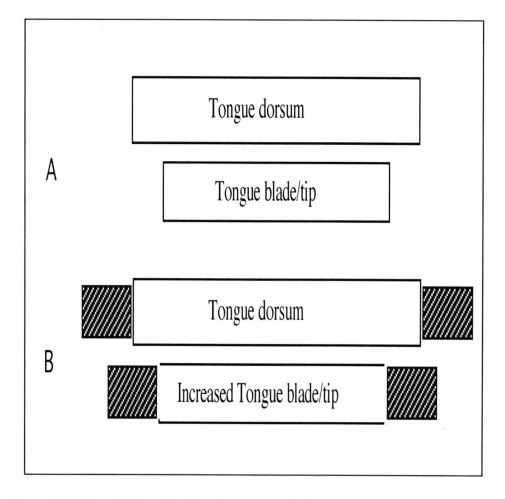

Figure 102: Schematization of the dependent model of click production. The figure shows that an increase in the tongue blade articulation also results in an increase in the duration of the total click duration.

In order to test these two models to determine which one is more likely to be in operation, simple linear regression was used to determine the strength of the correlations between the following variables: onset latency, seal duration, total click duration (the same as the tongue dorsum closure duration), and offset latency. The following correlations were done: total click duration vs. onset latency, total click duration vs. seal duration, total click duration vs. offset latency, onset latencey vs. seal duration, onset latency vs. offset latency, and seal duration vs. offset latency. Regressions were done on normalized data to remove the effect of differences of speaker vocal tract size, as previously described in the SPG and aerodynamic portions of the study. Only regressions significant at the p< .01 level are considered. Table 24 shows the results of these correlations.

The regressions show two different patterns, one for the lateral click and another for the non-lateral pair. For the dental and palato-alveolar clicks, seal duration and total click duration covary. This is highly suggestive of the 'dependent model' of click organization, where we supposed that an increase in the tongue blade/tip would necessarily entail an increase in the tongue dorsum duration as well. We also found that onset latency does not covary with any of the other phases, again, suggesting that cavity formation has, in addition to having a fixed order, a specified duration as well.

In the case of the lateral click, there was a significant positive correlation between the offset latency and the total click duration and a negative correlation between the seal duration and the offset latency. Any increase in the seal duration of the lateral click did not result in an increase in the total click duration because the offset latency decreased, such that the total click duration was not changed. However, an increase in the offset latency increased the total click duration, as these variables were positively correlated. Possible reasons for the differences between the lateral click and the other click types is the difference in the rarefaction strategy for this click type and the fact that three releases are involved. Recall that rarefaction can continue even after the lateral release has begun which aids in sustaining frication for a longer time period. Given that the tongue dorsum is not released until after the frication of the lateral click has been completed, it is thus possible to get shorter seal durations and longer offset latencies, resulting in a negative correlation between these two variables. An increase in the total click duration would also result from the delay in tongue dorsum retraction/release.

Overall, the results indicate that, for all clicks, the lack of strong negative correlations, especially in the case of the dental and palato-alveolar clicks suggest that click gestures are not independent. The results point more towards the dependent model of click production, as the durations of the dorsal and coronal gestures vary proportionally, especially for the centrally released clicks. The lateral case presented special circumstances due to its lateral nature, and therefore required a different explanation.

Table 24: Phase Correlation Results

Click Type⇒ PHASE⇓	**Dental**	**Palato-Alveolar**	**Lateral**
OL vs. OFL			
OL vs. SD			
OL vs TCLD			
SD vs. OFL			S, p<.005 R2 = .258 negative correlation
SD vs. TCLD	S, p<.0009 R2=.202	S, p<.004 R2 = .173	
TCLD vs. OFL			S, p<.003 R2 = .294

Given that we have adopted the dependent model of click production, we can consider that all voiceless unaspirated clicks are *minimally* composed of three gestures—a dorsal gesture, a coronal gesture and a rarefaction gesture. (Clicks with more complex accompaniments would obviously be composed of more gestures). Following Fowler (1993) and Saltzman and Munhall (1989), we had earlier adopted the definition of a gesture as a target-intentioned combination of articulatory movements. In this definition it was made clear that not all movements are considered gestures and not all gestures are composed of one articulatory movement effected by a single articulator. In fact, each of these gestures are composed of several articulatory movements. For example, the rarefaction gesture can be composed of both tongue center lowering and dorsal retraction, as noted for the palato-alveolar click.

6.3 Primary versus Secondary Articulations

It has been argued that, in multiply-articulated consonants having the same stricture degree, one articulation should be considered "primary" while the other is deemed "secondary" (Anderson 1976). Anderson's test for which articulation should be deemed primary is mainly a phonological consideration. He shows, using various assimilation processes, that labial-velars pattern like simple labials in some languages and as simple velars in other languages. If we consider the phonological patterning of IsiZulu clicks, we might consider the nasal assimilation rule to be relevant. In IsiZulu, a nasal prefix preceding a click consonant becomes a velar nasal. If Anderson is correct, we would consider the velar articulation to be primary given that assimilation occurs with the back closure. However, intuitively we know that this result is incorrect, given that there are three distinct click types in IsiZulu. Anderson's approach may be valid for labial-velars, especially given that Maddieson (1993) has shown the labial and velar gestures of the simplex consonants and the complex compound consonant in Ewe to be similar gestures, offset in such a way as to produce the intended acoustic effect. However, in the case of clicks, there is little to be gained by adopting Anderson's viewpoint.

Of course, it is useful, for the sake of descriptive adequacy, to classify one articulation as "primary", but this should not be interpreted to mean that the role of the non-primary articulation is not central to the production of the consonant. Overlapping coronal and dorsal articulations are both required to create and maintain a seal, and without either movement, cavity formation and rarefaction would not be possible. An analogy might be to say that the dorsal articulation is as important to the production of a click as the abduction of the vocal cords is to the production of $[t^h]$.

6.4   Future Research

This study has provided credible evidence that clicks do indeed coarticulate. However, much work still remains to be done on this segment type before their articulation is fully understood. It should be emphasized that the results of this study apply only to clicks in IsiZulu; and it is not clear to what extent these results are generalizable across all click languages. For example, Ladefoged and Traill (1994) have argued for five general click types—bilabial, dental, alveolar, palatal and lateral. The palato-alveolar click in IsiZulu would likely be considered an "alveolar" click using Ladefoged and Traill's nomenclature. Traill's x-ray study of clicks in !Xóõ showed that the alveolar click in this language is not produced in the same manner as seen here for /q/ in IsiZulu. In !Xóõ alveolar click production did not involve retraction of the tongue tip and the tongue dorsum as in IsiZulu. The comparison of the production of these two types of alveolar clicks demonstrates that a similar click type may have different production strategies. One possible reason for this difference may have to do with the difference in the set of contrasts that exist in a language. Production patterns have been shown to differ based on the types of contrasts employed in a given language (e.g. Cohn 1990). This study showed that palato-alveolar clicks in IsiZulu are uvular at the release. !Xóõ has two types of basic alveolar clicks that contrast solely on the dorsal component of the gesture, which may be either velar or uvular. Obviously if the velar dorsal gesture were to retract to a uvular position, the distinction between the two types of alveolars would be obscured. From this example we see that much research remains to be done on clicks as they are produced in other languages. Specifically, we suggest that aerodynamic data, especially intraoral pressure, would be most useful in delineating coproduction and coarticulatory strategies in click production, as it produced a wealth of new information in this study. To this end, more development in the area of field research techniques for measuring intraoral pressure in coronal segments is needed.

The results in this study regarding tongue body movement are based on inferences made from data drawn from several different techniques. Studies which *directly* track tongue body movement, such as x-ray microbeam or articulography would be advantageous in confirming results from this study as well as elucidating new data on the details regarding rarefaction strategies of the different click types as they are produced in any given language.

More work also needs to be done in order to analyze the effects of various other contexts on clicks. For example, this study did not analyze the temporal organization of clicks to the surrounding vowels nor their response to changes in speech rate, prosody or other changes or perturbations in timing. Work by Byrd (1994) predicts that the timing structure of multiply-articulated segments should not be altered by changes in context due to speech rate, for example. However, we have seen that clicks, while being well-organized, highly structured units, were shown to be highly adaptable to contextual modification.

6.5 Concluding Remarks

We have adopted a dependent model of click production. Within this framework is the assumption that clicks are target intentioned gestures whose composite movements are lexically specified to overlap. These overlapping tongue dorsum, tongue center and tongue blade/tip movements are combined into higher-level organized structures representing gestures. Several gestures are combined to create a particular click. Comparison of clicks and simple pulmonics showed that some aspects of the dorsal and coronal gestures were quite similar, supporting the notion of gestural economy (Maddieson 1996), but click-specific requirements oblige other aspects to differ from those found in non-click segments.

Much experimental work has been done which shows that vowels and consonants are produced separately but overlap in time to produce smoothly flowing speech (Fowler 1983). This study provides further evidence that context dependent influences on an intervocalic consonant may result from the mechanism of overlapping consonant and vowel gestures, thereby lending support to "coproduction" and "gestural" models of speech production. One might ask, "why coproduction?" The answer: Smoothly-flowing speech necessarily entails early preparation of upcoming intentions.

However, regardless of the model chosen from which to view and understand the articulatory dynamics of speech, one outstanding generalization may be drawn from the empirical evidence presented in this study. It is that, regardless of the complexity of a segment, if it is spoken, it must be integrated into the stream of speech. To this end, coarticulation is indeed a phenomenon that *must* necessarily exist in spoken human language.

Appendix A: Corpus

The corpus consisted of 4 syllable words of the following shape, /bV-bV-CVbV/, where 'b' is a bilabial consonant and 'V' is a vowel, either /a/, /e/ or /o/. 'C' is one of the following consonants—c, q, x, th, t, kh, g, hl or kl'. Each click was placed in the penultimate (stressed) syllable in the symmetrical vowel contexts of /a/, /e/ and /o/. In IsiZulu the penultimate prepausal syllable is realized with increased duration on the vowel. All speakers showed increased vowel duration of the penultimate syllable in this context. Seven of the nine test utterances consisted of real words, while two test utterances, although morphologically consistent with real IsiZulu words, contained nonsense verb stems. These two stems are clearly labeled in the table. Nonsense stems are marked by an asterisk.

The test utterances were constructed by combining the 3rd person plural pronoun /ba/ 'they' with either the past tense morpheme /be/ 'were', or the conditional morpheme /bo/ 'should.' These concatenated morphemes produced /babe.../ 'they were', /beba.../, 'they were' and /babo/ 'they should'. (The 3rd person plural morpheme and the past tense morpheme can be concatenated in either way without changing the meaning of the utterance). These morphemes were combined with disyllabic verb stems beginning with the test consonant followed by—/a/, /e/ and /o/. (In the SPG data, /a-/ was used to replace word initial /be-/, but see chapter 2 methodology for an explanation). The disyllabic verb stems are shown in Tables A1 and A2. .

Each verb stem was combined with /beba-/ 'they were', /babe-/ 'they were' and /babo/ 'they should' to generate a corpus which placed each of the click types in symmetrical vowel contexts /a___a/, /e___e/ and /o___o/. During EPG and aerodynamic data collection, all words were said in the carrier phrase, /bathi _____/ 'they say _____'. Sentences exemplifying each test utterance were given to the speakers prior to the recording session in order to clarify the meanings of the test utterances. These sentences are detailed on the following pages.

TABLE A1: Disyllabic Verb Stems: Clicks

dental click	palato-alveolar click	lateral click
-caba: tidy up	-qapha: stare intently	-xaba: to block
-ceba: set up one's home	-qeba: *	-xeba: *
-coba: cut meat	-qoba: slice meat	-xova: pound

Table A2: Disyllabic Verb Stems: Non-click Consonants

tongue blade articulation	**tongue dorsum articulation**
-thaba: happy	-kabha: split wood
-tefa: whining	-geba: bend down
-thoba: use warm compress	-goba: bend over

lateral articulation	**velar ejective lateral**
-hlaba: stab	-klaya: cut strips of cloth
-hleba: gossip	-kleza: squirt milk into the mouth
-hloba: clean	-kloza: salivate

Sentences exemplifying test utterances

Click Consonants

1.   bebacaba

Abafana bebacaba umuzi uma umama wabo efika.

Abafana	bebacaba	umuzi	uma	umama	wabo
efika.					
The boys	were setting up	a home	when	mother	their
arrived.					

The boys were setting up a home when their mother arrived.

2.   babeceba

Abafana <u>babeceba</u> amantombazane uma begangile.

Abafana	<u>babeceba</u>	amantombazane	uma	begangile.
The boys	were telling on	the girls	when	they
misbehaved.				

The boys were telling on the girls when they misbehaved.

3.   bab<u>oco</u>ba

Tshela abafana ukuthi babocoba inyama kababa kahle

Tshela	abafana	ukuthi	<u>babocoba</u>	inyama
Tell	the boys	that	they should cut	meat

ka	baba	kahle.
of	father	well.

Tell the boys that they should cut father's meat well.

4.   beb<u>aqa</u>pha

Abafana <u>bebaqapha</u> amaphoyisa ukuthi angababoni.

Abafana	<u>bebaqapha</u>	amaphoyisa
The boys	were watching	the police

ukuthi	angababoni.
so that	they (the police) didn't see them.

The boys were watching the police so that they (the police) wouldn't see them.

5.   bab<u>oqo</u>ba

Abafana baboqoba inyama masisha.

Abafana	<u>baboqoba</u>	inyama	masisha.
The boys	should slice	the meat	quickly.

The boys should slice the meat quickly.

6.   beb<u>axa</u>ba

Abafana <u>bebaxaba</u> umgwago ngamatshe namuhla ukuze amaphoyisa angadluli.

Abafana	<u>bebaxaba</u>	umgwago	ngamatshe
The boys	were blocking the road		with stones

namuhla ukuze	amaphoyisa	angadluli.
so that	the police	could not pass.

The boys were blocking the road with stones so that the police could not pass.

7.   bab<u>oxo</u>va

Tshela abafana ukuthi <u>baboxova</u> loludaka namuhla.

Tshela	abafana	ukuthi	<u>baboxova</u>	loludaka	namuhla.
Tell	the boys	that	they should mix	the mud	today.

Tell the boys that they should mix the mud today.

8.   ab<u>aca</u>ba

Abantu abacaba eduze komfula badliwa izikhukhula.

Abantu	abacaba		eduze komfula	badliwa
izikhukhula.				
People	those who set up a house		near the river	they are eaten by
floods				

Those people who set up a house near the river will be swept away by floods.

9.   ab<u>aq</u>apha

Onesi abaqapha izigulane ebusuku batelegile.

Onesi	abaqapha	izigulane	ebusuku	batelegile.
The nurses	those who watch	patients	at night	are on

strike.

The nurses who watch patients at night are on strike.

10.   ab<u>ax</u>aba

Abafana abaxaba umgwago ngamatshe baboshiwe.

Abafana	abaxaba	umgwago	ngamatshe	baboshiwe.
Boys	those who block	road	with stones	they should be

arrested.

Boys who block the road with stones should be arrested.

Non-click consonants

11. beb<u>atha</u>ba

Abantwana <u>bebathaba</u> kakhulu uma badla.

Abantwana	<u>bebathaba</u>	kakhulu	uma	badla.
The kids	became delighted	very	when	they played.

The kids became very delighted when they played.

12. bab<u>ete</u>fa

Ubaba wabashaya abantwana ngoba <u>babetefa</u>.

Ubaba	wabashaya	abantwana	ngoba	<u>babetefa</u>.
The father	spanked	the children	because	they were fussy.

The father spanked the children because they were fussy.

13. bab<u>otho</u>ba

Abafana <u>babothoba</u> uma kufika inkosi.

Abafana	<u>babothoba</u>	uma	kufika	inkosi.
The boys	should be humble	when	arrives	the King

The boys should be humble when the king arrives.

14. beb<u>aka</u>bha

Abantu <u>bebakabha</u> izinkuni zababa.

Abantu	<u>bebakabha</u>	izinkuni	zababa
People	were chopping	wood	Dad's

People were chopping Dad's wood.

15. ba**be**geba

Abantwana bami babegeba amakhanda balale njalo nje uma siya eThekwini.

Abantwana	bami	babegeba	amakhanda	balale njalo nje
	uma			
children	my	used to bend	their necks	and sleep all the time
	when			

| siya | eThekwini. |
| we went | to Thekwini. |

My children used to bend their necks and sleep all the time when we went to Thekwini.

16. ba**bogo**ba

Tshela abafana ukuthi <u>babogoba</u> lemithi esizokwakha ngayo lendlu ka gogo.

| Tshela | abafana | ukuthi | <u>babogoba</u> |
| Tell | the boys | that | they should bend |

lemithi		esizokwakha		ngayo	lendlu		ka
	gogo.						
the twigs that		we are going to build		with	house		of
	grandmother.						

Tell the boys that they should bend the twigs that we are going to build grandmother's house with.

17. be**bahla**ba

Abafana bebahlaba imbuzi.

| Abafana | bebahlaba | imbuzi |
| The boys | were slaughtering | the goat. |

The boys were slaughtering the goat.

18. bab**ehle**ba

Abafana babehleba izintombi.

Abafana	babehleba	izintombi.
The boys	were gossiping about	their girlfriends.

The boys were gossiping about their girlfriends.

19. bab**ohlo**ba

Abafana babohloba uma beya esontweni.

Abafana	babohloba	uma	baya	esontweni
The boys	should dress up	when	they go	to church.

The boys should dress up when they go to church.

20. beb**akla**ya

Abafana bebaklaya izimpahla zokugida.

Abafana	bebakl'aya	izimpahla	zokugida
The boys	were cutting	strips of cloth	for dancing.

The boys were cutting strips of cloth for dancing.

21. bab**ekle**za

Abafana babekl'eza izinkomo ethafeni.

Abafana	babekl'eza		izinkomo	
	ethafeni.			
The boys	were squirting milking into their mouths from	cows	in
the veld.				

The boys were squirting milking into their mouths from cows in the veld.

22. bab**oklo**za

Abafana babokloza uma bosa inyama.

Abafana	babokl'oza	uma	bosa	inyama
The boys	should salivate	when	they roast	meat.

The boys should salivate when they roast meat.

Appendix B: Pseudopalates

Appendix B shows scanned images of the pseudopalates for all four speakers. All images are to scale and are twice their original size. The impression of the underside of the front incisors is visible at the top of each diagram, and the name of each speaker is on the upper left side of the palate. The electrodes are depicted by white circles, and the front region is demarcated by a black line, and contains the same number of electrodes for all subjects.

Speaker NT

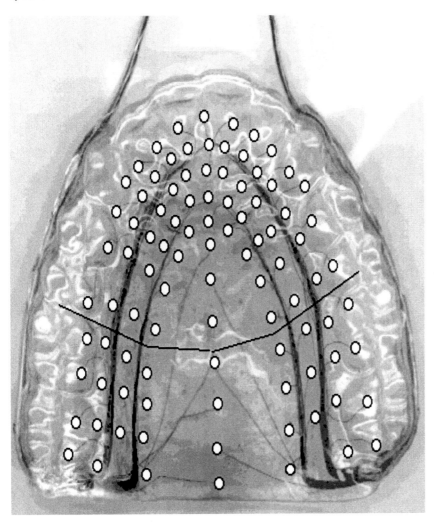

Speaker GV

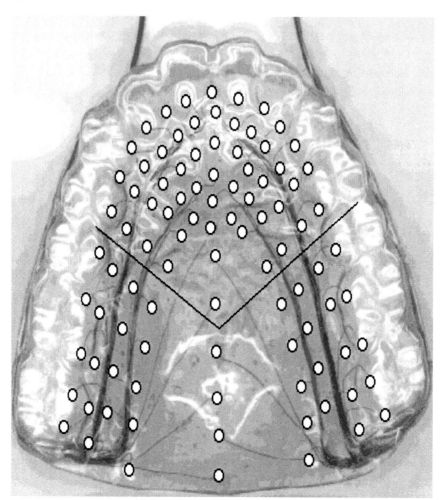

Speaker NK

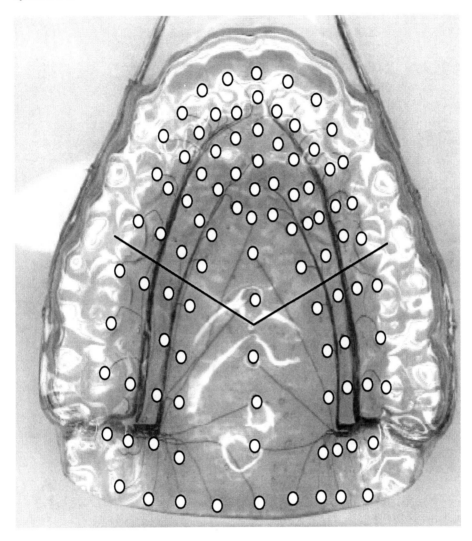

Speaker KK

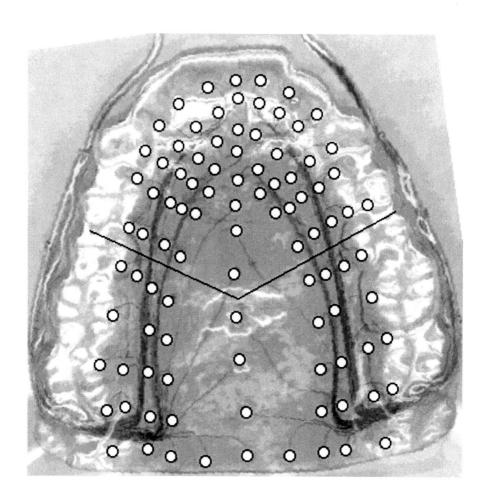

Abbreviations

The following abbreviations were used to refer to the measurements in this study. It is the author's hope that the listing here may facilitate understanding of the precise nature of the measurements involved in this study of IsiZulu clicks. All measurements are indexed. Please refer to the text in order to obtain an exact definition for each measurement.

Chapter 2: SPG-Static Palatography

ABCWd.	Absolute cavity width difference
CA.	Cavity Area
CL.	Total cavity length
CWd.	Cavity Width Difference
CW.	Total cavity width
TBLp.	Tongue Blade Position
TBLw.	Tongue blade width
TDp.	Tongue dorsum place

Chapter 3: EPG- Electropalatography

ABASI.	Absolute Asymmetry Index
EAI.	Anteriority Index
ECAI.	Cavity Area
EMAI.	Median Anteriority Index
EMAWI.	Width Index
EPI.	Posteriority Index
ONL.	Onset Latency
OFL.	Offset latency
SD.	Seal Duration
TCLD.	Total Click Duration
%MAX.	Peak linguopalatal contact

Chapter 5: Aerodynamic Measurements

ARVEL.	Average Rarefaction velocity
BDL.	Tongue blade/dorsum latency
INGAFmax.	Maximum ingressive airflow
IOBRL	Peak intraoral pressure/burst latency
IOPRmax.	Peak negative intraoral pressure
OFL.	Offset latency

OFVEL.   Average Offset Velocity
ONL.   Onset Latency
PHPRmax.   Peak pharyngeal pressure
PNEG.   Peak negative intraoral pressure
SD.   Seal Duration

Bibliography

Abercrombie, David. (1957). Direct palatography. *Zeitschrift für Phonetik*, 10: 21-25.

Abercrombie, David. (1967). *Elements of General Phonetics*. Edinburgh: Edinburgh University Press.

Anderson, Stephen. (1976). On the description of multiply-articulated consonants. *Journal of Phonetics*, 4, 17-27.

Barry, M. (1985). A palatographic study of connected speech processes. *Cambridge Papers in Phonetics and Experimental Linguistics*, 4: 1-6.

Barry, M. (1991). Temporal modelling of gestures in articulatory assimilation. *Proceedings of the XIIth International Congress of Phonetic Sciences*, vol 4, 14-17.

Beach, D.M. (1938). *The Phonetics of the Hottentot Language*. Cambridge: W. Heffer & Sons.

Browman, C. and L. Goldstein. (1986). Towards an articulatory phonology. *Phonology Yearbook*, 3: 219-252.

Browman, C. and L. Goldstein. (1990). Tiers in articulatory phonology, with some implications for casual speech. In J. Kingston & M.E. Beckman (eds.), *Papers in Laboratory Phonology I: Between the Grammar and the Physics of Speech*. Cambridge: Cambridge University Press, 341-376.

Browman, C. and L. Goldstein. (1992). Articulatory Phonology: An Overview. *Phonetica*, 49: 155-180.

Butcher A. and E. Weiher. (1976). An electropalatographic investigation of coarticulation in VCV sequences. *Journal of Phonetics*, 4: 59-74.

Byrd, Dani. (1994). *Articulatory timing in English consonant sequences*. UCLA dissertation. In *UCLA Working Papers in Phonetics*, 86.

Byrd, Dani, Edward Flemming, C. Mueller, & Cheng Cheng Tan. (1995). Using regions and indices in EPG data reduction. *Journal of Speech and Hearing Research*, 38: 821-827.

Byrd, Dani. (1996). Influences on articulatory timing in consonant sequences. *Journal of Phonetics*, 24: 209-244.

Catford, J.C. (1939). On the classification of stop consonants. Le Maître Phonétique, Third Series 65: 2-5. Reprinted in W.E. Jones and J. Laver (eds). *Phonetics in Linguistics: A Book of Readings*, London: Longman, 43-46 (1973).

Catford, J. C. (1977). *Fundamental Problems in Phonetics*. Bloomington: Indiana University Press.

Cohn, Abigail. (1990). *Phonetic and Phonological Rules of Nasalization*. Ph.D. dissertation, UCLA. In *UCLA Working Papers in Phonetics*, 76.

Daniloff, R.G. and R.E. Hammarberg. (1973). On defining co-articulation. *Journal of Phonetics*, 1: 239-248.

Dart, Sarah. (1998). Comparing French and English coronal consonant articulation. *Journal of Phonetics*, 26: 71-94.

Dart, Sarah. (1991). Articulatory and Acoustic Properties of Apical and Laminal Articulations. Ph.D. dissertation. In *UCLA Working Papers in Phonetics*, 79.

Doke, C.M. (1923). Notes on a problem in the mechanism of the Zulu clicks. *Bantu Studies* 2(1): 43-45.

Doke, C.M. (1926). The Phonetics of the Zulu Language. *Bantu Studies*, 2:123-137.

Doke, C.M., and B.W. Vilakazi. (1958). *Zulu-English Dictionary*. Witwatersrand University Press, Johannesburg.

Doke, C.M. (1925). An Outline of the Phonetics of the Language of the Chu: Bushmen of the Northwest Kalahari. *Bantu Studies*, 2:129-165.

Farnetani, E. (1988). Asymmetry of Lingual Movements: EPG data on Italian. *Quaderni del Centro di Studio per le Ricerche di Fonetica del C.N.R.*, 7, 211-228.

Farnetani, E., W. Hardcastle and A. Marchal. (1989). Cross-language investigation of Lingual Coarticulatory Processes using EPG. *Eurospeech '89, European Conference on Speech and Technology*, 2; 429-432.

Farnetani, E. (1990). V-C-V lingual coarticulation and its spatio-temporal domain. In W.J. Hardcastle and A. Marchal (eds.) *Speech production and Speech Modelling*. Kluwer Academic Pulishers, Dordrecht, 93-130.

Farnetani, E. (1997). Coarticulation and Connected Speech Processes. In *The Handbook of Phonetic Sciences*. (Hardcastle, W.J. and John Laver, eds.), pp. 371-404. Oxford, Blackwell.

Farnetani, E., Kyriaki Vagges, Emanuela Magno-Caldognetto. (1985). Coarticulation in Italian /VtV/ sequences: A palatographic study. *Phonetica*, 42: 78-99.

Fletcher, S., M. McCutcheon and M. Wolf. (1975). Dynamic palatometry. *Journal of Speech and Hearing Research*, 18, 812-819.

Fowler, C.A. (1980). Coarticulation and theories of extrinsic timing. *Journal of Phonetics*, 8: 113-133.

Fowler, C.A. (1983). Converging sources of Evidence on spoken and perceived rhythms of speech: cyclic production of vowels in monosyllabic stress feet. *Journal of Experimental Psychology: General* 112: 386-412.

Fowler, C.A. and E. Saltzman. (1993). Coordination and Coarticulation in Speech Production. *Language and Speech* 36 (2,3): 171-195.

Gibbon, Fiona, William Hardcastle and Katerina Nicolaidis. (1993). Temporal and Spatial Aspects of Lingual Coarticulation in /kl/ sequences: A cross-linguistic investigation. *Language and Speech*, 36(2, 3): 261-277.

Hardcastle, W.J. (1981). Experimental Studies in Lingual Coarticulation. In R.E. Ashe and J.A. Henderson (eds.), *Towards a History of Phonetics*. Edinburgh University Press, Edinburgh.

Hardcastle, W. (1972). The use of Electropalatography in Phonetic Research. *Phonetica*, 25, 197-215.

Hardcastle, W. (1984). New methods of profiling lingual-palatal contact patterns with electropalatography. *Speech Research Laboratory Work in Progress, University of Reading*, 4: 1-40.

Hardcastle, W. (1985). Some phonetic and syntactic constraints on lingual coarticulation during /kl/ sequences. *Speech Communication*, 4: 247-263.

Hardcastle, W., W. Jones, C. Knight, A. Trudgeon and G. Calder. (1989). New developments in electropalatography: A state-of-the-art report. *Clinical Linguistics and Phonetics*, 3(1), 1-38.

Hardcastle, W.J., F. Gibbon, and K. Nicolaidis. (1991). EPG data reduction methods and their implications for the studies of lingual coarticulation. *Journal of Phonetics*, 19: 251-266.

Hardcastle, W and P. Roach. (1979). An instrumental investigation of coarticulation in stop consonant sequences. In H. Hollien and P. Hollien (eds.), *Current Issues in the phonetic sciences* (pp. 531-540). Amsterdam: John Benjamins.

Hammarberg, R.E. (1976). The metaphysics of coarticulation. *Journal of Phonetics* 5:353-363.

Henke, W. (1966). *Dynamic articulatory model of speech production using computer simulation*. Ph.D. dissertation, MIT.

Jakobson, R. (1968). Extra-pulmonic consonants (ejectives, implosives, clicks), *RLE Quarterly Progress Report, MIT*, 90, 221-227.

Jessen, Michael. (2002). An acoustic study of contrasting plosives and click accompaniments in Xhosa. *Phonetica*, 59: 150-179.

Johnson, Keith. (1997). *Acoustic and Auditory Phonetics*. Oxford: Blackwell.

Kagaya, Ryohei. (1978). Soundspectrographic Analysis of Naron Clicks-A Preliminary Report. Research Institute of Logopedics and Phoniatrics, Faculty of Medicine, University of Tokyo, *Annual Bulletin* 12:113-125.

Keating, P. (1993). Fronted Velars, palatalized velars and palatals. *Phonetica* 50:73-101.

Khumalo, J.S.M. (1981). *Zulu Tonology*. M.A. Thesis, University of Witswatersrand, Johannesburg.

Ladefoged, Peter. (1957). Use of Palatography. *Journal of Speech and Hearing Disorders*, 22: 764-774.

Ladefoged, Peter. (1968). *A Phonetic Study of West African Languages*. Cambridge: Cambridge University Press.

Ladefoged, Peter. (1971). *Preliminaries to Linguistic Phonetics.* (Midway Reprint 1981). University of Chicago Press, Chicago.

Ladefoged, Peter. (1980). Instrumental Phonetic Fieldwork. *UCLA Working Papers in Phonetics*, 49:28-42.

Ladefoged, Peter. (1993a). *A Course in Phonetics. (3rd ed.)* Harcourt, Brace and Jovanovich, New York.

Ladefoged, Peter. (1993b). Linguistic Phonetic Fieldwork: a practical guide. *UCLA Working papers in Phonetics,*

Ladefoged, Peter. (1997). Instrumental Techniques for Linguistic Phonetic Fieldwork. In *The Handbook of Phonetic Sciences.* (Hardcastle, W.J. and John Laver, eds.), pp. 137-166. Oxford, Blackwell.

Ladefoged, Peter and Ian Maddieson. (1996). *The Sounds of the World's Languages* Oxford: Blackwells.

Ladefoged, Peter and Anthony Traill. (1984). Linguistic phonetic description of clicks. *Language 60:* 1-20.

Ladefoged, Peter and Anthony Traill. (1994). Clicks and their accompaniments. *Journal of Phonetics* 21: 33-64.

Ladefoged, Peter. (2003). Phonetic Data Analysis: An Introduction to Fieldwork and Instrumental Techniques. Malden, MA: Blackwell.

Maddieson, Ian, Siniŝa Spajič Bonny Sands, and Peter Ladefoged. (1993). Phonetic Structures of Dahalo. *Afrikanistische Arbeitspapiere* 36: 5-53. (see also *UCLA Working Papers in Phonetics*, 84)

Maddieson, Ian. (1993). Investigating Ewe Articulations with Electromagnetic Articulography. *Forschungsberichte, Institute für Phonetik und Sprachliche Kommunikation*, Universität München, 31: 181-214. (Also see *UCLA Working Papers in Phonetics* 85, 22-53)

Maddieson, Ian. (1984). *Patterns of Sounds.* Cambridge: Cambridge University Press.

Maddieson, I. and P. Ladefoged. (1989). Multiply-articulated segments and the feature hierarchy. Paper presented at the Annual Meeting of the LSA, Washington D.C. Printed in UCLA Working Papers in Phonetics 72: 116-138.

Maddieson, Ian. (1996). Gestural Economy. *UCLA Working Papers in Phonetics*, 94: 1-6.

Marchal, A. (1988). Coproduction: Evidence from EPG data. *Speech Communication*, 7:287-295.

Marchal, A. and R. Expresser. (1987). L'asymétrie des appuis linguo-palatins. Communication aux 16e journées d'études sur la parole. *Hammamet. Soc. Franc. d'Acoust.* 116-119.

Miller-Ockhuizen, Amanda. (2003). The phonetics and Phonology of Gutturals: A case study from Ju| ʼhoansi. (Outstanding Dissertations in Linguistics). New York and London: Routledge.

Miller, Amanda, Levi Namaseb & Khalil Iskarous. (2007) Tongue body constriction differences in click types. *Proceedings of Laboratory Phonology 9*. Eds. Jennifer S. Cole & José Ignacio Hualde. Berlin: Mouton de Gruyter. pp. 643-656.

Miller, Amanda. (2008). Click cavity formation and dissolution in IsiXhosa: Viewing clicks with high-speed ultrasound. In Sock, R., Fuchs, S. & Y. laprie, Eds., Proceedings of the 8th International Seminar on Speech Production, December 2008. Available online at http://faculty.arts.ubc.ca/amiller/paper 116.pdf.

Miller, Amanda, Johanna Brugman, Bonny Sands, Levi Namaseb, Mats Exter & Chris Collins. (in press). Posterior place of articulation differences and airstream contours in ǀNuu lingual stops. *Journal of the International Phonetic Association.* (second issue, 2009)

Nakagawa, Hirosi. (1995). A preliminary report on the click accompaniments in ǀGui. *Journal of the International Phonetic Association*, 25:2, pp. 49-63.

Nakagawa, Hirosi. (1996). A first report on the click accompaniments of ǀGui. *Journal of the International Phonetic Association*, 26 (1): 41-54.

Nakagawa, Hirosi. (1996). Aspects of the Phonetic and Phonological Structure of the ǀGui Language. Ph.D. thesis, University of Witwatersrand. Johannesburg.

Nolan. F. (1992). The descriptive role of segments: Evidence from assimilation. in G. J. Docherty & D.R. Ladd (eds.) Papers in Laboratory Phonology II: Gesture, Segment, Prosody. Cambridge: Cambridge University Press, 261-289.

Öhman, S.E.G. (1966). Coarticulation in VCV utterances: spectrographic measurements. *Journal of the Acoustical Society of America* 39: 51-168.

Öhman, S.E.G. (1967). Numerical Model of Coarticulation. *Journal of the Acoustical Society of America* 39: 51-168.

Recasens, Daniel, Jordi Fontdevila, Maria Dolors Pallarès and Antoni Solanas. (1993). An electropalatographic study of stop consonant clusters. *Speech Communication*, 12: 335-355.

Roux, J.C. (1993). An electropalatographic study of Xhosa clicks. Paper presented to the 7th ALASA conference, Johannesburg.

Saltzman and Munhall. (1989). A dynamical approach to gestural patterning in speech production. *Ecological Psychology* 1: 333-382.

Sands, Bonny. (1991). Evidence for Click Features: acoustic characteristics of Xhosa clicks. *UCLA Working Papers in Phonetics*, 80: 6-37.

Sands, B., Ian Maddieson and Peter Ladefoged. (1996). "The Phonetic Structures of Hadza." *Studies in African Linguistics*, 25-2:171-204. (see also *UCLA Working   Papers in Phonetics*, 84: 67-97).

Sands, Bonny, Johanna Brugman, Mats Exter, Levi Namaseb & Amanda Miller. (2007). Articulatory Characteristics of Anterior Click Closures in Nǀuu. Proceedings of the International Congress of Phonetic Sciences XVI, Saarbrucken, Germany, August 2007. Pp. 401-404. Available online: http://www.icphs2007.de/conference/papers/1540/

Shaiman, S. (1989). Kinematic and electromyographic responses to perturbation of the jaw. *Journal of the Acoustical Society of America*, 86: 78-88.

Smith, Caroline. (1995) Prosodic Patterns in the coordination of vowel and consonant gestures. In Phonology and Phonetic Evidence. Papers in Laboratory Phonology IV (Connell, Bruce and Amalia Arvanti, eds.), pp. 205-222.

Stevens, Kenneth. (1998). *Acoustic Phonetics*. Cambridge: MIT Press.

Stone, Maureen. (1997). "Laboratory Techniques for Investigating Speech Articulation." In *The Handbook of Phonetic Sciences*. (Hardcastle, W.J. and John Laver, eds.), pp. 11-32. Oxford, Blackwell.

Taljaard and Snyman. (1990). *An Introduction to Zulu Phonetics*. Hout Bay: M. Lubbe.

Traill, Anthony. (1985). *Phonetic and Phonological Studies of !Xóõ Bushman*. (Quellen zur Khoisan-Forschung, 1.) Hamburg: Helmut Buske Verlag.

Traill A. (1993). Doke's description of clicks. Paper presented to the 7th ALASA Conference, Johannesburg.

Traill, A. (1994). The perception of clicks in !Xóõ. *Journal of African Languages and Linguistics*. 15: 161-174

Tucker, A.N., Margaret Bryan, and J. Woodburn. (1977). The East African click languages: A phonetic comparison. In W.J.G. Mohlig (ed.), *Zur Sprachgeschichte und Ethnohistoire in Afrika: Neue Beitrage Afrikani-stischer Forschungen*, pp. 300-322. Berlin: Dietrich Reimer.

Wright, Richard, Ian Maddieson, Peter Ladefoged and Bonny Sands. (1995). A phonetic study of Sandawe clicks. *UCLA Working Papers in Phonetics* 91: 1-24.

INDEX

Breinigsville, PA USA
16 November 2010
249440BV00003B/4/P